Yan Lianke was born in 1958 in Henan Province, China. He is the author of numerous novels and short-story collections, including *Serve the People!*, *Dream of Ding Village*, *Lenin's Kisses*, *The Four Books*, *The Explosion Chronicles*, *The Day the Sun Died* and *Hard Like Water*. He has been awarded the Hua Zhong World Chinese Literature Prize, the Lao She Literary Award, the Dream of the Red Chamber Award and the Franz Kafka Prize. He has also been shortlisted for the International Man Booker Prize, the Principe de Asturias Award, the Independent Foreign Fiction Prize, the FT/OppenheimerFunds Emerging Voices Award and the prix Femina étranger. *The Day the Sun Died* won the Dream of the Red Chamber Award for the World's Most Distinguished Novel in Chinese. He lives and writes in Beijing.

Yan Lianke's cover artwork features the work of leading contemporary Chinese artists. Turn to the final pages to learn more about them.

Carlos Rojas is professor of Chinese cultural studies at Duke University. He is the author, editor and translator of numerous books, including the English translations of ten books by Yan Lianke.

By the Same Author

Serve the People!
Dream of Ding Village
Lenin's Kisses
The Four Books
The Explosion Chronicles
The Years, Months, Days
The Day the Sun Died
Three Brothers
Hard Like Water

This book has been selected to receive financial assistance from English PEN's PEN Translates programme, supported by Arts Council England. English PEN exists to promote literature and our understanding of it, to uphold writers' freedoms around the world, to campaign against the persecution and imprisonment of writers for stating their views, and to promote the friendly co-operation of writers and the free exchange of ideas. www.englishpen.org

Heart Sutra

Yan Lianke

Translated from the Chinese by
Carlos Rojas

Chatto & Windus
LONDON

13 5 7 9 10 8 6 4 2

Chatto & Windus, an imprint of Vintage, is part of the Penguin Random House group
of companies whose addresses can be found at global.penguinrandomhouse.com

Copyright © Yan Lianke 2023
Translation copyright © Carlos Rojas 2023
Papercut illustrations © Shang Ailan

Yan Lianke has asserted his right to be identified as the author of this
Work in accordance with the Copyright, Designs and Patents Act 1988

Heart Sutra was originally published in 2020 in Hong Kong as *Xinjing* by
City University of Hong Kong Press.

First published in the UK by Chatto & Windus in 2023
First published in the US by Grove Press in 2023

penguin.co.uk/vintage

A CIP catalogue record for this book is available from the British Library

TPB ISBN 9781784744663

Printed and bound in Great Britain by Clays Ltd, Elcograf S.p.A.

The authorised representative in the EEA is Penguin Random House Ireland,
Morrison Chambers, 32 Nassau Street, Dublin D02 YH68

Penguin Random House is committed to a sustainable future
for our business, our readers and our planet. This book is made
from Forest Stewardship Council® certified paper.

Supported using public funding by
**ARTS COUNCIL
ENGLAND**

Heart Sutra

Foreword

Buddha gazed at Jesus on the cross and said, "Your blood has all bled out. Would you like to come down? I'll help you."

Dao gazed at Jesus on the cross and said, "One always wants to go higher. Do you want to go higher? I'll help you."

Jesus gazed back at Buddha and Dao and replied, "I am at this location that is neither high nor low, and when people see me, they see the suffering people must endure."

The Virgin Mary went up to the cross and said, "Haven't you have already endured enough suffering on humanity's behalf?"

Muhammad went up to the cross and said, "If you don't do this, will humanity's suffering decrease?"

Jesus on the cross gazed down at Mary and Muhammad and said, "If I am here, then when people see me, they will see the suffering humanity must endure."

At this point, a group of people approached, and they chatted and drank next to the five deities—as though the deities were just like them. With a laugh, they said to the deities, "Hey, this is good wine, why don't you come and have a drink with us? You shouldn't stop until everyone is drunk!"

Part I

Preface

1. A womb like a flower, with the Bodhisattva Guanyin inside.

2. A womb like cattails and scallions, with Laozi inside.

3. When Guanyin is born, her delivery bed consists of a jade rabbit, the moon, and several villagers.

4. When Laozi is born, his delivery bed consists of an ox, crows, and a straw hat in the sunlight.

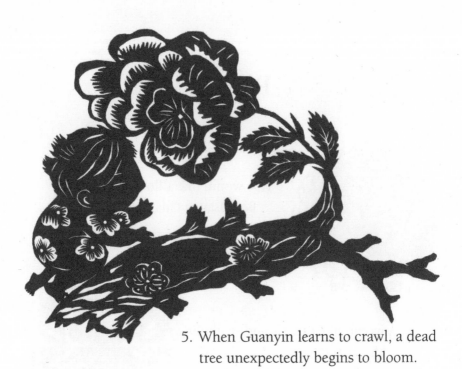

5. When Guanyin learns to crawl, a dead tree unexpectedly begins to bloom.

6. When Laozi learns to crawl, a dead tree unexpectedly begins to bud.

7. Guanyin's first dream is of a lotus blossom and a divine beast.

8. Laozi's first dream is of an enormous lotus-shaped leaf and a patch of wild weeds.

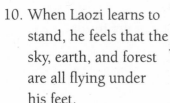

9. When Guanyin learns to stand, she feels that there is a black mass and a hand asking for help under her feet.

10. When Laozi learns to stand, he feels that the sky, earth, and forest are all flying under his feet.

11. Guanyin dreams again, dreaming of her future . . .

12. Laozi dreams again, also dreaming of his future . . .

01 Yahui

The Buddha has as much faith in fate as the Bodhisattva has in the power of her own finger.

Yahui, however, suspected that mortal affairs were not necessarily determined by fate. Take, for example, tug-of-war, where it is assumed that there will always be winners and losers, the same way that there will always be black and white. However, when two of China's five major religions compete in a tug-of-war, they cannot simply be divided into winners and losers. In a competition between teams composed of Buddhists, Daoists, Protestants, Catholics, and Muslims from China's northwestern Ningxia and Gansu Provinces, the losers will always be the competitors, while the winners will always be those who organized the competition itself—the same way that there are casinos everywhere, where gamblers experience excitement and frustration around the clock, but at the end of the day all the money goes into the pockets of the casino owners.

One of these tug-of-war matches took place in late September. At the religious training center on the campus of Beijing's National Politics University, everyone felt as though they were being boiled alive, with the campus, the streets, and the entire city stewing in the heat. Today's match was between the Protestant and Catholic teams. The Protestants had selected five disciples for the competition, as had the Catholics. The contestants were all wearing undershirts, underwear, and sneakers with a good grip. The court had a red rubber surface, which resembled a Buddhist temple cook's fat face and was set up in the school's badminton court, with the Catholic team positioned on one side and the Protestant team on the other. To determine which team was winning, Director Gong, the competition's organizer, had painted a white line on the ground, and it was across this line that the competition unfolded. The members of the Protestant team were not ordinary apprentices or missionaries but rather pastors, just as the members of the Catholic team were not ordinary monks and nuns but priests. Only high-ranking religious figures like pastors and priests were qualified to attend this advanced religious research program and participate in these tug-of-war competitions. The spectators sitting around the court included Daoist masters, Buddhist abbots, Protestant pastors, and Muslim imams— all either religious masters or master candidates.

This was a competition between master and master, deity and deity, human and human, and deity and human. It was part of one of the religious training center's classes, and consequently all the disciples were required to attend. Even Yahui, who was at the center merely as an auditor, had no choice but to attend.

But today she was late.

She was late because she had spent too much time fashioning intricate papercut images in her dormitory room's temple, after which she had spent some additional time admiring herself in the mirror. On her way to the competition, she looked at the school's tallest building and thought how nice it would be if this were a Buddhist convent. She looked at the school's new library and thought how stylish and powerful it would be if this were the convent's sutra depository. As she was thinking this, she tripped over some pieces of sandstone in the middle of the road. She looked down and thought, *Yesterday these stones tripped a small child, and today they've tripped me. What might they do tomorrow?* She resolved to move two of the stones to the side of the road, but after several attempts she found she was unable to budge them. A young Daoist came over to lend a hand, and he easily picked up the stones and moved them out of the way—but because he was afraid of crushing the grass by the side of the road, he instead placed the stones in a dusty area where there was no vegetation. When the Daoist returned, Yahui thanked him by clasping her hands together and chanting *Amitābha*. The Daoist didn't reciprocate with a heart palm salute, but rather, in a very secular fashion, he simply grinned and said, "Don't mention it. My name is Gu Mingzheng."

Then he walked away.

Yahui was surprised that a Daoist would respond to her in such a casual manner. She stood by the side of the road and watched him walk away as though looking at an unannotated page from a sutra. Meanwhile, at the tug-of-war court, they had already conducted the opening ceremony, and the Protestant and Catholic teams were already debating on which side of the white line the rope's red tassel would ultimately land. They argued until the flesh had almost fallen from their faces—as though debating who was God's most powerful presence on earth, Jesus or the Virgin Mary.

By that point, it was already three in the afternoon and the sun was burning brightly overhead, heating everything into a murky soup. Everyone felt like they were steadily boiling alive, and after they started the competition and began huffing and puffing, it sounded as if the earth were being rocked by thunder. Yahui finally entered through a small gate on the side of the court and stood quietly behind the Buddhist team. The first thing she saw were the bald heads of the senior monks, including one whose hair had already turned gray and whose close-cropped scalp resembled wheat stubble left in a farmer's field. Then she turned and saw the young priests and pastors divided into two groups, who glared at each other resentfully, like sports fans divided into two irreconcilable camps. Meanwhile, the Daoist and Muslim fans were casually laughing and chatting. The air was filled with shouts of "Go, go!", though it was difficult to tell which shouts were cheers directed toward the competitors, and which were simply spectators making a commotion.

As the temperature rose, the ground began to split open. Yahui watched for a while, until she began to feel similar cracks appearing in her own cheeks. Sweat poured out of these fissures, flowing like worms crawling down toward her chest. She was gazing up at the September sky when the shadow of a tree suddenly drifted overhead like in a myth. She turned and saw that the young Daoist master Gu Mingzheng had found a branch of an umbrella tree and was holding it over her head. With a smile, he said, "I'd like to treat you to an ice pop from that cold-drink shop."

02 Laozi

1. A young Laozi is herding cattle in the mountains.

2. Laozi is riding an ox to ford a river and ascend to the sky.

3. As confused as an ox in the cloudy sky.

4. Laozi discovers that behind the night sky there lies a vast expanse of stars.

5. Laozi discovers that the sky must also have shooting stars.

6. Laozi wonders: *Can I speak to this expanse of stars?*

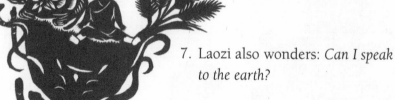

7. Laozi also wonders: *Can I speak to the earth?*

8. Leading the ox and walking on the earth, Laozi tries to reach the highest peak, where the mountains touch the sky.

9. On this peak, Laozi manages to touch the sky.

10. Laozi sees an eagle resembling the sun, and also sees an eagle-like sun and universe.

11. Laozi also sees Guanyin riding a divine beast through the sky and heading toward him.

03 Yahui

The fact that Yahui, an eighteen-year-old "jade nun," would soon become the object of the Daoist Mingzheng's love was something neither the school's religious masters nor the deities themselves possibly could have anticipated. Yet Yahui didn't even feel this was love. Instead, she simply regarded it as the kind of secular attachment her religious mentor, or *shifu*, had once mentioned—like the mud that sticks to your shoes on a rainy day. Once, as Yahui was going down the hall to dump her scraps from making papercuts, she happened to see Mingzheng at the bottom of the stairwell waving at her—like a boy wanting to give something he had just stolen to a girl. At the entrance to the building's seventh floor, there was a wooden placard that read: "Male disciples must stop here!"

He came to a stop.

The placard's interdiction stopped Mingzheng in his tracks. The female disciples were all housed on the seventh floor, the same way that all the female students at this university were assigned to the seventh floors of their respective dormitories—to prevent male students from visiting freely, and to block their amorous and lascivious impulses. In the religious training center, however, commandments were even more powerful than rules, and disciples crave commandments the way a starving person craves three meals a day.

The religion building's first floor contained the religious training center's administrative offices, as well as the offices of its faculty and instructors. The second floor was the Buddhist dormitory, the third was the Daoist dormitory, the fourth, fifth, and sixth were the Catholic, Protestant, and Islamic dormitories, respectively, and the seventh was reserved for the school's female disciples. Each floor had a study room with newspapers and journals, but none had a chapel or a Mass room.

Every religious master and disciple who came here for training attended under the arrangement of the nation's School of Spirituality and Faith. This wasn't a foreign religious academy, nor was it a church or mosque, or a Buddhist or Daoist temple. Instead, it was an advanced religious research program that had been established with government support at Beijing's most prestigious university. A short-term appointment was for three months, a medium-term appointment was for six months, and a long-term appointment was for a full year.

The religious training center consisted of a single building, which the school called the religious belief building, or the religion building. The building's exterior was just like that of the school's other buildings, but inside everything was completely different. Not only were male and female disciples forbidden from mingling with one another, but even disciples of the same sex and belonging to the same religion rarely walked together or spoke to one another. Each disciple's religious practices—such as worshipping, attending Mass, burning incense, and chanting sutras—were conducted in the privacy of their own rooms. Every student had a room, every room had a temple, and every disciple had a church—though the Buddhist temples were rather small, as were the Daoist temples and the Islamic mosques. The young Daoist Mingzheng, meanwhile, yearned to see the Buddhist nun Yahui in person—the same way he might be able to recite the Daodejing by heart yet still yearn to see the real Laozi, or the way Yahui might burn incense and chant sutras every day yet still yearn to see the real Buddha.

Deities and humans must always maintain their distance from one another, because it is only with distance that there can be deities in the first place.

However, although most foreign deities reside in the distant heavens, many of China's deities are located closer to humans, down on earth. Foreign deities mostly attend to people's spirit and soul, while China's deities attend not only to their spirit and soul, but also to more mundane matters such as food and clothing, life and death, jealousy and hatred, money and wealth, aristocracy and bureaucracy, marriage and reproduction. Often, when people are walking along, they may suddenly look up and see a deity.

Now this young Daoist was at the center searching for deities. After repeatedly failing to speak to Yahui at the entrance to the seventh floor, Mingzheng figured he would probably run into her at the entrance to the building at mealtime. He decided he would join her when she emerged to take a stroll around campus, so he waited for her both on the path leading to the canteen and at the entrance to the campus store.

One day, Yahui had her period and went to the campus store to buy sanitary pads, which even nuns need to use. She bought the Comfort and Treasure brand, which had a blue sky, white clouds, and a female model smiling and dancing on the box, and on her way back to her room, she was as happy as a drifting cloud. With a relaxed heart and light steps, she strolled through the campus garden and began to wonder, *Does the Bodhisattva also have periods? And if she does, what kind of pad does she use?* At this thought, Yahui immediately stopped and silently chanted *Amitābha*. Then she smiled and saw a pair of feet with pointed-toe shoes and gray socks to protect the ankles. The stitching along the bottom of the robe resembled withered grass, but it was also as neat as cracks in a wall. This was a Daoist robe, and like a Buddhist robe it was wide at the bottom and narrow at the top. A row of cloth buttons extended diagonally across the left side of the robe, like a river flowing through it.

"I just knew you were going to pass by here," Mingzheng said.

Yahui stopped in surprise and reflexively hugged her sanitary pads to her chest.

"Tomorrow, there will be another tug-of-war competition. However, if your *shifu* is opposed to these inter-sect athletic competitions, I can ask for the center to stop including them in its athletics classes!"

Yahui stared at the young Daoist in disbelief.

"Ours is a program for religious masters, and it is as selective as the Summer Palace's Communist Party School. If you aren't a Buddhist abbot or Daoist master, or a priest, pastor, or imam, then you are not qualified to enroll. I know you have come to look after your *shifu* and audit some classes on her behalf, but do you know why I, a twentysomething-year-old Daoist, was able to enroll?"

Lips pursed, Yahui continued staring at him.

Without answering his own question, the young Daoist approached her and took her hand. "Let's go over there!" As though giving her an order, he led her toward the garden on the west side of the campus. The perimeter of the garden was lined with willows, while the interior was filled with dead cypresses. Students looking for a secluded site to either study or chat flirtatiously usually didn't go there. This, however, was precisely where Mingzheng was leading her. Yahui wasn't sure why she was following him, but when they arrived, he said solemnly, "I know that the reason you weren't ordained when you turned eighteen is because your *shifu* wanted you to return to secular life."

" . . . "

"But who could maintain their faith while enjoying a secular life? I also want to return to secular life, so why don't we take the opportunity provided by this training program, return to secular life, and get married?"

Yahui stepped back in shock. With her gaze fixed on his face and her hands clasped in front of her chest, she repeatedly chanted

Amitābha, then turned and walked away. The young Daoist stepped forward and grabbed her, blocking her way like a wall.

"I really can arrange for the center to stop the tug-of-war competitions. Do you know about my family's relationship to the center's Director Gong?"

As Yahui listened, she took a step back, and then another. The entire time, her hands remained clasped in front of her chest as an interminable thread of sutra chants emerged from her mouth. After Yahui had taken several steps back, she turned and rushed out of the garden. As she ran off, she heard him calling after her, "I'm telling you that tomorrow, on behalf of your *shifu*, I'll ask the center to remove tug-of-war competitions from its athletics courses!" She turned to him in surprise, then hurried away even more quickly than before. When she reached her room, she dealt with her period. She didn't know why she kept feeling a surge of delight and wondered why Laozi and Guanyin hadn't ever fallen in love. She reflected that if Laozi and Guanyin had in fact fallen in love and gotten married, it would have been a beautiful, divine marriage!

04 The Bodhisattva Guanyin

1. You know? The flower bud
   waiting for its season is the
   Bodhisattva Guanyin.

2. A picture of a lotus cloud.

3. *Ah-ya-ya, ah-ya-ya*, it
   turns out that the young
   Guanyin is the most beautiful
   person in the world.

4. When a boy grows up, he will marry someone, and when a woman grows up, she will be married to someone. Guanyin grows up, the divine matchmaker arrives, and a pair of moons are born out of nothing.

5. However, there is only one beautiful Guanyin, and ten thousand suitors. What to do? Fortunately, no matter how many roads there may be, Guanyin will always be at the center.

6. Guanyin wonders: *Whom should I marry?*

7. Guanyin thinks: *Yes, yes, whoever is everyone, that is whom I'll marry.*

8. Guanyin was born so that she could marry everyone—men and women, young and old.

9. But thousands of people curse her, crying, "Whore, whore!" Then her suitors depart, and the roads are left empty.

10. By the time her parents arrive, the beautiful Guanyin has already left, heading in the direction of the sage. Her parents, meanwhile, see the world's largest lotus blossom.

11. Guanyin, soaring up to your auspicious cloud, where is your distant region?

12. Guanyin sees the river to heaven.

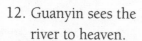

13. Guanyin also sees Laozi in the sky calling out to her: *It turns out that the sage is here waiting for me!*

14. An image of Laozi's and Guanyin's first date.

05 Jueyu

The ridge on the roof of Yonghe Temple could be seen from the Yonghe Missionary Hospital, as though it were printed on the window, like a feather stuck inside a copy of *Records of the Grand Historian*. Today, there was an unprecedented absence of the usual morning bells and evening drums, but now the silence was obliterated by a loud ruckus. In Beijing, the city's noise was as great as the silence of the prairie or of Qinghai Lake—as distant and vast as eternity.

Yahui was about to arrive.

For more than twenty days, Jueyu *shifu* had been waiting in the hospital for Yahui to come visit. A sickroom, white walls, transfusions, and injections—Jueyu *shifu* was propped up to eat and listen as the volunteer nurses and nuns chanted several lines from the sutras. She gazed at Yahui's papercuts, which covered the bed and the walls. As she did so she would let herself think, or else she would just look at the papercuts and not think at all—letting her mind remain as empty as a white cloud, completely devoid of content. She had suffered a stroke and could no longer speak or walk, and although her mind remained as clear as a beautiful scene, she had no way of communicating this scene to others. She had been checked into the hospital less than ten days after arriving at the university's religious training center in Beijing, where she had never anticipated that she would have to witness inter-sect tug-of-war competitions.

When these competitions reached their peak, she collapsed and was brought to this sickroom.

The sun slowly sank from the second-highest window to the second-lowest one. Back in Jing'an Temple's Jingshui Convent, in Xining Province, where Jueyu *shifu* had lived for forty-seven years, the sunlight at this time of day resembled red paper immersed in clear water, but here the light appeared as though it were flowing out of muddy water. There was a major thoroughfare outside the hospital, and the sound of traffic resonated like rain flowing through a bridge's drainage hole. The sound was initially distracting, but now the cacophony of cars honking, people talking, and objects colliding made Jueyu *shifu* feel as though she had a companion in her solitude. A nurse entered her room and placed several pills by the head of her bed. Maybe the nurse also said something to her, or maybe she didn't—in any event, as the nurse left, she shut the door behind her. After a while, the door began to creak open again, followed by the sound of someone exclaiming "*Shifu!*" Before Jueyu *shifu* had a chance to shift her gaze from the window, she heard someone placing several objects in the cabinet at the head of the bed. Jueyu *shifu* turned and saw the sweat on the back of Yahui's robe, then watched as Yahui placed some apples and bananas in the cabinet. Lastly, Yahui placed a thermos in the cabinet, as ripples of joy spread on her face. Jueyu *shifu* looked directly at Yahui and saw that she did not appear as precise and orderly as usual. She realized Yahui had been struck by a surge of joy, resembling a girl delightedly standing in front of her mother.

"*Amitābha.*" Yahui held her finished papercuts of Guanyin's and Laozi's birth and their subsequent meeting. She happily told her *shifu*, "Someone spoke to Director Gong, and he agreed to discontinue the tug-of-war contests!"

Jueyu *shifu*'s eyes brightened.

"Director Gong wouldn't listen to us, but there is a Daoist with an impressive background, whose father might even be a minister or governor. Director Gong will definitely do whatever he asks." As she was saying this, Yahui pulled over a chair and sat down next to the bed. She lifted her *shifu's* stick-thin hand, but suddenly remembered that she hadn't shut the door behind her. She got up to close the door, and as she was returning to her seat, she accidentally knocked over a broom behind the door. Then, as she was picking up the broom, she kicked over a trash bin, and as she was picking up the trash bin, her robe got snagged on a bamboo basket. Finally, smiling, she returned to the bed and once again grasped her *shifu's* hand. "You were hospitalized before you had a chance to meet this Daoist master. No one knows his family's background, or why he left his family to become a priest. In principle, he shouldn't have been able to join this program for religious masters, but when someone invited him to come, he did. When others said that the religion school's athletics class shouldn't have tug-of-war competitions, Director Gong ignored them, but when this Daoist master made the same point, Director Gong immediately agreed to discontinue the competitions." Yahui said this with a smile, as though she had accomplished a very difficult task. Yahui massaged her *shifu's* hand in her own, and as Jueyu *shifu* gazed back at her, her lips trembled and she seemed to whisper something. Then Jueyu *shifu* moved her body toward the head of the bed and sat up while supporting herself with her arms. She tried to lift her left arm but couldn't. Instead, while holding her right hand to her chest, she chanted *Amitābha*.

Yahui stared in surprise. Before, her *shifu* couldn't even move her hands, which hung limply from her arms like frost-covered grass, but now she could prop herself up and sit at the head of the bed. She could even use her left hand to make a Buddhist hand gesture, or mudra, in front of her chest. Yahui exclaimed, "*Shifu*, you're able to sit up?!"

Yahui once again clasped her hands in front of her chest and said loudly, "*Amitābha*, my *shifu* has sat up in bed on her own!"

Then she immediately rushed out of the sickroom into the hallway, shouting "Doctor! Doctor!"

In the hallway, which was not very long to begin with, there were no doctors or nurses. Instead, poking out of a doorway, there was the bald head of a young monk who was also there to visit someone. Yahui turned and ran back into the sickroom, then stood in front of the bed gazing at her *shifu*, who was rail-thin with snowy-white hair and wrinkles so deep that you could braid them. With tears in her eyes, Yahui exclaimed, "*Shifu*, I'll make sure the school stops organizing those tug-of-war competitions . . . Gu Mingzheng said that he has arranged for the center to discontinue them tomorrow."

With tears in her eyes, Jueyu *shifu* smiled and gazed at Yahui. She seemed to want to say something, but no words came out. Instead, she gestured with her right hand, and Yahui approached the head of the bed and once again grasped her hand. Jueyu *shifu* removed her hand from Yahui's and slowly ran her fingers over Yahui's body. She lightly stroked Yahui's chest, shoulder, and face. She caressed Yahui's chin, then brought her fingers up to Yahui's lips and the tip of her nose, before finally stopping at the bridge of her nose. Trembling, she caressed Yahui's nose, whereupon from the mouth of this woman, who almost a month earlier had been in a vegetative state, there emerged several halting words: "You . . . you have grown to resemble . . . to resemble a bodhisattva!"

Upon hearing this, Yahui burst into tears.

Jueyu *shifu* also burst into tears.

Jueyu *shifu* and Yahui hugged each other like a mother and daughter, or like someone embracing a loved one who has just returned from the dead. They wept until it sounded like the room was filled with a swarm of bees.

06 Director Gong,
Professor Huang, and Pastor Wang

Before class on Monday, the religion building felt as though the followers of each religion had been battling one another and the deities'
faces were covered in curses and slaps.

When the students returned from the dining hall after breakfast,
they entered the auditorium and saw a professor shoving a book in
Director Gong's face and shouting, "Damn it, I'm not going to take
it anymore!" He said this angrily, as though no one recognized his
talent.

Associate Professor Huang was forty-one or forty-two years old
and was handsome and learned. He knew Christianity as intimately
as a father knows his own son, and his articles were always published
in leading religious studies journals. Three years in a row, however,
each time he was considered for promotion to full professor, he was
mysteriously passed over. This inevitably made him furious, and he
would throw down his textbooks and the journals containing his
articles. On that day, he even threw down a computer mouse and
stomped on it. No one knew what exactly Associate Professor Huang
and Director Gong said to each other in the auditorium that day, but
it seemed as though the professor's outburst was not aimed solely at
the director. However, the encounter did leave Director Gong feeling so embarrassed and helpless that all he could do was exclaim,

"Why bother? Why bother?" In the end, the men simply glared at one another, as though they intended to do battle with their eyes.

By this point, a crowd of disciples had gathered around. Because the disciples didn't know what the issue was, they just stood there and watched the commotion. The female disciples were so shocked that their words got caught in their throats, while the male ones waited for an opening in the fight. The Buddhists and Daoists put their hands together in prayer, though it wasn't immediately clear whether they were praying that Associate Professor Huang and Director Gong would start fighting or that they wouldn't. More and more people arrived, making Director Gong and Associate Professor Huang feel as though they couldn't leave without first starting a fight. Director Gong picked up the computer mouse Associate Professor Huang had stomped on and kicked it back to him, shouting, "What's the point of getting angry at me for something the school committee did? You should go complain to them!"

Associate Professor Huang put his hands on his hips and laughed coldly. "Do you think I wouldn't dare?!"

Director Gong shouted back, "Then do it!"

Associate Professor Huang glared at Director Gong one final time, kicked the computer mouse back against the wall, then strode through the crowd and out of the building. The disciples formed a path for him, allowing him to drift by like a specter. When the door opened, sunlight surged in and filled the building. Associate Professor Huang waded through the disciples' expectations and the divine light, and, panting, proceeded outside. The students watched him leave. Associate Professor Huang pushed the door with such force that it was as if he were opening the outer gate of the imperial court. By the time the light-yellow glass door closed behind him, Director Gong was already several meters away.

This appeared to mark the end of the dispute. The disciples turned back to Director Gong, who seemed to be about to say something, but then the auditorium door opened a crack and

Associate Professor Huang's face reappeared. The disciples heard him announce, "Director Gong, as of this moment, I, Huang Qiudong, officially resign! After leaving this damned religious training center, I'll become my own master. You'll no longer have to worry about my career, my home, or where my child will go to preschool!" Then, his face bright red, he stepped outside and slammed the door. Through the door's glass window, the disciples could see him standing with his back to the sun, as the sunlight streamed down over his head and shoulders, before finally reaching his face.

Everyone waited for Director Gong's reaction. To their surprise, however, he turned to them and shouted, "What are you staring at?! You are all believers and God's children. Is there anything in this mortal world that you haven't already seen before?" As he said this, he cast his gaze over the crowd, making them feel as though they had become debased and secularized. Everyone left the auditorium quickly and rushed toward the stairwell and elevators. Even the old bishop and Monk Dade felt that they had let down Director Gong and the deities, and so when they passed in front of Director Gong, they bowed deeply to express their remorse.

The auditorium once again fell silent. As Director Gong was turning to leave, he saw the class monitor of the Protestant class, Pastor Wang Changping, standing next to him. Pastor Wang said quietly, "Associate Professor Huang is a talented individual, isn't he?"

"So what if he is?" Director Gong glared at Pastor Wang. "Rain will still fall from the sky and women will still get married. There may be nothing I can do to help Associate Professor Huang get promoted—that is, of course, unless you can arrange for God to issue me two more faculty lines for full professors."

Pastor Wang reflected for a moment, then said, "Even without the new faculty lines, he could still stay." Director Gong gazed at Pastor Wang, evaluating him as he would a believer who had suddenly come to perform penance. Pastor Wang was more than a decade older than Director Gong and was also taller and thinner. He was the head resident pastor of Guangxi Province's famous Jialan Church, and therefore had been assigned to serve as the Protestant class's class monitor. Because of this position, Director Gong treated him more respectfully than he treated the other disciples.

Director Gong stared at Pastor Wang for several seconds, and then, in a voice that was simultaneously hard and soft, asked, "How can I get Associate Professor Huang to stay?"

Pastor Wang laughed, then looked around and replied, "You have to use money. In this era, money can resolve anything that the gods cannot."

Director Gong also smiled and asked, "And where exactly would I find this money?"

"In this religion building you oversee."

Director Gong looked up at the ceiling and then glanced in the direction of his own office, as though he were about to go work. For the sake of politeness, however, he invited Pastor Wang to sit with him for a while.

Director Gong's office was located at the northern end of the hallway. It was room 106, and had a steel plaque with the words *Director's Office* printed in yellow. The office was sixteen square meters—somewhat larger than the offices of the other instructors. Upon entering, visitors would see a huge chart labeled "Tug-of-War Regular Season and Playoffs" posted over the window, beside which there was a bookcase, a table, a sofa, and a small fountain. There was also a copy of the journal *Chinese Athletics* as well as several religious magazines and newspapers—all prominently displayed.

Director Gong invited Pastor Wang to sit on the couch and poured him a glass of hot water, then proceeded to steep a cup of the *maojian* tea that one of his students had given him. Director Gong explained apologetically that the religious training center was considered marginal by the university, like an extra thumb on a hand with six fingers. However, even if it was completely useless, it still couldn't be removed. It was very difficult for lecturers at the center to be promoted to associate professor, just as it was difficult for associate professors to be promoted to full professor. As a result, the instructors came and went, prepared to leave at any moment. They were like people squeezing into a temple to view deities. Inevitably there would come a day when the temple would collapse and the final deity would depart, after which not a trace of a visitor would remain.

Pastor Wang listened attentively, as though in a confessional listening to a saint. When Director Gong finished, Pastor Wang, like a saint gazing at the window in the back of the confessional, looked at him and asked, "And what about you?"

"Of course, I am thirty percent heat and seventy percent light." Director Gong returned the conversation to the topic of dignity, adding, "How could I let down those who appointed me here? Not only would I like to promote every instructor and give each of them a house, I also want to convert this temporary religious training center into a formal religious studies institute."

"Would that be difficult?" Pastor Wang asked.

Director Gong replied, "It depends on whether or not the deities are inclined to help . . . After all, if it weren't difficult, I wouldn't have been assigned to work here."

"Do you have a plan?"

"This is National Politics University. A good university must have academic monographs and national research achievement awards. With these, it may be possible for our religious training center to become elevated to an institute, whereupon all of our problems would be resolved."

Pastor Wang then asked, "Would we need anything else?"

Director Gong replied, "Yes. For instance, we would need more talented individuals. You can see that we already have some, such as Associate Professor Huang. But damn it, when he gets angry, he's perfectly capable of smashing something right in front of me."

Pastor Wang took a couple of sips of tea, spat the tea leaves back into his cup, and shook it until they sank to the bottom. Then he returned the cup to the table and proceeded to say something divine and mysterious. He could see that the center's problems were a question not only of monographs, articles, and talented individuals, but also of money. He asked, "If we had money, would we be worried about being able to retain our talented individuals? If we had money, would we be worried that those evaluators won't promote our lecturers to associate and full professor? If we had money, would we be worried about not having sufficient monographs and academic awards? Would we be worried that the higher administration doesn't respect our religious training center and doesn't include it within the university's formal establishment?"

Pastor Wang asked Director Gong several more "would we be worried" questions along these same lines, until eventually a trace of a smile emerged in the corner of Director Gong's mouth. Director Gong gestured at Pastor Wang and said, "But tell me, where can we find these additional funds? Do you know how much the university gives the center every year? It's not even enough to cover the cost of a few student meals."

Pastor Wang took another sip of tea and replied, "Everyone who comes to this high-level religious training center is either a religious master or a master candidate. Usually, they only look after their own churches, temples, and mosques, but do you think that they are all penniless? Don't they all have at least some savings?"

Director Gong fired back, "Then take some money from the pockets of those believers. Who cares if they write a letter of complaint to the higher-ups! You religious people are as exquisitely sensitive as a woman's hymen, aren't you?"

"But what if the believers *are* willing to donate?" Pastor Wang gazed at Director Gong for a moment. "I can take the lead and donate a hundred thousand yuan, which could then be used to improve everyone's material and cultural life. What do you think?"

Director Gong simply stared at Pastor Wang. Eventually he laughed and said, "What if you try to report me for accepting a hundred-thousand-yuan bribe?"

Pastor Wang turned pale. Staring intently at Director Gong, he asked, "Does this mean you don't think I'm a believer?" Without waiting for the director's response, Pastor Wang got up and excused himself, then headed out of the room. When he reached the doorway, he glanced at the "Tug-of-War Regular Season and Playoffs" chart that Director Gong had posted over the window. Just as he was about to open the door, Pastor Wang heard Director Gong say, "Pastor Wang, before you became a believer, did you ever serve in a national institution?"

"I was briefly a civil servant," Pastor Wang replied with a smile, and added, "But I felt that going to the office every day was pointless, so I transferred to the church."

Director Gong laughed. "I can certainly understand that."

Then Pastor Wang opened the door and saw students of different faiths on their way to class. As he was about to head over to the church, he turned and shook Director Gong's hand, then disappeared into the crowd of fellow believers.

07 Director Gong, Pastor Wang, and Imam Tian

Director Gong originally worked at the Athletics University, but later transferred to the National Politics University because it was closer to his home. His former specialty was folk athletics, but now he simply incorporated this interest into his religious teaching. Given his many years of experience teaching folk athletics, he had decided the previous year to produce a volume titled *Synthetic Treatise on Tug-of-War and the Contradictions Between Religions.* As a result, tug-of-war became the center of this year's athletics course, just as an ordinary monk might become the abbot of an entire monastery and preside over everything within it.

This Friday's competition was between the Protestant and Islamic teams. The previous Friday the Protestant team beat the Catholic team, which helped transform the Protestant team's belief into faith. Moreover, Pastor Wang donated a hundred thousand yuan of his own savings to the athletics course, thereby ensuring that all future winners would receive a prize of five hundred yuan. Although five hundred yuan might not sound like a lot, it was enough for students to buy some beer and snacks after class, while those who didn't drink could instead purchase candy, cigarettes, and pastries. These prizes made the competitions even more exciting. If the athletics class started at two o'clock, the competition could begin by two-thirty. The sun would be shining directly onto the field, transforming the court's rubber surface into a thick red bean soup. All the regular students were present, and even Yahui, a mere auditor, attended. Anyone who didn't attend would be reported as truant, and anyone with too many truancies would have difficulty graduating. Meanwhile, some graduates of this national class of religious masters could be promoted to the position of vice chairman of the provincial- or municipal-level Chinese People's Political Consultative Conference, while others could become national representatives or directors of the National People's Congress, which met in Beijing every year in the Great Hall of the People. So, who would want to be truant? Even an eighty-two-year-old Protestant elder and an eighty-one-year-old Catholic bishop obediently came to sit in the stands.

The sun continued to shine down onto the court's rubber surface, which reflected the sun's rays back into the sky, such that an even greater amount of heat could again be projected to the earth. The iron railing around the court became so hot that it could brand the flesh of anyone who touched it. The pastors and imams participating in the competition wore only their undershirts, underwear, and sneakers, and like everyone else they desperately wanted to win. Not only would the victorious team of this best-of-three competition take home five hundred yuan in prize money, but furthermore, after one team won, everyone would be able to return to their dormitories.

The crowds on the sidelines were all holding newspapers, journals, and their religion's sacred scriptures over their heads, as though suspended overhead was a miniature universe over which they maintained complete sovereign control. One Daoist leader was balancing a copy of an Annotated Daodejing on his head, the cover of which had a portrait of Laozi that, in the heat, had been reduced to a pile of ashes in a distant desert. In the sports field, different athletic courts were separated by fences. Some disciples were shooting baskets while others were playing volleyball, and even farther away an empty soccer field was waiting for someone to come play. On the campus's streets, some students were carrying parasols while others were wearing sunscreen.

Director Gong—who was not yet fifty, had shoulders that were as broad as a board, and was wearing athletic pants and a tank top—was serving as the competition's referee. The five imams on the Islamic team were all middle-aged, as were the five pastors on the Protestant team. This was a relatively youthful competition, and if you looked carefully, you might notice that the imams were a bit thinner than the pastors, their skin was darker, and they all smelled of loess soil. Meanwhile, the pastors were, on average, several years younger than the imams, and most were from the Zhejiang region. They appeared calm and relaxed and—combined with the fact that they had already defeated the Catholic team the previous week—especially determined, like a rich person entering a supermarket. Headed by their class monitor, Wang Changping, the Protestant team entered the court first, after which Tian Dongqing led the Islamic team in and to the other side. The brand-new competition rope was grayish-white, and the red tassel had three gold-colored wood beads attached to the end, like the ones that hang from either side of a pair of regal curtains. Director Gong was standing next to the tassel, with a satisfied and excited expression. He was more than one-point-seven meters tall, and when his shoulders shook it seemed as though leaves and fruit were about to fall to the ground. He was holding a red flag and took out a copper whistle, then nodded to the two teams, whereupon the Protestant team's Wang Changping stepped forward and offered the Islamic team's Tian Dongqing his hand, saying, "Friendship comes first."

Tian Dongqing, however, did not reciprocate, and instead replied coldly, "Competition comes third."

Then Tian Dongqing returned to his team. This was a very minor matter, but beneath Imam Tian's icy response Pastor Wang heard a hint of excitement and was reminded of the fierce competition. He clenched his fist, looked at the referee, then returned to his own team.

Director Gong observed this interaction and heard Imam Tian's response, which was not the standard "friendship comes first, competition comes second." Director Gong didn't believe that the Islamic team would really put friendship first and competition second or third. He knew that although they said competition comes third, in reality they believed competition didn't have a trace of friendship.

After Director Gong transferred from the Athletics University just outside Beijing's Fifth Ring Road, to this religious training center at National Politics University, he was promoted from associate to full professor and finally to director, and no one was more familiar with each religion's collective nature than he. The Buddhist classes' gentle and secular attitude, the Daoist classes' pride and worldliness, the Islamic classes' egotism and competitiveness, and the Catholic and Protestant classes' emphasis on harmonious mediation, combined with their apparent unity in public but fierce rivalry in private— these all collectively represented the character and temperament of China's five great religions, the same way that a variety of fruits and leaves might represent a vast forest.

The sun had already begun to set, and the sunlight had shifted from a chaotic amalgam to a set of clear rays—except that when each ray approached another, they became bundled together, and as these bundles rained down from the sky, they piled up in the afternoon of this final Friday in September.

After wiping the sweat from his brow, Director Gong blew his whistle, whereupon each team picked up its end of the rope. Each team's leader was positioned two meters from the rope's center tassel, and the other teammates were positioned at set distances behind them—all gripping the rope as though it were an enormous snake. Some of the spectators who had come to watch the competition were standing in the back and were using their sutras, textbooks, and magazines to fan themselves, while the esteemed older priests, abbots, imams, and pastors were positioned in front, where they watched with delight. Yahui was in the rear of the Buddhist group.

She wasn't particularly interested in who won or lost, and instead was scanning the stands behind the Daoist team to try to catch a glimpse of Gu Mingzheng.

"Hey, Gu—didn't you say there wouldn't be a competition today?" As Yahui was heading to the court, she had pulled Mingzheng to the side of the road and forced her question on him, the way one might grab a fleeing thief. However, this thief appeared very innocent, and he replied, "Director Gong did indeed say that there wouldn't be a competition today, so how could I have known he would still host one?" Mingzheng promised that after class, he would find Director Gong and ask him again to cancel the competitions. He would definitely get him to cancel them! With this, Yahui had proceeded unhappily to the tug-of-war court. But where was Mingzheng now? A moment earlier, he had been standing behind the Buddhist team's spectators, on her side of the court, and he even gave her a mischievous grin. In the blink of an eye, however, he disappeared—and now was with neither the Daoists nor the Buddhists. Yahui wanted to go look for him, but she also wanted to stop at the cold-drink store across the road and have an ice pop. Before she had a chance to leave the court, however, a burst of laughter erupted. She turned and saw that the Islamic team, on a signal from their team captain, Tian Dongqing, had suddenly released their grip on the rope, such that the Protestant team immediately toppled over like dominoes. Drops of sweat fell to the ground, splattering droplets everywhere. As this was happening, the court came to resemble a theatrical stage. Although the Protestant team quickly picked themselves up and shouted at the laughing imams, "You lost! You lost!" they nevertheless still felt they had been tricked. Moreover, the spectators' roars of laughter suggested that the Islamic team, in their performative failure, were in fact the true victors.

At this point, Director Gong blew his whistle, pointed at the Islamic team with his flag lowered, and then pointed at the Protestant team with his flag raised, announcing the match's winners and losers.

However, Wang Changping protested that the Islamic team's trickery reflected not only a lack of respect for the athletics class, but also a mockery of Protestantism itself.

When Director Gong heard this, he said to Tian Dongqing, "Don't mock the school's other religions, OK?"

Tian Dongqing was almost forty years old, and although he was much shorter than Director Gong, his shoulders were almost as broad. As he stood in the sunlight staring at Director Gong, he suddenly wiped the sweat from his brow and then looked over at his teammates, sending them a message with his eyes. The Islamic team responded as though they had received a direct order from Muhammad. They stood straight and chanted, "For Allah, and for the Quran—" as they made the sign for Allah in front of their chests. Then they stood next to the rope and arranged their skullcaps, as though by doing so they would be able to receive God's power and message.

The Protestant team prepared for the next match.

Director Gong squatted next to the rope to make sure the tassel was positioned directly over the center line, then he stood up and looked around. Before he blew his whistle, the competitors adopted their competition stance. The rope was pulled taut and the tassel swayed over the white line, and eventually stopped moving. The contestants braced themselves, and the competition began.

The contestants concentrated all their strength in their thighs, waists, arms, and the hands with which they were gripping the rope. After blowing his whistle, Director Gong raised his flag halfway, then brought it down like a cleaver. The tassel shifted back and forth, again and again. The rope became so taut that someone could sit on it. In fact, if at this point, someone had said something about the difference between one religion and another, the competition could easily have escalated into a full-blown religious war. Director Gong leaned over and stared intently at the tassel. From its movements, he could assess each team's strength and determination. He regretted having told Imam Tian to treat the Protestants with more respect. What he should have said was simply, "I'd like for you to treat your opponents with more respect." But he had already made the first remark and couldn't take it back, so he had no choice but to let Allah and Christ use the tug-of-war competition as a proxy to determine who was more powerful. Sweat poured down his forehead, through his eyelashes, and into his eyes, to the point that he needed to keep wiping away the sweat in order to continue staring at the tassel. The sun seemed to be burning a hole in his head, and while part of him wanted to put out the flames, another part of him simply didn't care. Noting that the members of the Islamic team were all wearing white skullcaps in the blistering heat, he wondered whether they felt as though their heads were in a stove. He looked to the left and saw that the spectators cheering for the Protestant team were shouting "Go, go!" so loudly it seemed as though their cheers could split bamboo, then he looked to the right and saw that those cheering for the Islamic team were not shouting "Go, go!" and instead were repeating the solemn and sacred syllables, "Al-lah, Al-lah! . . ."

Startled by this invocation of religion, Director Gong abruptly stopped blowing his whistle. He turned and saw that the Islamic team's skullcaps were soaked with sweat. Their faces were no longer sallow and melancholy, but rather were so flushed that it seemed as though blood would gush out if you so much as touched them. Director Gong was certain that the Muslims would win the match because they were able to draw on the strength of Allah and Muhammad. He turned back to the tassel, and as he watched it move slightly to the right of the center line, he seemed to hear the Protestant team's feet being pulled forward. A second later, however—because the Protestant team either deployed a new tactic or else managed to draw on a new reserve of strength—the tassel came to a stop and then slowly started to move back to the left.

The spectators assembled on the right included not only Muslim disciples but also Buddhist ones, while those on the left included not only Protestant disciples but also Catholic ones. The Daoist students were idly standing around, but the shade of the trees behind the spectator stands on the left was like a deity beckoning people over, and most of the Daoist masters and disciples eventually drifted over to that side. As a result, it seemed as though the cheers coming from the left side easily drowned out the ones from the right. One person stood up with his fist raised and began cheering, like a secular person screaming bloody murder. There was no laughter on the court; instead, there were just turbulent emotions flying through the air. The religious masters were no longer masters in the religious world, nor were they deities or representatives of deities. Instead, they had all returned to the secular world of winners and losers. Even the elderly monks, bhikkus, priests, and pastors had stood up in the front row and were supported by the younger disciples as they shouted "Go! Go!" as though welcoming the arrival of their respective deities.

The tassel was pulled to one side by the pastors and to the other side by the imams, then it was pulled to one side by the imams and to the other side by the pastors. It paused, moved, paused, and moved again—as time seemed to slow to a crawl. Some disciples, after using pages from a book to wipe away their sweat, threw the balled-up paper to the ground. There were water bottles on either side of the spectator stand, and although no one was seen drinking water, the pile of empty bottles nevertheless kept growing and was kicked by people walking around. The sun seemed to make the sound of footsteps as it moved across the sky, but when you looked up, it appeared frozen in place. By this point, the earlier breeze had subsided but the heat persisted, as the cicadas sounded like birds being roasted alive. The sound of a bell announcing a break in one of the classrooms drifted over, after which there emerged a crowd of students so young that they still had their infant birthmarks. As these students went to buy cold water or iced coffee, they passed the tug-of-war court and saw the competition, then joined in the cheering.

The cheering became a solid wall of sound, as waves of "Go, go!" surged from the court.

The moment of truth had finally arrived. The faces of the five pastors on the Protestant team were deathly pale, as though they had just realized that Mary was about to have a very difficult birth. The pastors had clearly pulled the imams over to their side, and the lead imam's left foot was only two inches from the center line. If the pastors pulled just a little harder, the imam's foot would slide across the line and his team would lose. In the end, however, the imams somehow managed to stand firm. Tian Dongqing's exclamations of "Allah, Allah!" were no longer shouts, but hoarse cries. As the lead imam's foot was about to cross the line, he suddenly knelt down, lifted his fist, and with a bloody shout asked Heaven, "Allah, why do you not help your children?"

At this moment, the imams' feet stopped moving and their bodies once again began to lean back. Meanwhile, the members of the Protestant team began to tire, as though God did not approve of their attempt to pull the imams forward. The competitors and other disciples behind them shouted, "Go, go! Just a little more! Just a little more!" Some rushed down to stand behind Director Gong, and as they watched the tassel approach the center line, they shouted, "Christ! Christ!"

Yahui wasn't sure whom to cheer for. She stood behind a group of nuns and monks, her clenched fists filled with sweat, and after she closed her eyes, an even louder sound surged toward her—as though people had just discovered that a church was on fire. They shouted, "Someone has collapsed! The old imam has collapsed! Stop pulling! The old imam has collapsed!"

By the time Yahui reopened her eyes, the lead imam who had been kneeling had already gotten up and joined the circle of people gathered around the seventy- or eighty-year-old imam Ren Xian, who was lying on the ground amid the crowd. Someone who sounded very experienced shouted, "Don't move him! Let him lie there for a moment!" Everyone quickly stopped shouting, praying, and calling for Allah and Christ. Only the disciples huddled around the old imam on the ground kept softly saying something, until eventually they heard his hoarse voice like wind in a forest, saying, "Children, this is a competition!"

Then Tian Dongqing carried the old imam back to the religion building. The other competitors dispersed, and in the blink of an eye Director Gong was left alone on the court. As Director Gong was about to leave, Pastor Wang, his face still covered in sweat, suddenly came up and solemnly gazed at him.

"I just heard that the real reason you organized this entire competition is for the sake of the book you are writing?" Pastor Wang said. "Director Gong, I could donate some funds to help you publish your book, so that you won't need to mobilize the crowd every week to participate in these competitions."

Director Gong gazed skeptically at Pastor Wang for a moment, then said, "Pastor Wang, you are not a true believer. If you were, you would understand how important it is for different faiths and denominations to become unified and integrated. If you understood how important this unification and integration is, you would recognize that these competitions and other activities that I organize are not merely for the sake of everyone's health." As he said this, he began walking contemptuously toward the area beyond the court, the same way that, several days earlier, Pastor Wang had begun to stalk out of Director Gong's office. However, after taking several steps, Director Gong suddenly stopped and said to Pastor Wang, "Thank you for showing me that the more the religious masters in our program cultivate themselves, the richer they will become. This knowledge is even more valuable to me than the money you have offered to donate. Let's walk back together—we can continue our discussion on our way back."

After saying this, Director Gong left. Pastor Wang initially hung back, like a tree waiting for a storm, but after a moment, he hurried to catch up. Their minds were both filled with different thoughts.

08 Nameless

1

"And, you are . . ."

"You don't need to know who I am; you can simply call me Nameless. As long as you know why I've come, that's sufficient."

"It's because you hope that our . . . that our temple will donate some money to the religious training center?"

"Not the temple. I hope that you yourself will donate."

"Me? . . . Well, I do have some savings."

"So how much will you donate?"

"I can donate ten thousand yuan."

"Do you think it would be worth my while to come find you for only ten thousand yuan?"

"Then how about twenty thousand . . . ? Although I'm an abbot, each month I only receive the frozen salary of a dead monk. Compared with all of you, I am virtually destitute, and although it is true that I don't need to support a wife and children, I still have almost no savings to speak of."

"Do you really not have any savings?"

"I brought my bank passbook with me to Beijing. If you want, I can get it and show it to you."

"Did you hide your passbook inside a sacred book?"

"*Amitābha . . .*"

"Do you really not have to support a wife and children? Do you really not have your own family?"

"*Amitābha . . .*"

"A hundred and twenty *li* east of Daxian Temple, there's a community called Big Li Village. Wasn't that your home before you joined the monastery? On the east side of Big Li Village, there is a small courtyard with a small three-story foreign-style house. Whose woman is the woman who lives in that house, and whose children are her children?"

"*Amitābha . . .*"

"I know you are the Buddhist disciple with the greatest sense of regret. It is only with a sense of regret that one can then cultivate a sense of piety, and it is only because of your sense of regret and piety that I've kept silent about this matter until now. That is, I've come to see you today not because I want Daxian Temple to make a donation, but rather because I want you to voluntarily make a donation on your own behalf."

"*Amitābha . . .* I'll do my best. I can donate all of my savings . . ."

2

". . . Oh! It's you!"

"You're very smart. You immediately recognized me, Nameless, and didn't mistake me for Zhuangzi or Laozi."

"I know why you've come . . . Would you like green or black tea?"

"Out of all the dormitories, yours is the only one with a pine-wood tea tray and tea set. From which of your ancestors did you inherit this purple clay teapot? And don't tell me it's from the Forbidden City, or that it was previously used by the emperor . . . If you were to sell this tea set, the proceeds could cover four years of tuition for ten college students. Even if you sold just the teapot, the proceeds could allow five students to pursue their doctorates at foreign universities."

"He-he . . . Why don't you first have some tea? When you've finished, I'll prepare some of my Da Hong Pao tea, which I've never served to anyone before. Once you've tried it, you'll be able to determine whether other fine black tea is real or fake. Of course, I'm not comparing my Da Hong Pao with the high-quality kind that you might find in the home of a governor or minister . . . If you take a sip, you'll understand. What do you think? Doesn't the taste resemble a thread being sewn through your tongue? I wouldn't exactly call it pain, but it's a kind of tingling. What would you call it? For years, I haven't been able to come up with a way of describing the way this fragrance sticks to the tip of your tongue. When Laozi asked those questions about the union of body and soul—*While you cultivate the soul and embrace unity, can you keep them from separating? Focus your vital breath until it is supremely soft, can you be like an infant? Cleanse the mirror of mysteries, can you make it free of blemish?*—perhaps he was sipping this tea, and as the earthly fragrance coursed through and aggregated in his body, it inspired him to come up with those six statements about virtue? *The Dao gives birth to all things and nurtures them. It gives birth to them but does not possess them. It rears them but does not control them. This is called mysterious integrity.* That is to say, it produces them yet makes no claim to possessing them; it carries them through their processes but does not vaunt its ability in doing so; it brings them to maturity but exercises no control over them—this is the great virtue of the far-reaching person. And if this is the case, why would I, a Daoist master, want to keep this tin of black tea hidden, drinking it only myself and not permitting others to enjoy it? You should take a sip, and another . . . That's right, take a sip, breathe, let it settle, then let the tea sit in your mouth for a moment . . . like this. When you swallow, you should raise your head and gaze up at the sky, the mountains, and the stars. Even if you are in a dark room, you should let your heart generate the sun, the stars, and the entire universe. Only in this way can you attain a true understanding of the tea . . . Wouldn't you like some more? Why don't you drink for a little while longer? You should definitely finish this second cup, because the flavor of the second cup is completely different from that of the first—it is soft and far-reaching, like standing at the edge of a precipice and staring down into the ten-*li*-deep abyss . . . Wouldn't you agree? Or do you think I'm wrong? *Soft fragrance that can be smelled from ten li away, and white clouds that can be seen from a great distance.* If you put it this way, it would be completely wrong to treat Bai Juyi as a Buddhist poet. I feel that his Daoist qualities exceed his Confucian and Buddhist ones. Wouldn't you agree? Could it possibly be otherwise? OK, OK, I'll listen to you. Go ahead."

". . ."

"Don't look at me that way. For better or worse, I'm the host of a famous temple, but when you look at me that way, you make me feel like a bad and lazy little Daoist."

". . ."

"What's wrong?"

". . ."

"The issue . . . Oh, the issue . . . is money. I'll do as you say, and if you tell me to donate, I'll do so. If you tell me to donate a certain amount, I'll do so. Thirty or fifty thousand, one hundred or two hundred thousand—I'll donate as much as you want . . . Right, right, I know that it's not that you are telling me to donate, but rather that I'm donating voluntarily. This is because previously I was of two minds when it came to belief. I coveted money, so now I'll voluntarily donate some. Completely voluntarily!"

3

"Thank you for telling me all this. With respect to the donation, I can offer any amount you like, but if the money is to be used to support inter-sect athletic competitions—and particularly if it is to be used for tug-of-war competitions—then I will adamantly refuse to donate, whether it be on my own behalf or on behalf of my church or my denomination."

"In that case, you won't donate anything at all?"

"Not a cent."

"And you aren't afraid I'll reveal your secret?"

"I'm not afraid . . ."

"If I were to reveal your secret, not only would it impact your ability to become a priest, it could also lead your church and disciples to lose faith in you."

"I know I've sinned . . . In fact, it was precisely because I sinned that I originally joined the church. I decided to become a priest precisely because I knew I had sinned, and this is also why the believers selected me to become their priest. If I didn't know I had sinned, the believers would not have selected me to serve as their priest and to explain the Bible's religious doctrine and its concept of original sin."

"It wasn't the believers who selected you, but rather the organization."

". . ."

"Did you not see that your priest certificate has the organization's stamp?"

"I did see that . . . but I view that stamp as a handprint left by the Pope and the Virgin Mary."

"Well put. However, if I were to retract that stamp, then the Pope's and the Virgin Mary's handprints would also be retracted."

". . ."

"A donation is not an issue of money, but rather of attitude. Do you understand?"

". . ."

"Go ahead and make a donation, even if it is only for ten thousand yuan. If you do, members of other religions will do the same. Protestants, Catholics, and perhaps even some Muslim imams—right now, everyone is watching you . . . Or you could *not* donate, but we'll still announce that you've donated a hundred thousand yuan . . . or fifty thousand . . . or let's just say ten thousand. The problem is not whether or not you donate, but rather whether or not every disciple will obey the organization."

"   . . . "

"How about this? You tell me whether you'll obey the organization, OK? If you say you won't, I'll immediately rescind your priest certificate, and you'll no longer be a priest in the church that is the most symbolically resonant religious site in China. You will no longer be able to serve as a bridge between disciples and the Virgin Mary, nor will you be qualified to stand inside the church and affectionately tell your disciples how much God loves them, how much Mary loves them, and how much Jehovah loves the world that lies beyond the reach of eight hundred bamboo poles . . . This is actually a very small matter, so why make it an issue? Even if God wants the world to be harmonious and people to be healthy, isn't this perfectly consonant with the spirit of the tug-of-war competitions? OK, OK, you don't need to donate much, just ten thousand yuan. Moreover, you don't even need to give us the actual money, because we can simply announce that you donated ten thousand yuan in your capacity as the eldest priest. If you do that, I'm sure I'll see other priests confessing in their rooms. OK, I'm leaving now, so that you can go up to your picture of the Virgin Mary and confess to her. I'm confident that God, Mary, and Jesus will certainly not be displeased with your donation. They are all righteous and broad-minded, and they understand that there is no inherent contradiction between the principle that friendship comes first and competition comes second, on one hand, and God's advocacy of humanity's healthy spirit, on the other. They understand that the principle that friendship comes first and competition comes second is the true covenant that God has given humanity."

"   . . . "

"I'll be leaving now. Given that you've agreed to make a voluntary donation, I'll be leaving . . . There's no need for you to see me
out. If anyone asks, you can just say that I'm Nameless."

". . ."

"There's no need for you to see me out . . . Goodbye."

". . . Goodbye."

4

After Nameless emerged from the religion building, he stood in
front of it for a while. He felt as though his energy were going to
explode right out of his body. He gazed out at the campus, then
went over to the flower pond next to the entrance to the religion
building. The pond was filled with bamboo, and in the mud below
the bamboo there was a mousehole the size of a man's finger. Meanwhile, in the corner of the flower pond there was a bottle of sulfuric
acid that a cleaner had been using to scrub dirt and rust from the
windows. The bottle carried a warning: DANGER! HIGHLY CORROSIVE.
Nameless stood next to the bamboo grove and gazed down at the
mousehole. He abruptly picked up the bottle, twisted off the cap,
and poured half of the contents into the hole. Then he replaced the
cap and put the bottle down, confident that the acid would kill the
bamboo, and gazed out at the field in front of the religion building.
Because the religious training center had money, therefore all the
disciples, under the direction of Director Gong, participated in athletic competitions—including shuttlecock, table tennis, badminton,
and tug-of-war. And because each event offered both a trophy and a
monetary prize, therefore all the disciples participated—including
men and women, young and old. The resulting scene was invariably
as tumultuous as a conference on world religion being held right
in front of the religion building, and the sound of applause and
laughter was always like this season's thunderstorms.

With a smile, Nameless headed over in that direction.

09 Another Nameless

This was a politics class, which no one was permitted to skip. The classroom was located on the first floor and was equipped with sleek, modern stadium seating, like in one of Beijing's five-star movie theaters. Each seat's base and back were made from real leather and sponge cushions, and the back of each seat contained a foldable writing table to be used by the person sitting behind it, like the sort of table on which people make offerings to deities. There was a stage and a screen, and the projection equipment featured the school's most modern technology. The professors and experts invited to the class could sit on the stage and lecture like political leaders, but they also had the option of stepping down from the stage and speaking to the students in a more casual fashion. Given that the students at the religious training center were all either religious masters or were about to become masters, visiting professors and experts would rarely sit on the stage.

October arrived and, with it, National Day. The center picked this national holiday to invite an expert to come lecture on the topic "Where Was New China Born?" Everyone attended, even the elderly religious masters.

The only student who didn't attend was Gu Mingzheng.

Yahui was sitting in a back row on the east side of the classroom, and the seat next to her, where Mingzheng would normally sit, was empty. In the classroom, the curtains were open and the air-conditioning was on, and in the sun's rays it was possible to make out the shape and color of each dust particle. It was the temperature typical of early spring or late fall. The Buddhist, Daoist, and Muslim disciples were all warm in their religious attire and headgear, while the Protestant and Catholic disciples felt a bit chilly in their summer clothing. Fortunately, the latter quickly acclimatized, and after just a few sneezes they were OK. The tree outside the window resembled a painting suspended in midair, and the birdsong was alternately subdued and urgent, like a river that changes flow, now leisurely, now rushing. The walls of the classroom were all a devout shade of white, and in front of each student there was a pen and notebook, as well as a cup of tea and a bottle of mineral water. There were also the computers that almost never left the hands of the younger disciples.

At 8:50, everyone took their seats, and at 8:55 Director Gong entered. At 8:56, he stood on the stage and took roll. At 9:00, he went up to Yahui and quietly asked, "Where is Mingzheng?"

"*Amitābha*," Yahui replied. "I haven't seen him since yesterday."

Director Gong stood in front of her for a moment, then slowly turned and, facing the crowd, announced, "All of the disciples have arrived. No one is missing."

At this point, everyone noticed that a man was standing in the shadows near the classroom doorway. He was thin and straight, in his seventies or eighties, and was standing there like an unearthed sword, with silver hair and a tight face. He was wearing a thin, woolen military uniform, and his chest was adorned with numerous medals arranged in three rows—red, yellow, and green—as though a rainbow had been straightened out and placed on his chest. Below the medals were several first-class gold badges and tags, which dangled from his chest like a crucifix from a Christian's neck. The man slowly entered the classroom, went up to the stage, and gazed out at the disciples who had assembled there. Smiling coldly, he asked, "Is it true that everyone has arrived?"

Director Gong hesitated, then replied with a smile, "Yes, everyone has arrived."

The old man once again gazed at the crowd assembled below the stage. He was silent for a moment, then suddenly shouted, "What about the young Daoist Gu Mingzheng? Gu Mingzheng, please stand up!"

Everyone immediately turned toward Yahui. A dead silence descended upon the classroom, and even the elderly imams, bhikkus, and pastors—who were all older than the expert in revolutionary history—were startled by this scene. They were surprised that this man not only knew Gu Mingzheng's name, but also could tell at a glance that Mingzheng wasn't present. Everyone sensed that something momentous was about to occur, and some disciples made the sign of the cross on their chests while others made Buddhist and Daoist mudras. Most of them, however, simply stared up at the old man and his military medals, as though those medals were the sacred histories and scriptures of his life and of this world.

"I don't believe there is anything more important than today's class." After a brief silence, the old man paced back and forth, then added, "If a young Daoist like Gu Mingzheng, who doesn't even have any rank, can skip class just because he wants to, does that make him more respected than all of the religious masters who are currently sitting before me?

"Does he think he is older than me and all of these religious masters?

"If he isn't coming, then we simply won't have today's class. I can't believe that, when even I, whom national leaders address as 'Teacher,' must attend, this young Daoist is allowed to skip for no reason at all!"

Muttering angrily, the old man gazed at Director Gong as if at a child. "And you dare to claim that not a single student is missing! If that is indeed true, then go find Gu Mingzheng for me. Even if his father really is a governor or minister, he still needs to attend class."

The old man suddenly sat down and shouted again, "Go look for him . . . Go find Gu Mingzheng for me!"

Director Gong turned pale and repeatedly wrung his hands, as though trying to extract something from his palms. "I'll go look for him. He's probably sick in his room. But even if he is sick, he still should have asked to be excused!" With this, Director Gong headed to the door. He kicked the doorframe and stepped outside, then crossed the hallway and proceeded toward the auditorium. When he reached the elevator outside the auditorium, he pushed the button, then took the stairs to the Daoist third floor. He went to room 309 and knocked, shouting, "Gu Mingzheng, Gu Mingzheng!" When there was no response, he continued knocking, and even kicked the door a few times.

"Gu Mingzheng, are you asleep? Are you so engrossed in your dream that you can't wake up?! Hey, Gu Mingzheng, aren't you afraid your beautiful dream might turn into a nightmare?"

10 Gu Mingzheng

Gu Mingzheng had gone to the Babaoshan Revolutionary Cemetery.

In Beijing, Babaoshan is as famous as Tiananmen Square and the Great Wall. The previous day, when the Islamic and Protestant teams were engaged in the tug-of-war competition, Gu Mingzheng had been sitting near the Protestant team's spectator stands. Next to the stands there were a couple of Chinese scholar trees, and in their shadows there were some bricks on which people had been sitting. On one brick there was a discarded newspaper, and when Mingzheng picked it up to fold it into a fan, he noticed that in the lower-right corner there was a short obituary and a photograph, below which there were four Chinese characters in bold:

Portrait of Gu Dongqiang

Because Mingzheng shared a surname with the deceased figure in the photograph, he quickly read the obituary. He learned that Gu Dongqiang had been a revolutionary who had served as both governor and minister, and when he died from illness at the age of ninety, he was the last surviving member of the Red Army, which had been active from 1928 to 1937. The obituary noted that during the period of the Eighth Route Army, Gu Dongqiang had served as the army's underground correspondent. During the War of Resistance against Japan, he was the youngest captain of a guerrilla brigade based in the enemy-occupied areas. During the War of Liberation, he served as the acting commander of the Southwest Theater's Reinforcement Regiment, and after the founding of New China, he served as county head, city mayor, and provincial governor, ultimately attaining the position of national minister and deputy director of some central committee. This illustrious experience attracted Mingzheng's attention, and he quickly finished reading the obituary. Then he looked again at the photograph above the text and felt a jolt of surprise, as though his eye had been pricked by a needle. He noticed that the figure in this black-and-white photograph bore a certain resemblance to himself—particularly the thick black eyebrows, long nose, and upturned smile. His hand began to tremble and blood rushed through his veins like water through a tunnel. As Mingzheng was watching the tug-of-war competition, he gazed up at the sky—feeling that humanity was so close, yet heaven was so far, even as the world continued to advance day by day. It was at that moment that he decided to leave the competition site. His first thought as he was departing was that he should go to the Babaoshan Revolutionary Cemetery to search for this Gu Dongqiang who, until a month earlier, had still been alive in the hospital. If only he could locate Gu Dongqiang, he would be as excited as if he had found his own father, birthplace, and home. Therefore, he left the court and headed toward the university's main gate, and then, relying on a local subway map and a municipal transportation card, he spent an hour and a half making three loops on the subway before finally arriving at Babaoshan in Beijing's Shijingshan District.

Babaoshan was not nearly as mysterious, divine, and inaccessible as Gu Mingzheng had imagined. Like everywhere else, the sunset left a red glow on the ground, walls, and streets, but as he emerged from the subway station and headed north, he felt as though he were entering another world. However, the pedestrians walking back and forth and the vehicles in the street were just as lively as before, as though they were all heading to the market. Mingzheng proceeded forward, and it was only after passing through a mottled and dusty gate that he noticed something unusual. The courtyard beyond the gate was very large and was paved in cement. The steam rising from the ground almost made him pass out. Because it was afternoon, the hearses in the garage were neatly arranged like coffins, and in the distance there was a series of numbered farewell rooms. The numbers ran from one to nine, each room identical to the others. There was a cypress by each entranceway, and above each doorway there was the couplet: "Born for the revolution, died for the people." This inscription was brilliant and meaningful, like a bright cloud hovering overhead. It was now time for people to get off work, but Babaoshan was always very hectic in the morning and leisurely in the evening, so the courtyard currently only had a few workers cleaning up that day's offerings while preparing for the next day's visitors.

Mingzheng headed over to a car parked in front of farewell room number two. Workers were picking up used wreaths that were still intact and placing them in a truck so that they could be resold the next day, while tossing the broken ones into a different truck. As Mingzheng approached, a young man holding a wreath walked over to him, noted his Daoist robe, and asked, "Do you want something?"

Mingzheng took out his newspaper, which was wet from the sweat of his hand, and showed it to the young man. The young man glanced at it, then silently carried the wreath over to the truck. He exchanged a few words with the worker in the truck, then returned and asked to see the newspaper again. He carefully read the obituary, and asked Mingzheng several questions as though interrogating him.

"What is your relationship to him?"

Mingzheng stared in surprise, unsure how to respond.

"I asked you," the young man said, raising his voice, "what is your relationship to him?"

Mingzheng said, "I'm his grandson."

"Where is your residency permit? Please show it to me."

"My grandfather and I were separated when I was young, and I've been searching for him ever since." As Mingzheng said this, he gazed at the young man entreatingly, hoping he would be able to see the resemblance between Mingzheng and the figure in the photograph. However, that young man didn't pay any attention to Gu Mingzheng's face, and instead he just laughed and waved the newspaper. "In this area of the cemetery, which is for provincial-level cadres and corps-level officers, someone like you comes every day to search for some lost relative. In the area for prefecture-level cadres and division-level officers, we get one or two visitors every couple of weeks, while in the area for county-level cadres and regiment-level officers, there may be only one visitor every few years." The young man stuffed the newspaper back into Mingzheng's hand, then turned and headed toward the farewell room. By this point, the sun was already setting in the west, and the light it produced was like life itself, with the final rays containing hints of warmth and softness. Mingzheng stood motionless like a tree. He wanted to leave, but he also wanted to burn some incense. In the end, he resolved to show the newspaper to someone else. He looked and saw a truck drive up and stop in front of the entrance to farewell rooms numbers four and five. This truck was also collecting and installing wreaths, and Mingzheng headed over to it. He heard someone shouting, "Hey, hey . . ." and when he turned around, he saw that it was the same young man who had been heading to farewell room number two. This time the young man approached Mingzheng with a much warmer expression than before.

"Are you a Buddhist monk or a Daoist master?"

Mingzheng took out his student ID, turned it to the first page, and handed it to the young man. The ID had its intended effect. The young man looked at it and then gazed at Mingzheng, as a gentle and kind expression enveloped his face like a velvet curtain.

"Are you really a Daoist master?" he asked. "Is it true that the living Buddha from Tibet is also at your religious training center?" Without waiting for an answer, the young man eagerly continued. "Because we interact with dead people every day, everyone here carries around a Buddhist relic. Tomorrow is National Day, and if you can give me a set of prayer beads consecrated by the living Buddha, I'll help you go to the provincial-level revolutionary households' columbarium to look for your grandfather."

This is what they agreed to do.

As though completing a commercial agreement, they proceeded with a negotiation, signing, and fulfillment. Then, as the man was leaving, he recommended that when Mingzheng returned the next day, he should wear his street clothes instead of his Daoist robes. More specifically, Mingzheng should wear a clean white shirt to look like a student or teacher. The next day was October 1, National Day, and Director Gong had invited an expert to come and discuss the history of the Party and the revolution. When Mingzheng returned to Babaoshan that morning, he was wearing black leather shoes, gray pants, and a white shirt. He resembled not so much a teacher or student, but rather a young person from the countryside who had changed his clothes to visit the city and expand his horizons. This time when Mingzheng saw the young man, he was under a tree in front of the funeral parlor. The young man noted Mingzheng's clothing and smiled, whereupon Mingzheng handed him a rosary bracelet that five monks had caressed until it was shiny. The young man weighed the bracelet in the palm of his hand, as though trying to assess the power of the five monks.

"It's oak," Mingzheng said, and the young man nodded.

Mingzheng then accompanied the young man down Funeral Road, and it was only when they reached a small garden at the end of the road that he noticed that it was a peach blossom garden that seemed to occupy a different universe from the hectic world outside.

There were rockeries, fountains, green plants, and flowers both seasonal and exotic, and on either side of the stone-paved paths there were neatly trimmed dwarf cypresses and holly bushes. The nearly ripe apples were as large as handballs, and as they hung from the trees, they pulled down the branches until they were nearly vertical. Meanwhile, the fruit-bearing branches of the late-ripening pear trees were sticking straight out. There were also various kinds of melons and other vegetables growing in the areas between the fruit trees.

After entering the garden, Mingzheng stood in shock for a moment. He didn't think the scenery was particularly nice, and instead he felt a sense of panic, as though he had gone to a Daoist temple and found a sincere and beautiful bodhisattva. He passed through this green area, and up ahead he saw a row of buildings resembling the Palace Museum, with a roof covered in row after row of glazed tiles, like a freshly plowed garden. Behind the buildings there was a mountain that nearly reached the sky, on which the vegetation appeared nearly black. There were several dozen children standing in line in front of the complex and, in accordance with their teacher's instructions, they were all wearing red scarves. The young man pointed at the group and observed that they were students from Beijing Cadres' Children's Middle School, who had been brought there to attend a revolutionary tradition class, and to search for their grandfathers and great-grandfathers. The young man added, "If you follow them, you'll be able to enter the columbarium and look for your own grandfather."

Like magic—or like glass shards in a kaleidoscope—the young man suddenly seemed to become a completely different person. After the young man finished speaking, he departed, making Mingzheng feel as though everything that had happened was a result of the fact that the prayer beads he had given the young man had not been sanctified by a real living Buddha. *If you don't foresee my Bodhi tree, I won't enlighten you; and if you don't foresee my dark valley, I won't be your Daodejing.* Watching the young man walk away, Mingzheng felt as though he had slipped into a daydream. However, the teacher and students in front of him were indeed real, and he could hear the teacher telling the students to straighten their scarves, take notes, and write a reflection essay after they returned to school. Mingzheng hesitated for a moment, then headed over to them. By this point, the students had already started entering one of the old buildings, so Mingzheng straightened his shirt and joined the end of the group, as though he were a teacher bringing up the rear. As the group entered the building, two students turned and looked at him. They both nodded politely, assuming that he worked in the cemetery.

This wasn't a Buddhist or Daoist temple, but rather the columbarium of the Babaoshan Revolutionary Cemetery. A few workers were inside, and they watched as the students in their white shirts and red scarves poured in and headed to the elevators. One after another, the two elevators sent the students down to the basement. As the women operating the elevators opened and closed the doors, the teacher and students didn't utter a single word during the entire process. Mingzheng was part of the last group of students to enter the elevators, and before he'd even had a chance to look at the propagandistic pictures of the Long March and the Eighth Route Army, the elevator noisily came to a stop. The door opened, and the students ran out to catch up with the rest of the group. Mingzheng was the last to emerge, and when he did, he stood in shock in front of the elevator door.

Constructed within a mountain, the columbarium for high-ranking cadres consisted of multiple terraced levels arranged in a semicircle and was as large as a hill, a mountain, or the Great Hall of the People. Each level was half a meter tall, and was connected to the next by four steps. It seemed as though the entire underside of the mountain had been excavated, leaving an empty dome. The inside of the dome was painted silver-gray, like a starry sky overhead, illuminating the entire columbarium in white light, to the point that even the water droplets on the ground were clearly visible. Mingzheng didn't know how far down the elevator had brought them, but when he looked upward he could see row upon row of tombs and steles, neatly arranged like an army marching toward him. The tombs were made from green marble and were eighty centimeters wide and a meter and a half tall, while in front of each one there was an urn sitting in a foot-high pile of sand and gravel. On each tombstone there was a row of golden, bowl-sized calligraphic characters, with inscriptions like *The Tomb of Department Director XXX* or *The Tomb of Bureau Director XXX*. Above each inscription there was a portrait of the deceased that was twice as large as the inscription itself. At the lower corner of each tomb there was a plastic flower, behind which there was another inscription detailing the deceased's biography and accomplishments in fighting for the revolution.

The columbarium was filled with a gentle humid scent, as the breeze from the air-conditioning blew on people's bones, and workers were erecting a ladder to replace some bulbs in the incandescent lamps overhead. The students accompanied their teacher along a curved path into the center of the structure, as Mingzheng followed ten steps behind. Then he stood at a fork in the path leading toward the tombs, gazing up in astonishment. He stood somewhat hesitantly next to a curved path with a trash can, and after the students distanced themselves from him, he proceeded alone along a path that stepped up the inside of the mountain. He kept looking at the photographs on the tombstones on either side of him. The tombs on the first ten levels all had flowerpots with plastic flowers, but when Mingzheng reached the eleventh level, he noticed that the tombs now had tile pots with specially grown orchids. Although these orchids were not as eye-catching as the plastic ones, they had the advantage of generating a fresh fragrance that permeated the entire area. At this level, the inscriptions on the tombstones no longer read *The Tomb of Department Director XXX* or *The Tomb of Bureau Director XXX*, but rather *The Tomb of Governor XXX* or *The Tomb of Major General XXX*. Despite these subtle changes, as Mingzheng kept his gaze fixed on the tombstone photographs, he began to feel as though the nose in one photograph or the chin in another resembled his own. He placed the newspaper photograph in front of one of the tombstone photographs and compared the two, but upon realizing that they were completely different people, he then headed toward the steps. Following a path through the tombstones and looking to both sides, he advanced several dozen meters until eventually he crossed over from one set of steps to another. In this new area he saw the same tombstones, inscriptions, and specially grown orchids, with the only difference being the numbering of the area and the tombstones—like a misnumbered row of seats in a movie theater.

Mingzheng saw the teacher and students in the distance, and could faintly hear the teacher telling the students to go look for the tomb of their grandfather or great-grandfather, or their grandmother or great-grandmother. The teacher told the students to "search for traces of your ancestors and follow the path of future revolutionaries." When Mingzheng saw the students fan out in search of their ancestors, he felt a hole in his heart. He stood among these tombstones with a vast sense of loss, as though searching for a needle in a haystack, and only after the students had dispersed into the wilderness like mushrooms did he finally pick himself up and head forward. After climbing another eight levels and thirty-two steps, he discovered a new secret. It turns out that on the lowest ten levels the deceased were all department-level officials, on levels eleven to eighteen they were all provincial-level officials and major generals, on levels nineteen to twenty-four they were all vice-ministry-level officials and lieutenant generals, and on levels twenty-five to twenty-eight they were all ministry-level officials and generals. What about above the twenty-eighth level? Would the deceased interred there all be national leaders like emperors and prime ministers?

Mingzheng wandered among the tombs with a mounting sense of excitement and shock. Alternately ascending and descending a few steps, he proceeded upward from the provincial and lieutenant-general area, ultimately reaching an area where not only were there real orchids in front of the tombs, but now each tomb had three or four flowerpots. In this area, the florists had managed to coax the plants into producing white and red blossoms whose fragrance wafted past your nose like a delicate thread. The steps here were no longer bare stone, but rather were covered in red carpet, with mahogany railings on either side. As Mingzheng continued climbing, what surprised him most was not that the titles of the deceased had become more elevated, nor that the size of the tombs and the number of flowers had increased in accordance with the titles of the deceased, but rather that the people appearing in the rare and luxurious photographs—regardless of whether they were graying or already fully gray, balding or already completely bald, whether they wore glasses or not, had a round or square face, a fat or thin face—all invariably bore a certain resemblance to him.

Standing in front of the funeral portrait of a deputy minister, Mingzheng had just noticed that the nose of the white-haired figure was just like his own—light yellow, sharp as a blade, and smooth as though it had just been polished. Just as he was wondering whether this deputy minister might be his own lost father or grandfather, he saw a lieutenant general's portrait right next to the deputy minister's portrait. It was positioned in the center of a tombstone that was one meter wide and one and a half meters tall. As Mingzheng viewed the photograph through the plexiglass frame, he felt the figure was looking at him as though he wanted to speak to him and reach out to him. As he was becoming excited by the figure's look, Mingzheng noticed with alarm that there was a black mole over the lieutenant general's right eye. He looked at the newspaper photograph, then quickly put it away and instead took out a card-sized photograph of himself. Although the backdrop of his portrait was Mount Laojun and the temple where he had lived for twenty years, which made his figure appear small by comparison, he was nevertheless able to make out the black mole over his right eye. His own mole was smaller than that of the lieutenant general, but it was in exactly the same location. Mingzheng reflexively caressed his mole, then touched the one in the photograph. As the cool glass pushed his warm finger away, he placed his own photograph next to the other one and noticed that not only his mole but also his features and skin tone were almost identical to those of the lieutenant general.

Mingzheng stared in shock.

He became convinced that he was in fact the lieutenant general's grandson. He circled around to the back of the tomb to check the lieutenant general's biography, résumé, and accomplishments. Beginning with the first sentence, "Zheng Rengui, from Hong'an County in Hubei Province, born on August 1, 1921," he proceeded to read the entire inscription, including the description of how, during the Long March, the lieutenant general had climbed a snowy mountain, and how, while in Yan'an, he learned how to weave cloth and plant corn. He learned how, during the War of Resistance against Japan, the lieutenant general engaged in guerrilla warfare and bombed many buildings. He learned how, during the War of Liberation, in the battle of Menglianggu in Shandong, the lieutenant general led a battalion and engaged nationalist troops in trench warfare until the battalion's more than three hundred men had all been killed and the lieutenant general himself had been hit by three bullets and fallen unconscious into a river of blood—though, fortunately, reinforcements arrived and he was rescued . . . When Mingzheng reached this point in the biography, he felt a chill run down his spine. He returned to the front of the tomb and once again placed his photograph next to the lieutenant general's. He now felt that his skin tone and the shape of his face actually were not very similar to the other man's after all. After repeatedly comparing the two faces, he eventually decided to go to another area of the columbarium to continue his search. Perhaps he'd be able to find his grandparents in the area for national leaders and officials?

When Mingzheng reached the ministry-level area, one level higher, his pace slowed. There was no fundamental difference between this area and the vice-ministry-level one, except that these tombs were somewhat larger—the same way that, before they died, the people buried here also lived in larger houses. The flowers and steps in front of the other tombs, together with the circular path and its moisture-resistant rubber red carpet, were all made to the same specifications and by the same brands—with the only difference being the area's spaciousness and the materials used for the tombstones. The tombstones in the ministry-level area were not made from domestic stones brought in from a Fujian quarry, but rather had been imported from a special mining district in Australia. The material used for the vaults was even finer than in the preceding level, and the granules in the surface of the tombstones were smaller than grains of rice. Mingzheng didn't know that the main difference between these different kinds of stone lay in their water resistance, nor was he interested in the fact that the marble used for the ministry-level tombs could be carved like jade into utensils and jewelry. Instead, he simply searched the ministry-level tombstones for a photograph to which he could compare his own. He decided that if he was unable to find his own likeness among the ministry-level tombs, he would continue his search at the twenty-eighth level and above. The higher he proceeded, the closer he got to the emptiness and solitude of the mountain peak, and the area of each level became smaller, even as the size of the tombs themselves continued to grow. What would it be like above the twenty-ninth level, or the thirty-second?

Mingzheng continued making his way upward, until he was more than halfway up the mountain. How many levels remained in the top third of the mountain? Whose tombs were at the very top? Could there be an area for national leaders? Given that on every level there were cadres and officials who resembled him, could there also be someone resembling him among the national leaders on the highest levels? Might he be a direct descendant of some national leader?

Perhaps he was a former leader's grandson, or even great-grandson? He felt like a lucky star located far from the center of a family compass; or perhaps he had been exiled altogether, to become a Daoist hiding out in the mountains?

Mingzheng resolved to continue making his way upward until he found someone who resembled himself among the national leaders at the uppermost level. He climbed from the twenty-fifth level to the twenty-sixth, where he saw a row of five ministry-level tombs, including three ministers and two army generals. He inspected them one after another, assuming that he most likely wouldn't find anyone who resembled him more than the lieutenant general on the twentieth level. However, just as he was about to proceed to the twenty-seventh level, he noticed that, on a tomb located next to a cement column connecting this area to the one above it, there was a female minister smiling in his direction. He slowed down and went over to examine her photograph with curiosity. Standing in front of that ministry-level section of the columbarium that was one-third as large as the tug-of-war court, he walked past an area with flowers and recently watered soil. He didn't see a resemblance to the woman, but in the left-hand corner of her one-foot-two-inch-tall photograph, there was a smaller photograph of a man. The latter image, which was only a few inches tall, buffeted Mingzheng like a typhoon. With a square face, large eyes, a straight nose, and lips that were caught between a smile and a frown, the figure looked just like Mingzheng's father.

Once again, Mingzheng stared in surprise. After a while he went around to the back of the tombstone and read a mysterious inscription:

Lin Cuiling, born in June of 1921 in Xiangtan County, Hunan Province, ultimately appointed to a ministry-level position. During the Long March, she was the Red Army's youngest female soldier. Her entire life, she sang, danced, and fought. After New China was founded, she never married. As one of

China's first generation of foreign diplomats, she accompanied
national leaders when they visited foreign countries, conduct-
ing hundreds of negotiations. She was praised by Mao Zedong,
Liu Shaoqi, and Zhou Enlai as "a Chinese flower blooming on
the world stage."

The inscription concluded with this florid line, which was as brief
as an epiphyllum bloom.

Mingzheng stood behind the tombstone, staring at that short
inscription that ended with the phrase "a Chinese flower blooming
on the world stage." He wondered—if she had been a ministry-level
figure, and furthermore never married, then what was her relationship to the man in the photograph attached to the left-hand side of
her funeral portrait, who resembled Mingzheng? What was the man's
name? What had been his occupation and position? What were his
birth and death dates? Although Mingzheng had hoped that this
"Chinese flower blooming on the world stage" could be his grandmother, he realized that something wasn't quite right. Although the
woman never married, there was nevertheless a man's photograph
where her husband's portrait ordinarily would be, and furthermore,
this man—whose name and occupation remained unknown—bore
an uncanny resemblance to Mingzheng himself. This made Mingzheng eager to leave the twenty-sixth level and ascend directly to
the twenty-seventh. Even so, he remained oddly and obsessively
convinced—for no real reason—that this man must be his father,
grandfather, or some other close relative.

Mingzheng wanted to find someone to confirm the name, age,
and origin of this man next to this ministry-level woman. He looked
around and saw that the workers who had been replacing the incandescent bulbs were now heading back down the mountain with their
ladders, tools, and electrical cords. One worker waved to Mingzheng
and shouted, "Hey, you there! Come carry this ladder."

Mingzheng headed over, but after taking a couple of steps, he suddenly thought of something and shuddered, then quickly turned and headed back down. He proceeded faster and faster, to the point that soon he was half running and eventually he could even hear the weight of his entire body pounding down on his knees as he ran.

11 Yahui, Mingzheng, and Jueyu *shifu*

Every day—every single day—nothing particularly notable happened in class. And yet, there was always something . . . and on this day, Yahui had to go to the hospital to visit Jueyu *shifu*.

Originally, Yahui had planned to go the previous day, but instead she had spent the entire day with Imam Tian preparing for an exam on the relationship between Chinese religion and Chinese society, and she didn't finish the examination essays until evening. Yahui had been attending classes at the center on Jueyu *shifu*'s behalf while her *shifu* was in the hospital, and although it was an open-book exam, Yahui still wanted to do as well as possible, so that she could present her scores to her *shifu* as a gift. In return for Imam Tian's help, she bought him some of the university store's most expensive chocolates. In exchange, Tian Dongqing not only explained to her the principle that, throughout history, Chinese religion has always been in the service of society, he also explained the reason—which was not appropriate for writing in her examination booklet—why Chinese religion cannot supersede governmental authority or political power. When it came to this exam topic, Tian Dongqing's knowledge was as vast as the sky, and even if you merely considered the reference books piled on his desk—which included works like *Marxism's Perspective on Religion, The History of Humanity and of Religion, The History of China and of Religion*, and *Chinese Religion's Spirituality and Secularity*—any of these texts could be used to complete three or five examination booklets, thereby allowing a student to become a master-level disciple in a single stroke. Yahui had previously thought that if it weren't for the fact that Tian Dongqing was more than twenty years older than she—and that his wife, Ruan Zhisu, had come with him to the center and was living with Yahui on the seventh floor—she would surely have preferred to spend all her free time with him rather than with Mingzheng.

But now that they were together, Imam Tian merely smiled and said, "For those who have come to study at the center, it's sufficient that they simply pass their exams."

"But I must do right by my *shifu*," Yahui replied. "While she is in the hospital, all the scores I receive will be listed under her name."

Imam Tian explained how the examination booklet should be filled out, and he even wrote the important parts on a sheet of paper and asked her to copy them into her exam booklet. She handed in her booklet in the evening, and the next morning she listened as Nameless, his chest covered in medals, lectured on the topic "Where Was New China Born?" That afternoon, Yahui learned that she had received a score of ninety-eight on the exam, placing first in her class. Meanwhile, Tian Dongqing himself just barely passed with a score of sixty.

Yahui took her first-place score and went to see her *shifu*, and as she was emerging from the religion building, she noticed that the sky was as blue as a three-year-old child's painting. Yahui stood in the courtyard, stared up at the sky, and noticed that the clouds resembled a herd of horses and a lotus pool, then she watched as they drifted away. When she reached the school entrance, she ran into Gu Mingzheng, who was descending from the skywalk. They both stood under the skywalk, and Yahui noticed that Mingzheng's face was flushed and, like a fool, he was wearing a coin-sized Mao badge pinned to his chest. The badge had a bright red base, out of which the golden Mao portrait shone like a picture of the Buddha. Yahui stared in astonishment at Mingzheng and his commemorative badge. Her eyes began to burn and she clasped her hands in front of her chest. After chanting *Amitābha*, she stared at him and asked, "Heavens . . . where have you been the past couple of days?"

Mingzheng patted his badge and replied, "You didn't go out? I went to see the Great Wall and the Palace Museum, and also visited Babaoshan and Tiananmen Square!"

Yahui continued staring at him. She seemed to want to say something, but no words came out. Instead, her lips trembled as she headed to the side of the road.

At this point, Gu Mingzheng turned and positioned himself in front of her, then removed his Mao badge and offered it to her. "Do you want this? They sell for one yuan each in Tiananmen Square."

Yahui continued staring at him without saying a word, then silently lifted her hand to hail a taxi.

"Here, take it . . ." Still smiling, Mingzheng handed her the badge. "Perhaps you might find it useful someday."

Yahui turned away and spat at the ground. She replied coldly, "Gu Mingzheng, the deities up in heaven are watching. Aren't you afraid they might punish you?" As she asked this, a taxi stopped in front of her. She opened the door, got in, and left Mingzheng standing in the school entranceway, like a wad of writing paper tossed out of the school window. Mingzheng gazed scornfully at her taxi, which was the color of a yellow Buddhist robe.

Half an hour after Yahui left Mingzheng, she arrived at Yonghe Temple. She got out of the taxi and stood for a moment in the entranceway, gazing at the palace. She thought how nice it would be if Jueyu *shifu* were the director of Yonghe Temple, because then she could spend her entire life in Beijing's oldest and most vibrant temple, right outside of which there were subways, stores, pedestrians, and the Second Ring Road. Moreover, just as incense smoke can reach the mountains and seas, the temple could collect several hundred, several thousand, or even several tens of thousands of yuan in the merit box every day. Yahui entertained these odd thoughts for a while, and then, as a wave of sadness welled up in her chest, she followed the temple's red wall toward Yonghe Hospital.

There was a small park in the entranceway to the hospital. Occupying a square plot that was over a *mu* in size, the grove contained poplars, elms, cypresses, and pine trees. A brick path wound through the trees like a wet ribbon, and as Yahui quickly walked along this path, she once again saw a miraculous sight, as though she had glimpsed the shadow of a bodhisattva in the sky. Astonished, she stared with her mouth open, and for the longest time she didn't say a word.

She saw her *shifu*, who had not gotten out of bed for more than a month, sitting on one of the garden's stone benches, and next to her there was a wheelchair, a water glass, a sutra, and a cloth for her to wipe her brow. The sun was shining down through a gap between two trees, landing on her face and shoulders, giving her thin and sallow face a red glow. Her *shifu* used one hand to massage the knuckles of the other, then used the other hand to massage the knuckles of the first. "*Shifu!*" Yahui came to a stop and, after staring for a moment, headed over. As she approached, she again stopped and quickly performed a Buddhist ritual and chanted a sutra. Then she knelt down in front of her *shifu*, grasped her hands, and gazed up at her.

"How did you manage to come outside?!"

Upon seeing her *shifu*'s recovery, the annoyance and resentment Yahui had felt toward Gu Mingzheng immediately faded. Up ahead there was another patient and a volunteer nurse, who were laughing and looking in the direction of Yahui and her *shifu*. Jueyu *shifu* turned to Yahui and exclaimed, "*Ya-ya, ah-ah,*" as tears streamed down her cheeks. At this point, Volunteer Nurse Wang—a layperson who had not yet joined the Buddhist order—walked over to Yahui. She warmly remarked that she didn't know what Yahui had told *shifu* the last time she came to visit, but perhaps Yahui had brought a spirit with her, because from that point on it appeared as though some force were protecting Jueyu *shifu*. Shortly after Yahui's previous visit, Jueyu *shifu* had been able to sit up in bed, and the next day she was able to sit up, hold her bowl, and grasp her sutra. By the third day, she was able to hold her own chopsticks and rice bowl and could even take a few steps while leaning against the wall. Now not only could she support herself by leaning against a wall, she could even stand and walk on her own—as though the spirit were supporting her.

As the nurse said this, she pulled Yahui over, and once they were several steps from Jueyu *shifu*, she asked Yahui earnestly, "So, what *did* you tell your *shifu* the last time you came?"

"I told her that the school would no longer hold tug-of-war competitions. I don't think I said anything else."

"Then you should continue speaking to her in the same vein today—because if you don't, all of the progress she has made may be in vain."

With this, the fifty-year-old volunteer nurse headed back to her patient. That patient was a Protestant and had crosses hanging from his neck and his IV bottle. His bottle needed to be changed, so Nurse Wang quickly pushed him back to the sickroom. As she was leaving, Nurse Wang nodded to Yahui, encouraging her to do as she had instructed.

Yahui returned to Jueyu *shifu*'s side, then pushed her and the wheelchair back into the shade. After pouring her *shifu* a glass of water, she suddenly thought of something, then half knelt in front of her, grasped her hand, and giggled like a child. "He-he-he . . . *Amitābha* . . . Such an important matter, and I forgot all about it! Director Gong asked me to send his regards. Last week, he not only discontinued the religious training center's tug-of-war competitions, he also arranged for all students to sing a religious song in their rhetoric class. He said that in this week's class, everyone will sing the Protestant 'Jesus's Hymns,' next week they will sing the Catholic

'Ode to the Virgin Mary,' the following week they will sing the Islamic 'In Heaven There Is Only You,' and the week after that they will sing either 'The Daoist Universe' or our own Sanskrit 'Great Compassion Mantra'!"

Yahui appeared girlish as she said this, as though she were Jueyu *shifu*'s daughter. Yahui repeatedly tapped her *shifu*'s legs with her hands, adding, "Director Gong also told me to ask you—when it comes time for the other disciples to sing our Brahma song, should they first sing the cheerful 'I Am a Lotus Next to the Bodhisattva or the sorrowful 'Great Compassion Mantra'?" Yahui stared at her *shifu*'s face and noticed that it was not only flushed but also slightly plump, and her eyes, which had previously been cloudy, had already started to clear up. In the corner of her eye a tear slowly swelled until it rolled down her cheek.

"I feel it would be best to first have them sing 'I Am a Lotus Next to the Bodhisattva.'" Wiping away her *shifu*'s tear, Yahui added in a childlike tone, "Once they observe the Bodhisattva's compassion and dignity and sing the sorrowful 'Great Compassion Mantra,' they will be able to appreciate the Bodhisattva's goodness, broad-mindedness, and compassion for the world."

Yahui asked, "*Shifu*, do you agree?"

She added, "Even if the world were larger than it is, it would still be no match for the Bodhisattva's compassion, and even if the universe were vaster than it is, it would still be no match for the Bodhisattva's broad-mindedness. We must help disciples from other religions understand the Bodhisattva's capaciousness and essence."

Then she asked, "Isn't that right, *Shifu*? Wouldn't you agree that this is in fact the Way of the Buddhist canon? If so, I'll go tell Director Gong. I'll tell him you recommended that the disciples first sing 'I Am a Lotus Next to the Bodhisattva.'"

Jueyu *shifu* wept, her tears falling like raindrops onto Yahui's head and face. She removed her hand from Yahui's grasp, then hugged her tightly. As if noticing for the first time that Yahui had grown up,

Jueyu *shifu* suddenly realized the spirit of the Buddha. As for Yahui herself, she was increasingly clear about what she should say and what she should do—so she obediently continued saying good things about the relations between the different religions represented in the center. By the time she had almost finished with these happy reports, the sun had again moved toward the west and its heat had begun to fade, as a chill descended on all areas of the hospital's clinic and sickrooms. A breeze blew through the trees in the courtyard, and the sunlight shifted from one side of Jueyu *shifu*'s body to the other, as patches of sunlight moved away from her body and shoulders and instead began to fall like sacred rays on her head—making her face, which had come to resemble a withered date, return to the appearance it had had back in July and August. Her face regained a jujube-colored glow and the corners of her mouth contained the hint of a smile. It looked as though she were about to say something, though no words escaped her lips. Instead there were just a few drops of spittle around her mouth. Yahui wiped her *shifu*'s mouth and smoothed back her hair. At this point, the hospital's holy bell tolled, and the sound melodiously drifted out and back again—as though a river were flowing through the sky next to the Second Ring Road. Yahui gazed up at the celestial river and said, "*Shifu*, you will recover soon, and if you were to remain in Yonghe Temple as a host, I would be able to stay in Beijing for the rest of my life." Jueyu *shifu* looked up, listened to the tolling of the bell, then turned in that direction. She uttered a string of *ah-ahs* and *ya-yas*, as her gaze fell on a small bag hanging from the right side of her wheelchair.

Yahui removed a pen and notebook from the bag and handed them to her *shifu*, who placed the notebook on her knee and proceeded to write a string of crooked characters—including some that were larger than a fingernail and others that were smaller than a bean. When she finished, Jueyu *shifu* handed the page to Yahui, who immediately turned pale.

"Really? Are you sure you want to do this?"

Yahui stared at her *shifu* for a moment and repeated the question a couple more times. Only after her *shifu* nodded emphatically did Yahui accept the fact that she had in fact made up her mind—like the Buddha deciding to give his sacred lotus pad to a member of another religion who had previously harmed him.

12 Yahui

Take 100,000 yuan from Jing'an Temple's 220,000 yuan and donate it to the religious training center. Director Gong may use these funds to support the singing of religious songs.

This is what Jueyu *shifu* wrote to Yahui, and now this sheet of paper was in Yahui's pocket. She didn't know how many years it had taken the temple to raise 220,000 yuan, or how much incense the temple had needed to burn in the process. The funds had originally been raised to help repair the temple, but now Jueyu *shifu* had decided to donate a hundred thousand of it.

At six that evening, Yahui had left her *shifu* and emerged from the hospital. She was still holding the sheet of paper with her *shifu's* messy writing on it, but she yearned to crumple it up and toss it into a roadside trash can. When she reached a trash can, however, she merely glanced at it and kept walking.

Usually, if Yahui wanted to eat something tasty, her *shifu* would ask her, "Have you forgotten that controlling one's appetite is Buddhism's most fundamental religious precept?" In Xining there was a restaurant that could prepare vegetarian fare that was indistinguishable from meat, but every time Yahui told her *shifu* she wanted to go there, her *shifu* would pull a long face, make a Buddhist mudra in front of her chest and, as though either cursing or praying, mutter,

"*Amitābha* . . . Pure heart! Pure heart!" It was as if Yahui had committed a great sin, or as though her heart were full of refuse.

The sun set in the west, and twilight slowly fell. In an alley off Yonghe Street, there was a lively area full of the smell of food. For some reason, while gripping that sheet of paper filled with horizontal lines, Yahui suddenly developed a strong urge to eat and drink something. She wanted to spend lots and lots of money, so that she could quickly spend down the vast sum that was written on the sheet of paper. Furthermore, as she thought about eating, her stomach began to rumble. She scanned the shops on either side of the alley, and although initially she only saw one or two small eateries, as she proceeded farther down the alley it seemed as though both sides of the road were filled with fragrant restaurants. The smell of food was as strong as in Kumbum Monastery during tourist season. As Yahui's pace slowed and her gaze remained fixed on the sides of the alley, she noticed a Lanzhou noodle restaurant, next to which there was a stall selling Xining meat buns. Seeing that there were also northwestern restaurants here, Yahui reflected for a moment, then stuffed the sheet of paper into the pocket of her robe and headed over to the stall. In a soft voice, this Buddhist nun asked, "Do you have any pork?"

"Well, we certainly don't sell human meat!"

"Pork is quite tasty, but actually this isn't for me. I'm getting it for someone else. Could you add some extra pork to the meat bun?"

"Do you want lean or fatty pork?"

"Please add some extra lean red pork to one of the buns, and some extra fatty white pork to the other. I'll pay for the extra meat."

The chopping of the knife sounded like the cheerful rhythm of Sanskrit music, and in the blink of an eye the block of lean meat had been diced into small cubes, while the slab of fatty meat had been reduced to paste. The fragrance was so thick Yahui could see it swirling around in front of her as it tickled her nose. However, even her nose didn't care how appealing the dish was—she simply wanted to gulp it down. There were some other customers at the stall, and as they ate their food they stared in surprise at her nun's robe and close-cropped hair. Yahui, in turn, repeatedly nodded to them and explained, "I'm getting this for someone else, I'm getting this for someone else," whereupon the other customers would apologize with embarrassment and look away. Yahui packed up the two meat buns, which were still hot to the touch, into a couple of plastic bags. Then she handed over twenty yuan, put the buns in her pocket, and left the stall.

Next, she entered the Lanzhou noodle shop next door, where there were fewer customers than there had been at the meat bun stall. Inside, the counter functioned as the cook's workspace, and the tables on the other side were the customers' eating area. Although the restaurant was rather simply decorated, everything appeared new and clean, and the yellow tables and chairs still smelled of fresh paint. Of the shop's eight tables, six were already occupied, but in the corner, where the light was dim, there was an empty two-person table. More than ten pairs of eyes were observing Yahui—curiously taking in her close-cropped hair, her nun's habit, and her baby face. Yahui gazed back at them and smiled, then she made a Buddhist mudra and bowed. She wasn't sure whether or not she uttered a Buddhist chant, but she certainly felt as though she had. Then she turned to the woman at the counter, who had been staring at her, and said, "Sister, could you give me a bowl of noodles, without meat? I only take vegetarian broth. I'll give you the money for the meat, and then you could give me some extra vegetables. OK?" The woman at the counter nodded, and the other customers seemed to relax as they resumed their meals. The customers looked away from Yahui as though pulling shut a row of curtains.

Yahui sat down at the table in the corner, and gave no more thought to the Buddhist scriptures, strictures, or the Bodhisattva, nor to the people behind her or the black flies on the wall in front of her. To avoid inviting company, Yahui discreetly pushed her table against the wall, making it appear too cramped for anyone else to sit there. When her bowl of noodles arrived, she saw that it was in fact a bowl of silk noodles with clear broth and extra vegetables, with green onions and vegetable leaves floating in the soup. The hot room was foggy and chaotic, as though the world were still in a period of confusion before the arrival of the deities. The sound of people behind Yahui sipping and slurping their noodles flowed like a spring. Sometimes the buzzing of the air conditioner drowned out those slurping sounds, and at other times the air conditioner was drowned out by the slurping. A man and woman behind Yahui were leaving the shop hand in hand, and as they passed they seemed to glance in her direction and say something. What they said was not important, but what *was* important was that now there was no longer anyone sitting directly behind Yahui. Given that now no one was watching her, no one would notice that, while eating her vegetarian noodles, this young nun was secretly removing a meat bun from her pocket.

The bun's fragrance was exquisite, and the steam had left a thick layer of condensation on the surface of the plastic bag—such that people outside wouldn't notice that this was actually a meat bun and instead they would only see a couple of baked rolls. To prevent other customers from smelling her meat buns, Yahui first ate the lean one. It was less fragrant, though the odor still escaped as soon as she opened the bag, so she hurriedly clasped it shut again, to trap the fragrance inside. She instinctively glanced behind her, but saw that all the other customers were either eating or chatting and minding their own business. She was reminded that the good thing about Beijingers is that almost nothing ever surprises them—which is why Beijing is the perfect place for a religious disciple wearing secular clothes. Yahui slowly reopened the bag and leaned over, but rather than bring the bun up to her mouth, she instead extended her lips into the bag until they touched the bun and the meat inside.

Yahui took a bite, then quickly closed her mouth and returned the bun to her pocket. The fragrance knocked against her teeth and leapt into her mouth, making her upper jaw tremble to the point that she had no choice but to place her tongue on the roof of her mouth to blunt the sensation. However, the fragrance ran along her gums like air flowing out of a deep valley and over the mountains. The fragrance was as dark red as the lean meat itself, like overflowing pink clouds filling her palate and throat. She couldn't bring herself to immediately swallow the bite she had taken, and instead wanted to let the flavor linger in her mouth until it permeated all the way to her scalp, like *qi* circulating through her body. She had bitten off a crescent-shaped piece and now her tongue pressed it to the roof of her mouth, like a screw and its corresponding nut or like a sacred text and its corresponding disciple. Everything was just right—sacred and solemn. After savoring the intense taste, Yahui began to chew, and the tips of her teeth began to tremble and her stomach began to rumble, as though several cracked wooden doors were opening up for her. Afraid that the other customers would hear, Yahui began devouring the bun as though she hadn't eaten anything in days. Without even waiting for her teeth and the bun to exchange a few polite words of greeting, she gulped down the first bite so that it would block the sound of her stomach rumbling.

Then she took a second bite.

And a third.

She leaned over and took another sip of the noodle broth, then turned and glanced behind her. Only then did she feel the world was safe and at peace. Although that evening the streets were full of people, everyone was busy doing their own thing and no one was particularly interested in what anyone else was doing. Yahui took one bite after another of her noodles and her meat bun. She repeatedly stirred her bowl with her chopsticks, then inserted her mouth into the bag in her pocket. Over and over, a gentle elegance, like the footsteps of students in a morning class outside the temple, slowly returned to her body. She would sip some soup, eat some noodles, and chew some of her meat bun, as though reciting each word of a sacred sutra. She paused when she had to pause, and resumed when she could resume. Only after she had finished half of the lean meat bun did she slowly close the first bag and open the second one.

Yahui devoured the large bowl of noodles and the two meat buns. By the time she finished she was stuffed, but felt that if she were to buy another meat bun, she probably could have eaten that as well. At this point, she suddenly remembered she was a jade nun—a Buddhist nun who had first entered the order as an infant eighteen years earlier. Controlling one's appetite is Buddhism's most important precept, and therefore, after Yahui emerged from the restaurant and took a taxi back to the university, she first walked around campus for a while, and only after her stomach had relaxed did she slowly return to the religion building.

13 Gu Mingzheng

That night, something rather unusual occurred.

Yahui returned to her room and proceeded to burn some incense for the Bodhisattva. After offering three prayers, she washed her face and brushed her teeth. As she was getting ready for bed, she heard footsteps in the hallway, as though someone were trying to ascend to the seventh floor but instead found their way blocked. She heard people arguing and jostling, together with shouts and prayers. The footsteps approached—*dong dong*—and then stopped right in front of her door. Just as Yahui was wondering what was happening, she heard a knocking sound. She opened the door and saw Gu Mingzheng, his lips purple with anger. Standing there as though about to rush inside, he shouted, "Yahui, you wear a nun's habit like an angel, demonstrating your respect for the Bodhisattva's compassion, but didn't I also wear that medallion on my chest even as you let others insult my Daoist faith?!"

Shouting loudly, Mingzheng blocked Yahui's doorway while drenching her face in spittle. A moment earlier Jueyu *shifu*'s fellow disciple and leader of the center's Buddhist nuns' group, Shuiyue *shifu*, had been struggling to prevent Mingzheng from coming up to the seventh floor, and now she—together with two Daoist nuns and Imam Tian's wife, Ruan Zhisu—was standing behind Mingzheng and staring at Yahui. Rather than chant *Amitābha*, Yahui instead asked,

"What's wrong? What's wrong?" In the ensuing tumult, Yahui learned that Mingzheng had gone to walk around the campus after lunch, and upon returning home he had found that hanging in his doorway there was a plastic bag containing several pieces of dog shit and a copy of the Daodejing. He now held out the bag—as though he wanted to throw it away as quickly as possible, but hadn't decided where to toss it. In the end, he simply stood in Yahui's doorway and demanded, "Who did you tell? Give me their names, so that I can throw this whole damned thing at them and their deities."

Yahui didn't reply. Instead, she simply stood there with a look of confusion. More and more people gathered in the hallway, as the "Male disciples must stop here!" rule had been effectively suspended. More than a dozen Muslim and Protestant disciples had come up from the lower floors and were now in the hallway watching this extraordinary confrontation between a Buddhist and a Daoist disciple. Eventually everyone fell silent, to the point that it almost seemed as though Mingzheng and Yahui were the only people present.

Yahui continued standing there motionless, as the smell of dog shit permeated the entranceway. She wanted to hold her nose, but also felt she should make a Buddhist mudra. In the end, she simply held her hands below her chest, neither raising nor lowering them. After a shocked silence, she seemed to remember something. She turned and looked at the women standing behind Mingzheng and saw that two of the Daoist nuns had turned pale, while Ruan Zhisu had a strange smile. Yahui looked away, then brought both hands up to her chest. After chanting *Amitābha*, she said something that astounded all the humans and deities in attendance: "If I did tell anyone, you're welcome to throw that bag in my face. However, you should be grateful to whomever hung this in your doorway, because they must truly love your religion!"

After saying this, Yahui took a step backward, glanced at Shuiyue *shifu*'s inscrutable expression and Ruan Zhisu's grin, then shut her door—effectively pushing the commotion out of her mind.

The lamplight bathed her room and the porcelain statue of the Bodhi-sattva in a half-golden light, and as Yahui stood in the light, like a willow in the middle of spring, it was unclear whether she was about to sprout a new set of leaves or continue angrily standing there, waiting for future wind and sunlight. After a while, she once again heard footsteps outside her door, and after the footsteps faded away she turned and walked back toward the deity, and toward her bed.

14 Tian Dongqing and Ruan Zhisu

Shortly after this incident concluded, there was another one.

The married couple Tian Dongqing and Ruan Zhisu had a disagreement. Originally, Allah had asked all Muslims to live as a single family, with disciples treating one another as brothers, and spouses treating one another as siblings—such that all fractures could be bridged by faith. On this day, however, Imam Tian contravened Allah's wishes and had an argument with his wife.

On the day in question, Tian Dongqing and Ruan Zhisu sat next to each other in class, and after class they left together. When they arrived at the halal canteen, however, they exchanged words. At this point, Ruan Zhisu was still smiling, as though she were telling a joke. Imam Tian, however, suddenly stopped in his tracks, his face purple with rage. He shouted, "Was it really you?" He stared at her for a moment, then angrily kicked a broken brick in the road. Finally, he turned and headed into the canteen.

Ruan Zhisu's smile faded, and her face turned sallow. She was already thin and petite, and always wore the sort of floral shirt favored by women in the northwest. Blue flowers on a white background framed her sallow face—as though some dead leaves had fallen into a clump of vegetation. She there for a while, before going in to join Imam Tian.

At the dining table, Tian Dongqing and Ruan Zhisu sat face-to-face. Ruan Zhisu moved a piece of mutton from her bowl to his, whereupon he moved it back to hers. Ruan Zhisu stared at her husband for a while, then pursed her lips, straightened her waist, and once again moved the mutton to his bowl.

Tian Dongqing angrily slammed down his chopsticks, whereupon Ruan Zhisu slammed hers down even more forcefully. All the imams and disciples turned to look at them. Old Imam Ren Xian, who was sitting next to the window, coughed and used his gaze to transmit the Quran's strictures and the word of Allah, in an attempt to stop the couple from quarreling in public. The entire canteen fell silent, as the other diners who had previously been eating and talking—including disciples of other religions and vegetarian students—all turned to stare. Others who were carrying over the food they had just purchased gathered around to watch the commotion, waiting for an even more dramatic outburst. The midday October sunlight poured in through the southeast-facing window, illuminating the canteen like sunlight illuminating Allah. The light shone down on Tian Dongqing and Ruan Zhisu and onto their table, making it look as though they were sitting in the middle of a stage. Even more people looked in their direction and crowded around. When the old imam saw the crowd growing in size, his gaze expressed the moral instructions of Muhammad as he looked sharply at Tian Dongqing again, transmitting Allah's meaning with his eyes. After receiving the imam's gaze, Tian Dongqing didn't say a word. Instead, he glanced at his wife, then got up and left the table.

This incident quickly passed, as though a couple's quarrel were a common occurrence. After Tian Dongqing left, everyone returned to their meals, and as they ate, they discussed topics such as which of the center's teachers and lecturers taught well, how Allah leads the masses in accordance with God's will, and how the Jews were driven out of Jerusalem. After everyone finished their lunch, the first disciples to return to the center's sixth floor heard Tian Dongqing in his room shouting, crying, and breaking things. They pounded on his door, shouting, "Imam Tian! Imam Tian!"

Tian Dongqing's room fell silent—as though there were no one inside. The students and disciples stood outside for a while, then eventually returned to their rooms.

That afternoon, Tian Dongqing went alone to the classroom. Although this class featured one of the center's experts lecturing on the origins and subsequent development of Islam in China and all the other students were present, Ruan Zhisu did not attend. During the break everyone went to their rooms to refill their teacups, while also taking the opportunity to bow and pray. For some reason, Tian Dongqing and Gu Mingzheng were silently walking together and, one after the other, they both proceeded upstairs. When they reached the third floor, Gu Mingzheng noticed a red plastic bag hanging on the door to his room. He stared in surprise, then carefully took the bag and opened it. Inside, he found some apples and oranges, as well as a new copy of the Daodejing. The smell of fruit resembled the breath of a spirit, leaving the Daodejing enveloped by the fragrance like Laozi sleeping beneath a fruit tree. Hurriedly looking back, Gu Mingzheng saw Tian Dongqing standing in the doorway to the stairwell, smiling oddly at him before heading upstairs.

15 Mingzheng and Director Gong

What followed was not quite orthodox, the same way that whenever the religious training center held its class on "Exchanged Reading of the Scriptures," Daoists would read the Bible, Buddhists would read the Daodejing, and Protestants would read the Quran. On the logic that reading encourages tolerance, every disciple was asked to read at least one sacred work from another religion. The center operated along a similar logic, so when there weren't enough people available to work, the center would simply invite one of the disciples to step in—and in this case it was Gu Mingzheng. It was said that Mingzheng wanted to serve as a secretary in the National Religion Association after he finished his training. Accordingly, his appointment in the training center's office could be seen as a kind of preparation for that future position.

Naturally, Mingzheng agreed to become one of the center's office workers.

Director Gong gave Mingzheng the key to an office right off the hallway, where he was expected to answer the telephone, take notes, and prepare a bottle of hot water for Director Gong before he came to work. Mingzheng was also expected to send signed receipts to the finance office and reimbursements to the teachers. Whenever someone needed to make some copies, Mingzheng would turn on the copy machine, and whenever Director Gong needed to draft an announcement or some other document, he would first use a fountain pen to write out the text by hand on a piece of A4 paper, whereupon Mingzheng would transcribe and print it, then stamp it with the center's official stamp—thereby making it legally binding.

The center had eighteen staff members in all. It didn't have an associate director, but it had five offices for the teaching and study of religion, each of which had someone who worked as both a teacher and an office director. When it was time for class, the teachers would go to class with their handouts, and when class was over, they would collect the handouts and leave. At the end of the month, when rice, cooking oil, towels, and bedsheets were distributed, the teachers could go to the center to chat and joke with each other, but the rest of the time they would remain at home reading and strolling around, taking their children to school, and buying and trading stocks, and they would rarely come to the center. Given that there weren't enough staff at the center, Mingzheng became Director Gong's assistant.

Mingzheng was officially transferred to the center in late October, and by November he was already as familiar with the center's work as he was with the rules of Daoism. One day, Director Gong was in his office writing his *Synthetic Treatise on Tug-of-War and the Contradictions Between Religions*, when Mingzheng entered and said with a smile, "Excuse me, Director Gong."

Director Gong looked up.

"Jueyu *shifu's* health has improved," Mingzheng continued. "I hear that now she can get out of bed and walk around."

Director Gong looked at him with a strange expression.

"She started to improve immediately after hearing that the center has decided to discontinue its tug-of-war competitions. If the center has really discontinued the competitions, and will no longer host inter-sect athletic competitions, then . . ."

With a frigid gaze, Director Gong threw his fountain pen onto his desk.

"Daoist Master Gu . . . Assistant Gu, this matter does not concern you."

Mingzheng's smile froze. He bowed, hesitated for a moment, then quickly withdrew from Director Gong's office.

16 Yahui

Time passed like smoke or water, and soon it was November eighteenth. Yahui's period came again, causing her considerable pain, but also a sense of comfort. She became fatigued, though she continued her daily routine: attending class, eating her meals, and making weekly trips to Yonghe Hospital to visit her *shifu*, Jueyu. Whenever she returned to her room she would burn incense, make papercuts, and ponder the volume *Encyclopedia of Chinese Papercutting Techniques*, from which she learned yin and yang papercutting techniques, as well as flowing-stream, ink-splash, and knife-slicing papercutting techniques. The topic of the papercut images, meanwhile, still revolved around Guanyin and Laozi, but because the papercutting lines were finer than before and involved multiple layers, Yahui's hand and the scissors became inseparable. She proceeded to produce a new story:

1. Oh, Guanyin has grown into a big girl.

2. Ah, Laozi has also reached adulthood.

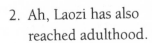

3. This way, they can each have the coming-of-age ceremony that they need.

4. Can two trees experience love at first sight?
   If not, then why does the world have forests?

5. Heading toward a tree is heading toward love.
   Therefore, when two trees fall in love, it is just like
   when Guanyin and Laozi fall in love.

6. If two trees can fall in love, why can't two people also experience love at first sight?

7. When they are supposed to hold hands, they hold hands, and it is only after they do so that their love begins to shine.

8. After coming together, it is necessary to separate, and it is at this point that the practice of using geese to deliver letters emerges.

9. After they exchange countless letters, it is time for them to marry. The act of escorting a bride to the bridal chamber is humanity's most beautiful event.

102

10. Because humanity has
    trees, it also has houses;
    and because it has houses,
    it also has villages and the
    world.

11. An ancient bridal chamber.

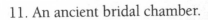

12. All marriages are simply a
    process of putting new wine
    into old bottles. New wine
    is very fragrant, and do we
    not grow up simply so that
    someday we might have a cup
    of this new wine?

13. Exchanging cups to drink and exchanging happiness to conjoin.

14. Exchanging happiness to conjoin, wedding chamber filled with candles. Such a beautiful life. Who doesn't think so? Everyone thinks so.

15. A happy blossom blooms.

17 Yahui, Mingzheng, and Director Gong

The day after her period ended, and just as Yahui was beginning to feel a bit better, she received a call from the hospital. The call was from a volunteer, who reported that not only was Jueyu *shifu* now able to get out of bed and walk around, she could also use the bathroom on her own and fetch herself hot water from the kitchen. She could even say a few words, and the utterance she repeated most often was, "Gong, Director Gong . . . is good, a good man . . . he, he stopped . . . he canceled the tug-of-war competitions!" The hospital recommended that Director Gong come and talk to Jueyu *shifu* about how he had decided to end the competitions. That way, in a few days—or at most a week or two—Jueyu *shifu* could hopefully be discharged and return either to the school or to Jing'an Temple to recuperate.

Yahui got out of bed, brushed her teeth, and washed her face. She applied some facial lotion, and while rubbing it in she proceeded to the first floor. There, she knocked on the door of the center's administrative office and asked where everyone was. Then she went to the conference room, where she found the center's director, instructors, and professors distributing rice and peanut oil, as well as red envelopes. The recipients were weighing their envelopes in their hands and giving Director Gong the thumbs-up. Yahui stood in the entrance to the conference room and bowed, clasping her hands to her chest and lowering her head, whereupon all the teachers stopped laughing and looked around warily. Yahui realized she had arrived at a rather inopportune moment, so she backed away while calling out to Director Gong, then returned to the first-floor hallway.

When Director Gong emerged from the conference room, Yahui told him about Jueyu *shifu*'s condition and the hospital's suggestion. To her surprise, Director Gong immediately agreed, like a flower blooming in season. "I'll go see her . . . In fact, I would have gone sooner if I hadn't been so busy." Director Gong added, "I'm happy to do anything I can to help Jueyu *shifu* regain her health." Then, holding a couple of books, he headed toward his office, as though preparing to leave with Yahui. He opened the door and went inside, leaving her standing in the doorway waiting for him. But after a while he waved to her, gesturing for her to enter.

This was Yahui's first time inside Director Gong's office, and as she stepped through the doorway, she stood there gazing curiously at the ten-square-meter room, which contained a black sofa and a large bookcase. In an empty space on the bookcase, there was a group photograph of the teachers, together with a trophy and certificate. Director Gong was sitting at his desk in the middle of the room, and when he saw Yahui he said: "It suddenly occurred to me—if your *shifu* recovers and returns to the center, I'm afraid you won't be able to continue attending class in her place."

Yahui stared at him.

"Do you want to remain in Beijing and stay at the school?"

Yahui nodded.

"Are you really a jade nun, and under the age of eighteen?"

Yahui replied, "I'm already eighteen."

Director Gong said, "I'm asking you seriously, do you want to join the Party?"

Yahui stared in surprise. "Which party?"

Director Gong laughed. "What other party is there?"

"But I'm a disciple." Then Yahui repeated more loudly, "Director Gong, I'm a disciple!"

The room fell quiet. It was as though the air had been sucked out of it, leaving everything frozen in place. Fortunately, this pause lasted only for a moment, whereupon Director Gong preemptively broke the silence. He smiled, leaned back, and proclaimed, "I'll just go ahead and say it—I think that if a disciple who has undergone religious training joined the Party, that would definitely be major news and that disciple would be our center's prized asset." Then, rather oddly, he added a few words complimenting Mingzheng, remarking that the young Daoist was young and smart, and that his heart was as lively as though it were mounted on a ball bearing. Director Gong stood up and cleared away the books on the table, placing a copy of *Religious Structures Under the Socialist System* on the bookshelf, then he leafed through a copy of *On the Possibility of Integrating All Religions* before placing it in his bag. He told Yahui to wait for him at the school's east gate, explaining that he was going to clean up and then would go visit Jueyu *shifu* in the hospital.

Yahui left Director Gong's office as though emerging from a cage.

18 Yahui, Mingzheng, and Jueyu *shifu*

Yahui was waiting for Director Gong in the school entranceway, but the person who arrived was instead Mingzheng.

Mingzheng walked over from a grassy area, passing two public education buildings. The early fall weather was very brisk, and as Yahui waited she looked west and saw the ink-colored Xiang Mountain ten *li* away. She reflected that at some point she should climb Xiang Mountain to see how Beijing's mountains differed from those in Qinghai. She had already visited the Great Wall and the Palace Museum, and now she wanted to visit Xiang Mountain's Biyuan Temple. As she was standing in the entranceway gazing at the trees on the mountaintop, she saw Mingzheng approach. He was wearing black leather shoes, gray pants, and a moon-colored Chinese jacket with a row of buttons on the front that were as bright as mirrors. A smile appeared on his face, as though the period since their squabble had disappeared in a flash of light.

"You're waiting for me . . ."

Surprised, she said, "But you're a Daoist and I'm a Buddhist—we need to remain separate like river and well water."

Mingzheng cracked a smile. "Have you forgotten that I'm the director's assistant? An assistant stands in for the director. Today the director is busy, so he sent me to visit your *shifu* on behalf of the center."

Yahui stared at Mingzheng in surprise, then glanced again to the side of the campus road and asked, "Is Director Gong really not coming?"

"Associate Professor Huang wanted to invite Director Gong out for a meal, to offer his apologies. Director Gong couldn't get out of it, so he sent me in his place."

Without replying, Yahui looked at the campus, at Mingzheng, and at the other people around them. A gloomy expression flickered across her face as she realized that Director Gong wasn't coming, and she became concerned that this might be because she hadn't confirmed that she would be willing to join the Party. She cast Gu Mingzheng an angry glance and, with a frown, asked, "Did Director Gong ask you whether you would join the Party?"

Mingzheng didn't say that he had, nor did he say that he hadn't. Instead, he glanced at Yahui as though to ask, *And what of it?*

"Did you agree?"

"I told him I would think about it."

They both fell silent, letting the flood of people sweep past them. There were some couples where the boy had his arm around the girl's waist or shoulder, and others who couldn't resist stopping in the middle of the road to kiss. The sky was high, but without a trace of a deity, and the clouds were sparse, without any discernible shape. Yahui and Mingzheng simply stood there, gazing at one another with a combination of warmth and coldness. Eventually a taxi drove up and someone got out, whereupon Yahui got into the taxi alone and headed toward Yonghe Hospital.

The trip to the hospital was uneventful, and it was as though the path had been cleared by the deities. Half an hour later, Yahui got out of the taxi in front of the entrance to the hospital and headed toward Jueyu *shifu*, who was exercising in the hospital's tree grove. Jueyu *shifu* was under a pair of cypresses with a volunteer nurse and her wheelchair, on the back of which there were a pair of crutches. Yahui had originally planned to explain to her *shifu* why Director Gong could not make it this time. She would claim that Director Gong had to attend a meeting, but that he would definitely come another day. She would explain that although Director Gong couldn't come in person, he nevertheless had asked Yahui to inform Jueyu *shifu* that the school's inter-sect athletic competitions had been halted and the tug-of-war competitions had been discontinued. As she arrived at the grove, she was still trying to figure out how to tell these lies as though they were the true word of the deities. She heard familiar footsteps behind her, and when she turned around, she saw Mingzheng rushing up with a couple of bags of apples and bananas. She was surprised that he had managed to catch up with her, given that she had left first and he had even stopped somewhere to buy some fruit.

And yet, somehow he was already there.

Yahui stopped and stood on the side of the road, gazing at the sweat on Mingzheng's brow. This time, Mingzheng didn't smile, and instead said in a soft voice, "No matter how fast the Buddhist's pace might be, it is no match for that of Laozi." He placed a bag of bananas in front of Yahui, then extended his words into the realm of the sacred: "The Bodhisattva walks with her feet, while Laozi walks with his heart." Seeing that Yahui was not accepting the bag, Mingzheng stuffed it into her hands.

"I can be reimbursed for this—now, I, too, get to apply for reimbursements."

What followed was like going up a series of steps, and no matter how many twists and turns there might be, one would inevitably continue proceeding upward.

With Mingzheng in the lead and Yahui behind him, they followed a stone-paved path into the grove. After going around a turn, they saw the pair of old cypresses in front of them. A volunteer nurse was supporting Jueyu *shifu* as she tried to walk, but when they saw Yahui and Mingzheng, they stopped and looked in their direction. With the bag of fruit in hand, Mingzheng went to greet them and announced, "Ah, *Shifu*, I always said that the Bodhisattva wouldn't leave you lying paralyzed in bed!"

Jueyu *shifu* and the volunteer nurse both stared at Mingzheng's young face, as though waiting for Yahui to introduce him. Before she had a chance to do so, however, Mingzheng took the initiative and introduced himself. He explained that he was a Daoist master and served as the assistant to the center's director. He explained that Director Gong had an important meeting that he couldn't get out of, and therefore had sent him, Mingzheng, to visit Jueyu *shifu* on behalf of the organization. He said that when the organization's students heard that Jueyu *shifu* was ill, they all felt as though their hearts had dropped. As he was speaking, Mingzheng pulled an envelope from his pocket, from which he removed a letter with an official stamp. Yahui initially assumed this was a condolence letter from the organization, but it turned out to be a notification announcing the abolition of inter-sect athletic competitions.

The situation was like a theatrical performance in which everything was fake and artificial, but also real and concrete. Yahui was both an actor and an audience member. She had not expected Gu Mingzheng would produce such an official-looking announcement, much less that he would stand in front of Jueyu *shifu* and read the announcement as though reciting an ode. His hoarse voice gushed forth like a partially thawed frozen river—

Members of the teaching and training sections, and of the religious training center:

To implement the Party's religious policy and maximize the friendship and harmony between different religions, the religious training center has resolved to abolish all inter-sect athletic competitions, as well as all competitions based on knowledge of religious policy and knowledge relating to the Party. From now on, the center's work relating to religious training will be exclusively for the purpose of elevating and respecting the principles of each religion's belief, independence, and freedom—such that, during this year of training, each disciple will come to believe more piously, deeply, and freely that his or her own religion's deity is the only creator. Each disciple will understand the birth, development, and flourishing of religion in China, and will be able to use a more powerful belief to disseminate their own religion's doctrine and faith to the masses.

Accordingly, as of today, we will permanently discontinue all the center's athletic activities, and particularly high-strength competitions like tug-of-war—with the exception of competitions between members of the same religion that serve to promote physical exercise. Moreover, the activities in question will also be permanently removed from the center's curriculum.

National Politics University Religious Training Center

The document had been signed two days earlier, and it seemed as though the ink was still wet. The notice was printed on a sheet of A4 paper, like an official notification, and at the top were the words *National Politics University Religious Training Center* in Song script, below which there was the religion center's red seal. Everyone found this very realistic and convincing, as though a deity were standing right in front of Jueyu *shifu*, Mingzheng, and the volunteer nurse. The only exception was Yahui—and although her eyes revealed a hint of skepticism, her expression nevertheless remained perfectly sincere and devout. The figurative curtains opened, whereupon everyone on stage had no choice but to perform their role. The result was pure theater, but at the same time was also as real as reality itself. As Mingzheng solemnly read the notification, the volunteer nurse burst into a victorious smile and Yahui gazed at Mingzheng with a joyous expression. Yahui circled around so that she was standing behind her *shifu* and gently massaged her shoulders and back like a filial child.

Mingzheng finished reading the announcement, after which the park became completely silent apart from the sound of autumn birds. Outside the grove, some doctors and patients were chatting in the sunlight. The sky was very high, like the deep and vast domain one finds in the scriptures, and it was in the deep stillness that Jueyu *shifu*, with tears in her eyes, asked in a trembling voice, "Is it . . . is it . . . is it true?"

As she asked this, she strode over to Mingzheng as though she were not sick at all.

Everyone stared in surprise, and the volunteer nurse cried out, "Ah, ah!" The nurse couldn't decide whether to help support Jueyu *shifu* or let her walk on her own, and therefore her hand paused in midair. Yahui also stood there stunned, watching Jueyu *shifu* walk back and forth. Her mouth opened, but she was unable to utter a single word. She had an astonished expression, as though she had just seen the Bodhisattva. Gu Mingzheng, meanwhile, was happily holding the announcement, his face radiating a powerful dawn light, as though he were Laozi come down to earth to direct the world and guide people's lives.

19 Yahui and Mingzheng

1

"Was it you who wrote this document?"

"I'm the director's assistant!"

"And did you add the stamp?"

"I'm in charge of that stamp, and can stamp whatever I want."

As Yahui and Mingzheng left Yonghe Hospital and stepped out into the afternoon sun, Beijing's streets resembled a freshly painted brick wall. They strolled together through the red light as though walking through a river. Now that Jueyu *shifu* was able to walk and talk again, the doctor suggested that she remain in the hospital to rest for another couple of weeks or a month. Then, if she still wanted to be discharged, she could leave. Yahui's feeling of resentment toward Mingzheng quickly dissipated. Walking shoulder to shoulder, they chatted like a pair of disciples leaving the scripture hall after class, discussing the texts and miracles on which the master had lectured. After passing through Yonghe Hospital's courtyard and tree grove, they proceeded to an alley off Yonghe Street, where they saw countless yellow leaves that had fallen like golden scrolls from the Chinese scholar trees lining both sides of the road. This was a footway, but there weren't many other pedestrians around. Yahui and Mingzheng strolled over those golden texts.

Yahui said, "I'm very grateful to you."

Mingzheng replied, "Then why don't you take me out to eat?"

Yahui stopped and noticed that up ahead were the meat bun stall and Lanzhou noodle shop where she had recently eaten. She asked hesitantly, "What would you like?"

"We Daoists don't have any dietary restrictions," Mingzheng replied. "I'll have a meat bun."

So Yahui and Mingzheng went up to the meat bun stall and ordered a bottle of cold beer and servings of pig's head, small fried fish, small river prawns, and peanuts. After they finished, Mingzheng approached the counter to ask for a receipt, explaining that he could get reimbursed back at the school.

2

In this way, Yahui and Mingzheng gradually were reconciled—as though Yahui's papercuts had succeeded in making Guanyin and Laozi a couple. They agreed to go to the zoo the following Monday. That morning, the center invited a professor from the literature academy to come lecture on *Dream of the Red Chamber* and Chinese Religions. However, Yahui and Mingzheng skipped class that day, like the novel's protagonists Jia Baoyu and Lin Daiyu—or like the work's third protagonist, Xue Baochai, and the maid Xiren—leaving the Grand View Garden to visit the wild garden.

The world that day was excellent, and the weather was also excellent.

The Bodhisattva Guanyin was up in the clouds, and the humans were down on earth. The campus was still the same campus as before, but Yahui was not the same Yahui. She had removed the nun's habit she used to wear all year round, and was now wearing an oversized yellow sweater with a collar so high that it brushed her chin. The Buddha was up in the sky and wasn't interested in what Yahui was wearing down in the mortal world. She had also removed the prayer beads from around her neck and hidden a crystal necklace in her pocket so that she could put it on after leaving the religion building. She was wearing a pair of gray straight-legged pants and low-heeled leather shoes, and had also put on some fragrant mint-scented perfume and blush she purchased at the imported-goods store. Were it not for her shaved head, no one would have ever guessed she was a nun.

Mingzheng was waiting for Yahui outside the school entrance, and they smiled when they saw each other. Under his breath Mingzheng exclaimed, "Beautiful, and fragrant too!" Then he led her over to a taxi.

Mingzheng and Yahui quickly left Zhongguancun Avenue behind. The street's buildings, trees, and pedestrians receded in the taxi's rearview mirror, and billboards flew past them like playing cards. The sky was deep blue, and the clouds were as white as piles of wool on the side of a field during sheep-shearing season. Yahui was reminded of Qinghai's desolate landscape, which gave her a more favorable impression of Beijing, with its countless cars, stores, pedestrians, and buildings. As Yahui looked out the window, Mingzheng placed his hand on her thigh and they proceeded to chat about nothing in particular.

Yahui said, "It's very strange, but last night I dreamed that Guanyin had come down with a cold and was running a fever."

Mingzheng stared at her in surprise, and said, "Heavens . . . I dreamed that Laozi was sick and running a fever!"

Yahui said, "I also dreamed that Tathagata was walking and broke his leg."

Mingzheng glanced at the taxi driver, then placed his hand over Yahui's mouth. Yahui realized she had said too much, and immediately fell silent. She looked out the window again, and upon seeing the houses and scenery, people and cars, she thought how nice it would be to have an apartment in Beijing. She turned to Gu Mingzheng and smiled.

"We already agreed that today you Daoists would treat us."

Mingzheng replied, "Yes, of course."

Yahui said, "I'd like for you to get me a couple scoops of ice cream."

"I could do that, if you like."

"I'd also like a couple bottles of sparkling water."

"As long as you can finish them."

Yahui thought for a while, then said, "I've heard that the zoo is very expensive?"

"How expensive could it possibly be?"

"Exactly, how expensive could it possibly be?" Yahui stared at Mingzheng and asked, "Do you have enough savings to buy an apartment in Beijing?"

Mingzheng leaned over and whispered in her ear, "Let's buy an apartment in Beijing!"

Yahui thought for a moment, then said, "OK, why don't you help me and my *shifu* purchase Yonghe Temple. That way, when she is discharged from the hospital, she and I can go live there!"

Mingzheng grinned at Yahui, and reached over to hold her hand. Yahui let him, and as they held hands their blood began to rush through their veins, even as they continued to stare straight ahead. The zoo was very close to the school, and no sooner had they begun to hold hands than the taxi arrived at the entrance to the zoo. Just as their blood was beginning to surge, the taxi stopped. It turned out that tickets to the zoo were, indeed, quite expensive—eighty yuan each—even though the entrance appeared as dilapidated as a northwestern shepherd's sheep pen. Once they went inside, however, the scenery changed completely. The trees were like a forest and the water was like a lake. Beijingers and others were crowded around with their children. Yahui and Mingzheng saw a mother and father with triplets who were attracting even more attention than the zoo's own displays. When they saw the triplets, Mingzheng glanced at Yahui's belly and smiled, whereupon Yahui kicked his shin. This was an expression of real anger, and afterward she went alone to check out the wolf pen. She also went to see the enclosure with the bald-headed and the red-beaked turkeys, as well as the one with the Siberian tigers. When Yahui arrived, the tigers were in the process of eating some meat, and the sight of the blood terrified her to the point that she immediately left. Mingzheng followed her out, and in order to look at her belly again he apologized. Pressing softly against her, he said, "Let me tell you a story. It begins like this . . .

"There was once a beautiful little white rabbit. The rabbit wanted some carrots, so it went to a store and asked the shopkeeper, 'Boss, boss, do you sell carrots here?' The shopkeeper looked at the rabbit, and replied, 'I don't have any carrots. You'll have to buy them somewhere else.' Disappointed and with drooping ears, the rabbit left the store. The next day, the rabbit returned, and once again went up to the shopkeeper and asked, 'Boss, boss, do you sell carrots here?' The shopkeeper looked at the rabbit with an odd expression, and replied, 'I've never sold carrots here. You should go somewhere else!' The little rabbit left again, very disappointed. The third day, the rabbit returned once again, and said, 'Boss, boss, do you sell carrots here?' This time the shopkeeper was genuinely angry, and shouted, 'I've never sold carrots. I only sell knives! If you want a knife, I can sell you one. OK?!' Trembling with fear, the little white rabbit didn't say another word, and instead turned and ran away.

"On the fourth day and the fifth day, the little rabbit didn't appear. The store's business returned to normal, but just as the shopkeeper was thinking that the rabbit wouldn't dare come again, he saw the rabbit standing in line with the other customers waiting to buy goods. When it was the rabbit's turn, the shopkeeper glared at it, thinking, *This guy has once again come to make trouble.* This time, however, the rabbit very politely said, 'My dear boss, today I would like to purchase a knife.'

"The shopkeeper was delighted and broke into a huge smile. In a very polite and friendly manner, however, he replied, 'I'm sorry, I've never sold knives here.'

"The rabbit stared in surprise, reflected for a moment, then said, 'You've never sold knives here? In that case, just sell me a bunch of carrots. OK?'"

Mingzheng suddenly stopped telling the story, like a car braking where it is not supposed to stop. Yahui looked at him and saw that he was standing there looking back at her. She said, "Go on!"

Mingzheng replied, "That's all."

Bewildered, Yahui stared at Mingzheng.

"That's it?"

"Yes, that's it."

After reflecting for a moment, Yahui squatted down and laughed. "That rabbit—what a stupid little rabbit!" As she said this, she laughed so hard her belly started to hurt and tears streamed down her face. Some passersby stared at her, having no idea why she was laughing. Mingzheng pulled her up and led her by the hand back into the crowd.

"Was that a funny story?"

Yahui nodded. "Tell me another one."

Mingzheng didn't tell her another story. Instead, he grasped her hand and walked to where there weren't very many people. He earnestly asked her, "Tell me the truth, shall we return to secular life and get married?"

Yahui gazed back at him without saying a word.

"We could buy an apartment in Beijing and spend our days there." Mingzheng's eyes flickered. "You know, I already have a residency permit to live in Beijing. If I haven't found my father by the time I graduate, I'll take a job as a secretary at the National Religion Association. By that point, I'll be a national cadre, and it would be wonderful if we could return to secular life and get married."

Yahui thought for a moment, then asked, "Would returning to secular life really be that wonderful?"

Mingzheng reflected for a moment. "It would be like lighting a warm fire on a cold day!"

"And getting married?"

"I'm not joking. Marriage would be like rescuing someone from a burning fire."

Yahui reflected for a bit longer, and said, "I'll need to ask the Buddha and the Bodhisattva . . ."

Mingzheng and Yahui fell silent, then they looked up at the sky. At this point, apart from some white clouds and dazzling sunlight, the sky above the zoo was as empty as Qinghai's Gobi Desert. Mingzheng asked Yahui, "What do you see?"

Yahui replied solemnly, "I see the Bodhisattva Guanyin."

Mingzheng asked, "What does she look like?"

"She looks like you and me, and like Guanyin."

Mingzheng once again craned his neck and gazed up at the sky, like a giraffe stretching its neck to reach some high branches and leaves.

Yahui asked, "And what do you see?"

Mingzheng replied, "I see Laozi."

"Does he really have so many white whiskers?"

"He looks like you and me, and like Laozi."

They looked away from the sky, smiled, then suddenly embraced and began kissing under the trees. Crazed, Mingzheng poked his tongue into Yahui's mouth, as their bodies trembled like mountains collapsing and the earth splitting open. In this way, they experienced the taste of returning to secular life and getting married, and of being rescued from a burning fire.

20 Shuiyue *shifu*

Someone mentioned they had seen Mingzheng and Yahui returning together at sunset, and that after entering the elevator and proceeding to the seventh floor, the couple entered Yahui's room together and didn't reemerge for a long time. Someone else mentioned that when Mingzheng finally emerged from Yahui's room, his clothes were partially unbuttoned and his face looked as though it had been lit on fire.

Given that Jueyu *shifu* wasn't around, her fellow disciple Shuiyue *shifu* had no choice but to attend to this matter herself. After all, wasn't she the class monitor of the school's Buddhism class, and hadn't Shuiyue *shifu* and Jueyu *shifu* joined Luoyang's Baima Temple together?

Evenings at the school were so carefree that everyone simply wanted to lounge about, as though relaxing on a beach. The large screen at the base of the religion building was projecting footage of some country's prime minister visiting campus, alongside a recording of his speech. On the screen, the prime minister was wearing a suit and a garland around his neck, and was greeting the school's officials. Below the screen, students were getting out of class and returning to their dormitories, and then emerging from their dormitories and going to the canteen.

Shuiyue *shifu* waited outside the canteen for Yahui. She knew that although Yahui didn't have class that day, she would still go there at dinnertime. When couples first fall in love, they always want to display themselves in public so that others might appreciate how beautiful love is, because otherwise the love birds might feel that their love would have been for nothing. Shuiyue *shifu* had previously experienced this same impulse, and she knew that Yahui would experience it as well. It turned out that Shuiyue *shifu* was correct, and Yahui emerged before the other disciples. She was wearing a yellow robe and a dark-red rosary, and in the light of the setting sun her face appeared as red as though a fire had been lit under it. When Yahui saw Shuiyue *shifu* standing beneath the screen, she immediately stopped in her tracks. She looked as though she wanted to hide, but Shuiyue *shifu* gestured to her: "Come here . . . Yahui, come here."

Yahui had no choice but to go over. The blush faded from her face, but her heart was beating even more crazily than it had been when she kissed Mingzheng at the zoo—although at the zoo her heart had been pounding from the heat of passion, whereas now it was pounding from chills of terror. When Yahui arrived, Shuiyue *shifu* glanced up at the giant screen, then pulled Yahui over to an area behind a roadside poplar tree. Shuiyue *shifu* waited until the sound from the screen's speakers had died down and a group of students had passed, then flipped Yahui's eyelids over and asked her to stick out her tongue. With the confidence of a physician, Shuiyue *shifu* said, "You have lust in your heart."

Yahui gazed silently at Shuiyue *shifu*, her face pale and her body frozen in place as though buried in snow.

"Who's the boy?"

With her mouth firmly closed and her head bowed, Yahui didn't dare look at Shuiyue *shifu*. She felt as though Shuiyue *shifu* was able to see straight through her clothes, exposing her naked body in the dusk light.

"Is it really that boy, Gu Mingzheng?" Shuiyue *shifu* kept her gaze fixed on Yahui, but after a while her voice softened and she said, "Tell me the truth, because if it is, I think it's really quite all right. Of the students here, Mingzheng definitely has the most potential. Everyone says that after he graduates, he'll be hired to work for the National Religion Association." Then she led Yahui over to a stone bench next to the roadside wall. After they sat down, Shuiyue *shifu* grasped Yahui's hand in her own and observed that nuns are women, too. She noted that women all have to go through this sort of thing, after which their hearts become enlightened and they can become a Buddha. If they don't go through this sort of thing, how can they really believe in the Buddha and become a Buddha?

As Shuiyue *shifu* alternated between asking and explaining, she removed Yahui's hand from her own and said, "Listen carefully. If you two do it, you must make sure you don't get pregnant, because then the Buddha would look down on you for the rest of your life."

Yahui blushed and bowed her head. As she did so, she grasped Shuiyue *shifu*'s hand. Shuiyue *shifu* looked in the direction of the road and smiled.

"Do you know why there is tension between me and your *shifu*? It is because when I got married, it was your *shifu* who reported me to the central temple. She was also the one who went to burn incense for the Buddha and the Bodhisattva, and told them about this."

Shuiyue *shifu* stopped and waited for Yahui to respond. Yahui, however, merely stared at her in wonder, as though observing some sort of serene scene. Yahui noticed that Shuiyue *shifu* kept smiling throughout this discussion, which made Yahui feel somewhat relieved, but also left her confused. When Shuiyue *shifu* raised the possibility that Yahui might become pregnant, Yahui wasn't certain whether she was presenting this as something desirable or something to be feared. Therefore, Yahui simply sat there in confusion, reflecting that she and Mingzheng were thousands of *li* away from any possible pregnancy. At the same time, however, she also felt that if she were to say this out loud it would surely sound insincere. So she merely stared at Shuiyue *shifu*, then bowed her head. Eventually, Shuiyue whispered into Yahui's ear, saying, "If it is fated that there will be sin, then so be it—as long as you can learn to keep a secret, it'll be fine. Being a woman is a dead end anyway, so as long as you eventually return to this side of piety, everything will be OK."

Then Shuiyue *shifu* fell silent and led Yahui over to the halal canteen.

21 Tian Dongqing and Wang Changping

The school's halal canteen adhered to all relevant religious regulations, and although it didn't serve pork, it did offer a wide assortment of delicious beef and vegetable dishes, as well as tofu dishes that tasted just like pork, fish, shrimp, and crab. As a result, all the center's disciples liked to eat there. At the entrance to the canteen there was a green vestibule with an arched dome, the walls of which were covered in Islamic-style paintings. Directly ahead there was a large dining room capable of seating two hundred people, the walls of which were covered in colorful slogans such as *All Religion Must Serve the People* and *The Relationship Between Religions Is a New Socialist Relationship!* Printed in red italic characters, these slogans were either hanging from the walls or printed directly on the walls themselves, making the canteen resemble a Beijing square. Regardless of whether they were actually Hui, all the cooks wore white skullcaps and all the servers were dressed in accordance with Hui customs.

Yahui entered the canteen with Shuiyue *shifu*. However, she didn't join her *shifu* in the Buddhist section below the slogan *Buddhist Nature Is Party Nature, and Buddhist Glory Is National Glory.* As Shuiyue *shifu* was serving herself, she said to Yahui, "Why don't you go over there and listen to what they are saying? Don't let them talk about us behind our backs." Then Shuiyue *shifu* took her plate and headed toward the *Great Unity, Great Harmony* section of the canteen. In that section there was a row of long tables, and all the students were facing one another.

Yahui, meanwhile, sat down next to Imam Tian Dongqing's wife, Ruan Zhisu. Sister Zhisu looked at Yahui's plate of stir-fried cabbage with mushrooms and, with a smile, proceeded to take one of the mushrooms from her plate and eat it. Everyone else at the table was listening to Tian Dongqing reflect on that day's class lecture on religion and *Dream of the Red Chamber*. When discussing *Dream of the Red Chamber*, literature professors often comment on the work's Confucian, Buddhist, and Daoist elements, but nothing has yet been said about its allusions to Allah and Islam. However, given that Islam was already flourishing in China from the Song to the Qing dynasties, and given that *Dream of the Red Chamber* is an encyclopedic reflection of Buddhist, Daoist, and Confucian components of Qing dynasty society, Tian Dongqing had long wondered: *Why does Allah not appear in the work? And if Allah doesn't appear, how could the work be considered an encyclopedic reflection of its era?* Tian Dongqing asked, "Who here has read *Dream of the Red Chamber*? Who has read this beloved novel of the Han people?"

None of the other imams had read the book, so they all bowed their heads and silently ate their rice and radish stew—like someone who knows the identity of a thief but lacks hard evidence. As the imams ate, the entire table was filled with the sound of their slurping and swallowing. No one paid much attention to Yahui, but neither did they avoid speaking to her. Instead, they acted as though nothing unusual had happened. Yahui ate her food with everyone else, calmly discussing some matters related to their class and asking about their forthcoming exams. When they finished their food, she announced she was going to get some more, then went to buy a dish of eggs and cauliflower, which she took to the southwest section of the canteen. This was where the Protestant and Catholic disciples usually ate, and the giant banner on the wall reading *All Belief Is for the Sake of the People and Society* made this area appear even brighter than the others. Yahui found an empty seat and remarked, "From a distance, I could hear Pastor Wang discussing the scriptures." As she said this, she put down the dish she was holding, and gestured for everyone to help themselves.

"Actually, we weren't discussing the scriptures. We were just chatting," said Wang Changping.

His section of the canteen abruptly quieted down. Several Protestant disciples looked at Yahui, as though she were responsible. Embarrassed, Yahui was debating whether to take her dish to another section of the canteen, but instead Pastor Wang waved her over. He took some food from her dish, remarking, "Don't worry, Yahui is her class's purest, most pristine disciple." Then he immediately returned to his previous discussion, as though reconnecting a severed rope: "Why is it that so many Westerners—and even some Chinese—hope China and the Party will soon collapse? When China and the Party fail to collapse, will this disappoint capitalist nations like the United States, Britain, France, Germany, Spain, and Italy?"

Wang Changping then looked at everyone and continued, "It is because China and the Party have a previously unrecognized connection to the Bible and to Jesus. Did you know that the Communist Party is actually one of Jesus's disciples?" Pastor Wang added, "You mustn't repeat what I'm about to tell you, because if you do, the Party and the nation would be most displeased. Everyone knows about the Bible's twelve apostles, and if you don't, you can't be considered a true disciple. You will also recall that, in the days after Jesus's resurrection, his apostles were still actively proselytizing. Jesus was crucified as a result of Judas's betrayal, and therefore Judas was stripped of his status as an apostle. At a subsequent meeting, the remaining eleven apostles resolved to select someone to replace him. They agreed on two candidates—and you'll recall that they were Barsabbas and Matthias. The apostles drew lots to decide which of the two would be selected, and in the end it was Matthias. But what happened to

Barsabbas? Like the apostles themselves, Barsabbas was one of Jesus's most devout followers, and if he had been selected rather than Matthias, perhaps things would have turned out completely differently?

"Just think, after Barsabbas, Jesus's devoted follower, was passed over, how could he not have been heartbroken? In fact, after Matthias replaced Judas as Jesus's twelfth apostle, Barsabbas left Israel to go proselytize on his own. He eventually got married, had a child, and continued disseminating the spirit of Christ to new generations and different places—like a seed being carried away by the wind. In this way, Barsabbas eventually reached Eastern Europe, Germany, and England. You all know that Marx was Jewish, as was Barsabbas, but did you know that Marx and Barsabbas shared direct blood ties? Did you know that Marx was Barsabbas's direct descendant?

"Let me ask you something. You know how we Chinese say that tangerines from the south are called tangerines, while those from the north are called oranges? In the end, however, they both come from the same soil and share the same root! The same could be said of Barsabbas and his descendants. Although there is no record that Marx, that great German Jewish thinker, was a direct descendant of Barsabbas, nonetheless Jesus knew that this would come to pass. So, when the eleven apostles cried out, 'Master, you know everyone's heart, so we beg you, please indicate whom you would choose,' the Master selected Matthias without hesitation, though he never forgot Barsabbas and always felt that he had let him down.

"This is also why the nation and the Party will never collapse. Indeed, how could they? After all, they are direct descendants of Barsabbas and Jesus. Furthermore, the Master always felt he had mistreated Barsabbas, and felt guilty about how he had treated this disciple who had been just as loyal to him as Matthias.

"It would have been better if the Master hadn't felt so guilty about Barsabbas, but he knew that this nation with its more than a billion people would be the result of Barsabbas continuing to proselytize after leaving him. Tell me, how could Jesus let our nation collapse, and permit its billion-plus citizens to be lost? And given that our nation enjoys the Master's protection, how could it collapse? Given the Master's protection, are not those other nations who are hoping for China's collapse merely rooting in vain?"

Upon hearing this, everyone stopped eating and stared at Wang Changping. They suddenly realized that this was his understanding of the relationship between the Bible and the nation, with the hidden principle resembling a meandering forest path. For centuries, this path had been obscured by a thick layer of leaves, but now it had been revealed by Pastor Wang Changping—and it appeared so straight and wide that a carriage of faith could ride down it, and people could see directly from one end to the other. The other disciples all stared at Wang Changping, and he stared back at them—like a teacher who, after finishing a lecture, uses his gaze to silently ask whether the students have understood what he has just said. The disciples nodded and, still reflecting on the Bible's hidden message, slowly resumed eating their food.

The entire time Wang Changping was speaking, Yahui stared at him while keeping her chopsticks suspended near her mouth—like someone who had gone in search of the Buddha and instead found Jesus and the Virgin Mary.

22 Believers

. . . attending class, eating meals, taking exams, and going to meetings. The week after hearing Pastor Wang's story about Barsabbas and China, there was an exam on the topic of "religious politics." Mingzheng took one of the examination booklets from the center's printing room and secretly shared it with Yahui, who then easily scored third on the exam. That night, after Yahui and Mingzheng watched a romantic movie together, Yahui returned to her room and had a dream. It was a wet dream in which she was masturbating, and when she woke up, her body was covered in warm sweat. She clasped her hands to her chest and repeatedly chanted *Amitābha*. In the dark, she lit three incense sticks in front of the room's Buddha portrait and, after kneeling before it, she finally went back to sleep.

After waking up again, Yahui invited Mingzheng to accompany her to Yonghe Hospital to visit her *shifu*. At the hospital, Yahui helped her *shifu* walk two full loops around the grove and discussed countless mundane matters inside and outside the school, as well as her *shifu*'s hopes and plans for after she was discharged. On her way back from the hospital, Yahui went to the same meat bun shop as before, after which she proceeded to the bamboo grove in Zizhu Park, where she and Mingzheng strolled hand in hand. After reaching a location deep in the grove, they almost did that sinful lusty thing, but fortunately someone happened to walk by and kept Yahui from proceeding into the sinful abyss. In the end, she didn't let Mingzheng enter her body's final destination.

A few days earlier, Shuiyue *shifu* had told Yahui, "If you have lustful desires, you should go ahead and fulfill them. Just make sure Mingzheng really is able to get a job at the National Religion Association after he graduates."

Yahui began having a series of secret rendezvous with Mingzheng, and any day they were scheduled to have a date, time would always rush by as though propelled by wind and water. Before they knew it, an entire week had passed, and then a month. During that span of time, there were many developments at the center. For instance, they originally had athletics class once a week, but the class was dropped whenever Director Gong was busy. Also, they originally had two classes with closed-book exams, but whenever Director Gong was in a good mood, the exams were made open-book. To help elevate the training class's material, cultural, and athletic life, Mingzheng wrote to each disciple who was about to graduate, asking whether they would be willing to donate to the center. These letters were printed in a standard format, with Mingzheng imitating the director's handwriting to write each recipient's name and title. Although the resulting Chinese characters were rather ugly, the center subsequently received numerous donations from alumni. It initially received several tens of thousands of yuan, then several hundreds of thousands, and within half a month it had raised over half a million. Furthermore, there were abbots, hosts, pastors, and priests who constantly sent money orders for thousands or tens of thousands of yuan, and each money order came with a note as beautiful as a Bodhi fruit, with florid wording such as, "Our temple has limited means, and although I cannot donate millions or tens of millions of yuan like a business tycoon, I am nevertheless donating twenty thousand yuan in appreciation of my alma mater's work in disseminating, cultivating, and supporting my religion."

To pitch his book, Director Gong showed some editors an outline and an excerpt, and although he originally simply wanted some feedback, in the end three presses told him that the work could be published only if he added more specific examples to the text—for instance, regarding how the disciples competed in the tug-of-war competition—while also providing a larger monetary subvention. Accordingly, when Director Gong reviewed the donation figures that Mingzheng gave him, he broke into a wide smile. He immediately stood up and pounded the table with his fist, exclaiming, "I want you to go organize another tug-of-war competition this afternoon on my behalf. Meanwhile, I'm going to visit the press!"

Standing in front of the director, Mingzheng replied softly, "Another competition? But none of the students really want to participate!"

"They don't?" After staring at Mingzheng for a moment, Director Gong slammed the donation sheet onto the table, and continued, "As they say, sheep wool grows on a sheep—we'll offer prize money for every competition. If a thousand yuan isn't enough, we'll offer two thousand; if two thousand isn't enough, we'll offer five thousand; and if five thousand isn't enough, we'll offer ten thousand. Then we'll see whether there are any disciples who are still unwilling to participate!"

That was how things were decided. That afternoon's athletics class did in fact include a tumultuous competition. At midday, Yahui returned to her dormitory to make some more papercuts and take a nap, and by the time she arrived back at the court, the other spectators had already assembled. As everyone was waiting for the competition to begin, it appeared Director Gong was offering some preliminary remarks. He was waving around an oversized replica check that measured five feet across and three feet high, and after hearing a roar of laughter and applause, he handed Mingzheng the check, said a few words, then also gave Mingzheng the whistle that had been hanging from his neck. At this point, the spectators began making a loud ruckus. Having heard that Mingzheng would be on the Daoist team, they asked, "Isn't this a case of someone being both a referee and a competitor at the same time? Isn't it like having a judge and an accused living in the same house?" The spectators continued arguing until Director Gong finally took the whistle from Mingzheng and handed it to Wang Changping, then left the field.

Wang Changping accepted the whistle with a smile, then removed his jacket, tucked in his white shirt, and adjusted his belt. With his whistle in his mouth, he took out a thick black pen and, after asking Mingzheng to hold up the replica check, proceeded to write "plus ten thousand yuan" after the original "ten thousand yuan." The spectators erupted in applause, and even the leaves of the evergreen trees around the court trembled and fell off.

Because this was an athletics class, Yahui deliberately arrived late. When she finally arrived, she picked a wildflower from the entranceway and sniffed it, as though smelling the Buddha's fragrance. Still sniffing the flower, she slowly walked toward the front of the court. She stood for a while outside the court, then circled around from the west side to an iron gate in the northeast corner. While she was standing there, she saw Director Gong biking over while shouting, "Congratulations to you and Mingzheng!" Without waiting for her to respond, he smiled and biked away.

When Yahui reached the tug-of-war court, the competition was about to begin. The Daoist and Islamic teams were preparing to compete, and the five members of each team were already on the court. The competitors periodically glanced at the spectator area, where Mingzheng was pacing back and forth like a monk holding an alms bowl, continually using his black pen to write updates on the check while making announcements such as "Protestant team: another ten thousand yuan!" or "Islamic team: another five thousand yuan!" Sometimes he would even identify the donors by name:

"Master Haifa: one thousand yuan!

"Abbot Yonghe: two thousand yuan!"

Every time Mingzheng added a new line to the check, he would announce the individual's name and title and the amount being donated. The result resembled television coverage of a charity concert for disaster relief, in which the combination of performances and donations ultimately renders the disaster a source of entertainment and the stage for the performance of happiness. The more devastating the original disaster and the larger the subsequent donations, the more joy the resulting applause would stir in people's hearts. Mingzheng was delighted with his role that day, and when the Protestant team donated eighteen thousand yuan, he wrote the amount on the check and shouted, "The Protestant team has donated a total of eighteen thousand yuan, which is eight thousand more than the Catholic team . . . At this point, the Protestant team has donated the most, and the total purse has grown to thirty-eight thousand yuan. Does anyone else want to donate? Who else wants to donate?!"

Each time a disciple raised his hand, Mingzheng would hand him the black pen, and in a blank area of the check the disciple would write his name or the name of his church or temple, together with a monetary amount. Then, Mingzheng would hold up the check and shout, "Baiyun Monastery has donated another ten thousand yuan, bringing the total to forty-eight thousand yuan. Shaolin Temple has donated another twenty thousand yuan, bringing the total to sixty-eight thousand yuan!"

The December sun was not cold at all, and the yellow sunlight mixed with the red rubber surface of the tug-of-war court to yield the color of a southern phoenix flower. The dense, humid air was filled with the scent of vegetation. When Yahui entered the eastern side of the court to watch the competition, she found that the spectators standing in front of her were blocking her view, such that she had to peer between them to see Mingzheng holding up his replica check. Mingzheng walked around the court, so that all the disciples could see the amounts written on the check, while also showing the disciples on the Daoist and Islamic teams that the purse had already increased to sixty-eight thousand yuan.

"Who else? Who else will donate?" Between the heads of the spectators standing in front of her, Yahui saw Mingzheng shouting with a bright smile like the afternoon sun on his face, like a son of God playing games in the mortal world.

"Father Wujun has donated another ten thousand yuan!

"Senior Monk Zhengdao has donated another ten thousand yuan!

"As soon as we reach a hundred thousand yuan, the competition will officially begin! When we reach a hundred thousand yuan, the competition will officially begin!"

As Mingzheng crossed from one end of the spectator stands to another, his shouts and whistles flew through the air. Both teams were energized by the rapidly growing purse. With his referee's whistle in his pocket, Wang Changping followed Mingzheng, shouting to the crowd, "Who will donate twenty thousand more? Who will donate twenty thousand more?!" As though receiving a divine order, someone raised their hand and donated five thousand yuan and someone else donated fifteen thousand—thereby pushing the size of the total purse just over the hundred-thousand-yuan threshold, to a hundred and three thousand. There was a wave of applause and laughter, while one disciple began whistling like a commoner. Given that this wasn't a sound that disciples should ordinarily be making, other spectators turned to look, whereupon the whistling immediately stopped.

Eventually, Wang Changping's own red-faced whistling marked the beginning of the competition.

The court immediately became very still, and the silence was broken only by the sound of disciples breathing. It was at this juncture, as Yahui was selecting a place to stand next to the Catholic and Protestant spectators, that she glimpsed someone's shadow through the red steel-mesh gate leading to the tug-of-war court. Like a cloud, the shadow appeared to hover there for a moment, then disappeared into the spectator stand. Yahui felt that the cloud that had blown in through the doorway resembled the Bodhisattva Guanyin walking out onto the court. Therefore, she gazed up at the sky and saw a misty and mysterious form half-hidden behind the clouds, and also perceived a transparent vastness in the sky above Beijing. In the distance, the black undulating ridge of the western mountains touched the sky. When Yahui first arrived, she had stared at the Guanyin cloud in the sky, and she now saw that it was still in the same location but instead took the form of a giant flower blossom. Only its original lotus shape was missing, and instead it had come to resemble a lake filled with pristine water. Yahui looked away from the cloud and turned back to the entrance to the tug-of-war court, where—apart from the white skullcaps on the heads of the Islamic team—there was virtually no trace of Guanyin. If Guanyin really did arrive, she would obviously proceed to the Buddhist section, because how could she possibly go to another religion's section?

Yahui turned to the Buddhists and saw that in this early-winter weather, the disciples were all wearing grayish-yellow monk's robes and crimson nun's robes. They were all squeezed together, their swollen faces a combination of red, purple, and yellow. The rope was suspended a meter above the ground, and all the disciples were excited that the competition was finally about to begin. Like real athletes, the members of the Islamic and Daoist teams had removed their robes and were now wearing only shirts and pants, and some had even stripped down to their undershirts and underwear. As they did so, Yahui could see that the fat, white pupa-like Daoist disciples had all led very comfortable lives, while very few of the thin, dark-skinned Islamic disciples had served as imams in mosques, and instead they mostly hailed from factories, mines, and northwestern plains, where they had farmed, harvested, and fasted. Meanwhile, Imam Tian, the captain of the Islamic team, had a face so dark that it seemed to glow black, like that of an imam from Africa. Seeing this, Yahui became certain that the Muslims were going to defeat the Daoists, the same way that someone accustomed to working in the fields would naturally be stronger than an office worker. On the other hand, Yahui also remembered that Mingzheng had once told her that everyone selected for the Daoist team had practiced martial arts and woke up every night to eat beef in secret. If this was indeed true, the Daoists could very well win the competition.

Finally, the battle began. The rope swayed back and forth for a moment but was then quickly pulled as taut as a steel pipe, as the tassel remained suspended right above the center line. Pastor Wang Changping was standing at the midpoint of the rope looking side to side and periodically blowing his whistle. Whenever he saw that the Islamic team had pulled ahead, he would shout "Go! Go!" to the Daoist team, and whenever he saw that the Daoist team had retaken the lead, he would yell "For Allah, for Allah!" to the Islamic team. He switched sides as easily as ivy growing along a wall, and whichever team he happened to be encouraging would inevitably respond by pulling even harder.

At this point, the Buddhist, Protestant, and Catholic teams were not competing, so they contributed to the raucous atmosphere. Given that everyone had already completed their exams, they were all as relaxed as disciples who had just finished their prayers and were leaving their churches and temples. Three days later they would have their end-of-term banquet, where they would drink Maotai-brand *baijiu* and eat delicious vegetable dishes, as well as imitation meat and fish dishes. Over the next few days, the disciples who were eager to leave Beijing would return to their homes, churches, and temples. During this period, everyone was feeling free and relaxed, and they also became very invested in other teams' wins and losses. As for the competitors themselves, they naturally also gave it their all, since whoever won would receive a hundred thousand yuan. The faces of the competitors were covered in sweat, and veins were protruding from their foreheads and necks. The Daoists and Muslims pulling the rope were all leaning backward, their faces contorted to the point that blood was almost flowing out, as their bodies resembled stakes impaling the ground. Although previously they could be differentiated based on the color of their skin, now they had all turned a purplish crimson as their blood rushed to the surface.

Yahui couldn't tell who the leader of the Daoist team was. She was standing in the area reserved for the Catholic and Protestant spectators, and because more than a dozen disciples were on their feet facing the court, cheering and waving, her view was periodically blocked. Furthermore, she wasn't completely focused on the competition, and constantly felt that her right eyelid was fluttering uncontrollably, as though it sensed an impending crisis. She repeatedly looked over at the Buddhist spectator area, as though the Bodhisattva had secretly entered and hidden among the disciples. Yahui felt as though her heart and soul were floating as she watched the competition, searched for the Bodhisattva, and remembered how she and Mingzheng would often sneak off to a restaurant in the Old Summer Palace neighborhood to secretly eat wild boar meat. She excitedly searched for Mingzheng, and after finding the oversized replica check on the side of the court, she eventually located Mingzheng standing by the entrance. He was holding two cans of her favorite drink and was gesturing to her like a beekeeper holding honey to lure bees. Yahui immediately headed over to him.

However, as soon as Yahui reached the corner of the spectator stand, she caught a glimpse of a shadowy figure—and clearly saw the Bodhisattva standing among the Buddhist disciples. The shadow flickered, as though a colored wind were blowing through the crowd. Then there was another disconcerting sound, reminiscent of the time when old Imam Ren Xian collapsed in the crowd during a competition and all the disciples immediately rushed over to him. This time, however, the competition had only just begun and hadn't even reached the exciting part. There weren't any shouts, nor was the match suddenly paused, but rather just one person looked over at the monks and nuns on the Buddhist team, then another, and another—and soon it seemed as though everyone was gazing in that direction.

Everyone saw the Bodhisattva.

The bright yellow glow contained a layer of dark red, and the red in turn had a shade of gold. That reddish-gold glow was shining down from above, and some of the nearby nuns and monks went to embrace it. Meanwhile, those who could not approach quickly clasped their hands to their chests while silently chanting the *Namo Amitābha* sutra. Then someone knelt by the side of the court and clasped his hands, whereupon ten or twenty other eminent monks did the same. Soon, all the Daoist, Catholic, Muslim, and Protestant disciples also turned toward the Bodhisattva and began kneeling and praying in accordance with their own rituals. Meanwhile, the Daoist masters and Muslim imams who were competing simultaneously relaxed their grip on the rope as they also turned to look in the direction of the Bodhisattva. The last person to notice what was happening was Pastor Wang.

He repeatedly asked the competitors, "What's going on? What's going on?"

Then he suddenly headed toward the crowd of monks and nuns and shouted to the crowd that was blocking his view, "Quick, call an ambulance! Call an ambulance!"

23 Jueyu

Jueyu *shifu* passed away.

She passed away because of the tug-of-war competitions, but not entirely because of the tug-of-war competitions.

When the hospital had said that she could be discharged in a few days, Jueyu *shifu* decided that after being discharged she would go directly to Xining's Jing'an Temple to recuperate. So who could have anticipated that, three days before she was due to be discharged, she would see a flock of white doves fly overhead while she was exercising in the grove in front of the hospital? The sky was dark blue that day and the doves were snowy white, like lotus petals overhead. Jueyu *shifu* suddenly wanted to return to the school and speak to her fellow students, so she changed back into the yellow robe she had been wearing when she arrived at the hospital, folded her blue-striped hospital gown and placed it at the head of her bed, then took a taxi back to the school. When she arrived at the religion building, she didn't see any other disciples. Upon learning that this was the final exam period and that, after finishing their exams, the disciples had all gone to the sports field, she clasped her hands together in prayer. She slowly proceeded to the sports field. There were clouds in the sky, and apart from the badminton court, which was full of people, the basketball court, tennis court, and soccer field were all completely empty. The grass field at the center of those ball courts was mostly yellow with a hint of residual green.

Jueyu *shifu* headed toward the badminton court and saw that disciples of all the center's religions were already there. Just as she was about to offer a prayer, she noticed Mingzheng shouting and waving the oversized replica check, as billows of laughter and applause drifted through the air—as though intended for the Bodhisattva of the Pure Realm to hear. When Jueyu *shifu* reached the court's metal fence, she heard Mingzheng shouting out the donation amounts, and after taking a few more steps she heard the sounds of the tug-of-war competition. Her heart shuddered as she peered through the fence at the heads and shoulders of the disciples who had gathered there. Pastor Wang was blowing his referee's whistle, and the disciples on the Daoist and Islamic teams were waiting for the competition to begin. She began to sweat profusely, and her heart was beating so fast that she almost collapsed. She took a few steps forward while leaning against the fence, ultimately reaching the court's west gate. As she was leaning against the gateway, she considered going back to find somewhere to lie down. At that moment, however, she glimpsed old Imam Ren Xian—who, like herself, had been opposed to the tug-of-war competitions. He was sitting on a stool in front of the Islamic team's spectators, watching the competitors as though watching a theatrical performance. His thin face now looked ten years younger, and he was beaming with joy.

Jueyu *shifu* wanted to retreat, but instead she advanced through the court's metal gate.

The competition began. In the early-winter light, there was a comforting smell of charcoal. Among the white clouds floating across the sky, it seemed as though each one held a pair of Guanyin eyes, and the swirls around them resembled a thousand Guanyin orchid fingers, beautiful, soft, and elastic. Everyone was on the ground, while the Bodhisattva was up in the sky, watching the competition from a distance.

The competition began, and the victor would be awarded the one-hundred-thousand-yuan purse. This money had been provided not by the school nor by the National Religion Association, but rather by the disciples themselves—as though they were collecting their own incense ashes and wax drippings from the area in front of the deities and consuming them. Jueyu *shifu's* breathing became irregular, as if her throat were blocked by ash and wax. The tug-of-war rope was swaying tautly in the center of the court, and Jueyu *shifu* felt as though a rod were impaling her chest. Sweat dripped from her head and face, splattering onto her hands clasped in front of her heart. She repeatedly waved her left hand as though trying to brush away something covering her chest, praying that a crack might open there and permit her to breathe. The other disciples were craning their necks to peer into the court, and none noticed that in the open space behind them Jueyu *shifu's* body was becoming increasingly contorted as she leaned against the gate, and her steps were becoming progressively lighter. As she walked over to the Buddhist section, her body resembled a pile of shrimp skins buffeted by the wind.

Jueyu *shifu* came up behind the crowd of disciples watching the Buddhist team, and when she turned, she saw Shuiyue *shifu* staring at the competition and grinning. The court again erupted with cries of "For Allah, for Allah!" At this point, Jueyu *shifu* realized that her body was failing, and that she didn't have the strength to support herself. She wanted to reach out and grab someone, or even just a vine, as the cries of the Islamic team began pounding in her ears: "Fellow believers, did you not eat meat and drink alcohol before the competition?"

Then, as the cries quieted down, Jueyu *shifu* saw the Bodhisattva appear before her, her dress dancing. Jueyu *shifu* stepped forward to grasp the Bodhisattva's hand, and by the time she reemerged from the Bodhisattva's lotus field, an entire day and night had already passed, and she was once again lying in her room in Yonghe Hospital.

She vaguely saw that the lamplight had become the color of sunlit water—bright yellow, like the lake in front of Jingshui Convent in autumn. On the table in the room, there was a bowl with chop-sticks and a half-filled medicine bottle, and the fluorescent lamp and cord hanging from the ceiling were swaying back and forth. Several shadowy figures were drifting from one side of the room to another. She heard a doctor say, "I'm afraid there's nothing we can do. Tonight, the two of you should stay here in the sickroom."

The doctor walked away pushing an emergency medical cart, leaving a distant silence and translucence. Eventually, there was the familiar sound of Yahui and Mingzheng's voices.

"Should we notify the organization?" Mingzheng asked Yahui.

"By organization, do you mean the school?" Yahui replied. "If so, then no need. This is a matter for our religion to handle, and if the organization interferes, will my *shifu* be able to have a Buddhist burial?"

Mingzheng was silent for a while, then asked her, "Could it be that you still hope to . . . to take Jueyu *shifu* back to Xining?"

This question was followed by a silence, as though the sickroom were empty apart from the solitude and white walls, lamplight, and other miscellaneous items. It was as though the air in the room had died, and the people in the room had also died. It seemed that Mingzheng sighed and sat down, but it also seemed that Yahui said something that immediately pulled him back to his feet. Either Yahui or Mingzheng flipped over the IV bag to look at the back and mut-tered something. They pushed the stool to one side, then pulled a wire bed out from beneath the sickbed. They unfolded the wire bed and placed it in the middle of the room, added sheets and a blanket, then made the bed and sat down, as the bedsprings made a screeching sound. One of them asked, "What time is it?" and the other replied, "Ten-thirty." Then Mingzheng said, "You should sleep. You were up all night caring for your *shifu*." So Yahui turned on the lamp at the head of the bed and turned off the overhead light, then returned to bed and lay down.

The sickroom was immediately filled with muddy yellow light, as though a crack had opened up in the still night and the light shining through had an immovable weight. There was the sound of a car driving down the road outside the hospital. In the hospital's courtyard something made a sound, after which everything fell silent again. Time became like mud, soft and heavy. There was a moment of stillness, followed by a moment of deathly silence. Originally it seemed as though the silence would persist, but then there was a noise, as though Mingzheng had been standing in the room for a while but then had come over to sit on the bed next to Yahui. It was unclear what happened next, but eventually Mingzheng got up and turned off the lamp at the head of the bed, leaving the room enveloped in darkness, as time seemed to fall into the darkness of an old well.

Jueyu *shifu* knew that Yahui and Mingzheng were lying together in bed like brother and sister, but also like husband and wife. A murky layer of moonlight was hanging over the window, and each of the windows in the building across the way was illuminated by lamplight that resembled so many sheets of paper. After a moment, or perhaps after a long while, Yahui suddenly whispered angrily, "Mingzheng, don't touch me!"

This was followed by silence, after which it was unclear what exactly happened—though the wire bed gritted its teeth as though it were about to collapse. It seemed Mingzheng wanted to do something, but Yahui wouldn't let him. They carefully tussled, and at one point it appeared Yahui had succeeded in pushing Mingzheng off the bed, but as he was rolling away he grabbed her clothes, filling the room with the sound of fabric ripping and buttons popping. After this, there was again silence. Then, someone gently slapped someone else's cheek, and the sickroom once again became as silent as a tomb. Eventually, Yahui hopped out of bed, cleared her throat, and said, "*Amitābha*, how can your religion have such hooligans?!"

Mingzheng didn't reply. He appeared unwilling to give up, and it seemed he made another move while standing in front of her.

Yahui again said angrily, "Gu Mingzheng, don't touch me. It was you who harmed my *shifu*. It was you who told her that the school had abolished its athletic competitions, and you even showed her proof. Yet you still proceeded to organize another tug-of-war competition and raised a ton of money!"

". . ."

Yahui said, "Gu Mingzheng, I haven't attained Buddhist enlightenment, but I have become enlightened with respect to your religion—*your* religion is a pile of plant ash that the people of Xijing make from fermenting vegetation. It isn't derived from heaven and nature, but rather it's a pile of compost derived from natural processes, like pig shit and dog shit!"

It was hard to tell whether Mingzheng said anything in response, but then he sighed and lunged toward Yahui. Soon he was lying beside her, as the bed was crushed under their weight and slid across the floor. Eventually, all that could be heard was the sound of tearing, pushing, and panting, combined with the rough sound of two people breathing heavily. Eventually Yahui appeared to accept Mingzheng's advances, but then Jueyu *shifu* suddenly reached out and knocked over the IV pole next to the bed.

With her final breath she said, "*Amitābha*, don't you know . . . that Guanyin and Laozi are . . . overhead? They are actually right here under your noses . . . this is a sin!" With this, the sickroom was struck by a silence like a bolt from the sky. Apart from Yahui and Mingzheng's hoarse breathing, there wasn't a trace of a sound.

Jueyu *shifu* passed away, her eyes becoming as pale as a snow-white lotus.

24 Guanyin and Laozi

1. Heavens, it turns out that firewood, rice, oil, and salt are essential parts of daily life!

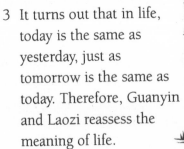

2. Heavens, it turns out that chickens, ducks, cats, and rabbits are also part of life.

3 It turns out that in life, today is the same as yesterday, just as tomorrow is the same as today. Therefore, Guanyin and Laozi reassess the meaning of life.

4. If they could conceive a child, their life would have new meaning. But why are they not able to conceive?

5. Fighting and smashing plates—is this what life is really about?

6. "Is it my fault we can't conceive a child?" Guanyin becomes so angry that she resolves to hang herself.

7. As Guanyin is about to hang herself, she suddenly sees a new world inside the noose.

8. "Can I be blamed for the fact that we can't conceive a child? Who doesn't dare to die?" Laozi is so angry that he climbs a mountain and prepares to leap off a cliff.

9. As Laozi is about to leap, he suddenly sees the distant sky and universe.

10. Actually, Laozi's and Guanyin's respective magical rides have been waiting for them in the Milky Way the entire time.

11. Now they need to separate, and the old ox is swallowing its final gulps of divine water.

12. After the divine beast also finishes its final gulps, it prepares to leave the old ox.

13. The old ox walks toward Laozi
and says, "Congratulations,
now you can finally leave
the mortal world."

14. The divine beast walks toward Guanyin and says,
"Congratulations, now you can finally leave the mortal world."

15. After bidding each other farewell, Guanyin and Laozi each
    head in different directions.

16. Guanyin heads
    toward spring.

17. Heads toward
    summer.

18. Heads toward fall.

19. Heads toward winter.

20. Laozi heads north.

21. Heads south.

22. Heads east.

23. Heads west.

24. Finally, Laozi, in the northwest, sees Hangu Pass in the distance, as though it has been waiting for him for thousands upon thousands of years.

25 Director Gong, Yahui, and Mingzheng

What followed was like a dream—a dream from which Yahui for the longest time was unable to extricate herself. It appeared the hospital was not at all surprised by Jueyu *shifu*'s passing. It was as if the hospital workers had already assumed she would die on that day, so they simply sent someone to the morgue and gave Yahui countless forms to fill out and sign. After Yahui had finally finished all the paperwork, she was informed that Director Gong wanted her to return to the school as soon as possible, because there was an urgent matter he needed to discuss. This is how she ended up standing in confusion in front of the hospital. Yahui paused for a while under the cypresses where Jueyu *shifu* used to do her exercises, before proceeding to the hospital's main entrance to catch a taxi back to the school.

Director Gong did not meet her in his office, nor in one of the school's cafés, but rather in a bar called Four Seasons Garden, which was in an alley across from the school. Yahui was vaguely familiar with the various residential quarters near the school, including Zhongguancun Avenue, Suzhou Street, and the Haidian university district, but as she was looking for Four Seasons Garden, she realized that Beijing's alleys were extremely peculiar—twisting and turning like a tangled ball of hemp. She made three loops around an alley called Willow Land and had to ask six different people before eventually discovering that beneath one family's house number there was a sign with four fist-sized characters that read *The Four Seasons Garden*. It was as though someone had intentionally made this bar difficult to find, and she had no idea why Director Gong had suggested that they meet there. As Yahui was hesitating, Mingzheng suddenly emerged, and when he saw her he exclaimed, "The director is waiting! Such an important matter, and now you've made him wait!"

Yahui glanced disdainfully at Mingzheng but allowed him to lead her in. The courtyard was separated from the outside world by a wall, inside which there was a gas stove and a beautiful garden. The courtyard had pomegranate and apple trees, together with two-meter-tall Chinese rose bushes. Although the fruit trees were out of season and only a few of the roses still retained traces of red, the courtyard's arrangement nevertheless reminded everyone of springtime. Next to each fruit tree there was an umbrella positioned so that raindrops would drip down onto the base of the tree, like someone continually reciting a poem. Tables and chairs were arrayed under the umbrellas along with heaters, and as customers enjoyed their drinks and coffee, it was as though they were listening to poetry while sitting next to a fire on a rainy day.

Murky water and misty poetry—just like a celestial courtyard.

Yahui entered the courtyard and stood beneath one of the trees, watching people sipping drinks under the umbrellas. The customers' glasses were as large as the ocean, yet they each held only a few drops—barely enough to cover the bottom of the glass. There was also the smell of coffee, like the scent of the tea that the Bodhisattva drinks in the legend. As Yahui followed Mingzheng inside, she saw that the entire room was decorated with wood paneling and was filled with European masks and African statues the likes of which she had never seen before, while the waitresses were all wearing uniforms that resembled floral pajamas. Yahui stood bewildered in the doorway, initially thinking they had come to the wrong room. She couldn't understand why the windows were tightly shuttered in the middle of the day, to the point that you needed a lamp to recognize people's faces. As customers drank and talked, they leaned close and murmured to each other as though plotting something. Mingzheng walked over and whispered into Yahui's ear, saying, "This is a bar, which is somewhat fancier than a café."

Attempting to stay out of sight, Yahui took a few steps forward, and saw that both the counter in the middle of the room and the cabinet behind it were full of bottles that were shimmering neon blue, green, and red in the lamplight. The room had a heater that was generating a sultry warmth. Yahui stood dazed in front of that crescent-shaped counter, feeling as though she had come to the wrong place. She had no choice but to wait for Mingzheng to lead her forward. Meanwhile, Mingzheng, smiling as though nothing had happened, came over and took her hand. "Christmas is around the corner, and Director Gong invited all the students in the religion class who are still around to come here to expand their horizons." As Mingzheng said this, he led Yahui to a private room, which had upholstered chairs and an old wooden table, a hanging lamp with a wooden lampshade, and chairs whose backs were inscribed with romantic phrases in English. As Yahui lifted the door curtain and went inside, she saw Director Gong and immediately slipped her hand out of Mingzheng's. Director Gong half stood up, nodded to Yahui, then gestured for her to have a seat in one of the upholstered chairs as he handed her a cup of coffee.

"I know I shouldn't have invited you and Mingzheng to meet me in a bar," Director Gong said with a laugh. "But people with Buddha in their hearts won't be afraid, regardless of where they are."

Yahui didn't immediately sit down. Instead, she clasped her hands in front of her chest and silently gave Director Gong a questioning look.

Director Gong gazed at her and said, "Mingzheng said . . . that your Jueyu *shifu* . . . is no longer with us?"

"She passed away," Yahui replied, as though correcting Director Gong's use of the phrase *no longer with us*. "The hospital just sent her body to the morgue."

"Oh . . . she passed away." After Director Gong apologetically repeated Yahui's phrase, Mingzheng brought in several meat, seafood, and vegetable dishes. The food was served buffet style. Mingzheng brought Yahui some salad and fruit, and brought Director Gong some meat, fish, and red wine. After serving himself cold crab, bamboo shoots, and fruit juice, he sat down across from Yahui. He pulled down a curtain decorated with assorted letters, stripes, and Christmas hats, which blocked out the outside noise and muffled the music to the point that it resembled clear water in a small stream.

It was time to eat lunch and discuss the matters at hand, so Director Gong swirled his wine glass, then put it down and said, "Yahui, it wasn't I who invited you here today. It was the organization."

Yahui looked at him again.

"Jueyu *shifu*'s death . . . her passing . . . is an important matter for the center, and it could create significant problems for us if the higher-ups were to learn she had a heart attack because of the tug-of-war competitions. All the effort we've put into the center over the past half year, the past year, and even the several years since I arrived, could end up being for nothing. Therefore, I don't want others at the center—including disciples and masters, not to mention the center's instructors and professors—to know that she has died. People die like a lamp being snuffed out, and not even a Buddha or deity can be reincarnated without having died first. Not even the Vedic deities! Not even Allah! Christianity's Easter came about when Jesus, after he died, was subsequently resurrected and became a god. But no matter what, Jueyu *shifu* wasn't going to survive . . . and given that, please help me keep the circumstances of her death a secret. Let's tell everyone she passed away after returning to Jingshui Convent. Afterward, you can devote yourself to your work at the center, and I'll make sure no one is sent to Jingshui

Convent to replace her as director—meaning that you'll be able to become the new director."

Yahui listened so attentively to what Director Gong was saying that her ears began to throb. As she was watching him speak, however, her gaze slipped away from his face and she instead found herself staring at his gray shirt. His shirt was the sort of handmade Chinese-style shirt that professors during the Republican era liked to wear. There was a loose thread wound around the second buttonhole, and although the air in the room was perfectly still, the thread was nevertheless swinging back and forth as though being blown by a breeze.

"Jingshui Convent . . . isn't very large, but it is, after all, a section-level temple." Director Gong thought for a moment, then added in a brighter tone, as though his voice now had a new layer of light, "Next semester you'll no longer need to come to class and take exams for your *shifu*. I'll tell the other disciples that your *shifu* is recuperating at Jingshui Convent, and that you are with her. This training session will end in six months, by which point no one will be thinking about her, whereupon you can take up the director position. Out of China's five major religions, you'll be the youngest section-level director."

Yahui remained silent and continued staring at that loose thread on Director Gong's shirt. She alternated between biting her upper and lower lips until they were both white.

"You're eighteen and will soon turn nineteen," Director Gong said. "If you become a director at the age of nineteen, your salary will be more than ten thousand yuan a month—which would be a true miracle within the religious world. This would be an unprecedented development for China, and perhaps even for the entire world."

Yahui had been clasping her hands together, but now she began picking at her robe with her left hand as though attempting to make a hole, while simultaneously rubbing the wooden table with her right. Her hands were covered in sweat and she tried to wipe them on the table.

At this point, Gu Mingzheng—who had been holding his chopsticks without eating anything—looked at Yahui, then turned to Director Gong. He suddenly asked, "Are you saying that next semester Yahui doesn't need to come to the religious training center?"

Director Gong replied, "Given that Jueyu *shifu* is no longer with us, on whose behalf would Yahui be attending class?"

Mingzheng stood up in shock, gazing first at Director Gong and then at Yahui. Meanwhile, Yahui also struggled to understand what exactly Director Gong meant—the same way that the Heart Sutra says that form is emptiness, emptiness is nothingness, and nothingness is existence and eternity, which allows people to understand that form, emptiness, nothingness, and existence are the subject of interminable teachings and allegories, even if it is impossible to explain them directly. Yahui stared at Director Gong, hoping he would explain his question to Mingzheng—hoping that he would explain with the same clarity that we know that clouds are clouds, rain is rain, and clouds, rain, and fog do not get mixed together. However, Director Gong simply held his cup and waved, like a missionary who has already explained his doctrines and has nothing more to say.

The air in the private room was as warm as a bamboo steamer, and the window was covered in a layer of condensation. Sweat was dripping from Mingzheng's face like water from the eaves of a house, and two drops fell onto the table in front of him. He wanted to say something, but he understood the implication of Director Gong's question and therefore remained silent. All he could do was wipe the sweat from his brow, look at Director Gong, and hope that someone would ask something or say something to disrupt that doctrinal meaning. However, Director Gong didn't say a word, and instead simply swished the wine in his glass, took a sip, then used the tip of his tongue to lick his lips and taste the air before returning his tongue to his mouth.

Given that Director Gong remained silent, Yahui couldn't very well say anything either. Nevertheless, she had to figure out the significance of the allusions to form, emptiness, nothingness, and existence in Director Gong's sacred utterance. So, she unclasped her hands and wiped her left hand on her robe and her right hand on the table. Then she asked, "Does my *shifu* need to be cremated?"

"This is Beijing, and no burials are permitted in the city," Director Gong replied in a loud voice. "Moreover, not only will she need to be cremated, but furthermore no Buddhist ceremonies can be performed at her cremation."

With this, everyone seemed to suddenly understand the implication of Director Gong's earlier question. All three of them were silent for a long time, and in the silence it was as though the spirit world were returning to the spirit world, and the human world were returning to the human world. Eventually Yahui looked at Director Gong and asked, "Would it be helpful to you if we don't tell others that my *shifu* has died?"

"Of course it would." Holding his wine glass, Director Gong stood up. "The center is a vice-bureau-level organization, and therefore I currently hold a vice-bureau-level appointment. The center's instructors and I have been working so hard precisely so that the center might be redesignated as an institute, which would make it a vice-department-level institution, which would raise my rank and help resolve our instructors' title and housing issues. If the higher-ups were to find out that someone from one of the training classes had died, the center might lose all hope of being redesignated as an institute. It is not particularly important that I might lose hope of changing my own rank, but what *is* important is that all of our instructors would have no hope of being assigned housing or of being promoted."

Upon hearing this, Yahui stared at Director Gong with her mouth closed, as though ruminating on the significance of what he had just said.

"You've been at the center for half a year now. Don't you understand that belief is only valuable when it helps *others* become better?

If believers were not attempting to benefit others and instead were only trying to benefit themselves, there wouldn't even be a rationale for religious belief."

Yahui continued to listen with her mouth closed. As she sat there gazing at Director Gong, it looked as though she understood, but then again it also looked as though she didn't.

26 Yahui and Mingzheng

When Yahui emerged from the bar, Director Gong still had some matters to attend to, so it was Mingzheng who saw her out. On the street corner in front of the bar, Mingzheng entreated her, "Let's return to secular life and get married. That way, you won't need to live in Xining all alone."

Yahui gazed at Mingzheng, then looked up at the sky and said, "Mingzheng, my *shifu* is still lying warm in the morgue." She was silent for a moment, then continued, "As for whether we should return to secular life and get married, I need to go to the morgue and ask my *shifu*. Let's see what she thinks."

At this point, Yahui fell silent again. She glanced at the passersby, then added, "As long as my *shifu* approves, I would be willing to return to secular life with you, even if you were a heretic or an infidel."

Mingzheng stood there, his face pale.

Yahui walked away. She turned and leisurely headed toward Zhongguancun Avenue and then the school, which was still on winter break. As she proceeded, she silently counted prayer beads as methodically as the pace at which she was walking. Only after she had gone a considerable distance did she hear Mingzheng cry out, "You'll regret this! I guarantee you'll regret it! If you don't return to secular life, you'll eventually die in that godforsaken Xining, where birds don't even take a shit . . ."

Yahui briefly slowed down, but didn't stop.

Part II

Preface 1

1. Laozi finally reaches Hangu Pass.

2. But what will he do now? Laozi is imprisoned by the guard Yixi at Hangu Pass, and pleads to write his book on world salvation.

3. Laozi begins composing the Daodejing at night.

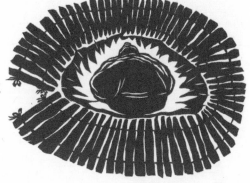

4. The book is five thousand characters long, and its light shines for five thousand years. After finishing the Daodejing, Laozi leaves Hangu Pass and proceeds west.

5. Laozi heads northwest, then continues even farther.

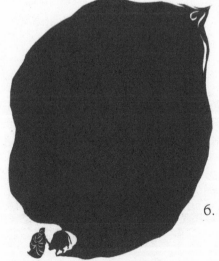

6. Up ahead there is a vast unknown, but there is also a vast known.

7. Oh! Ah! Ha-ha . . .
  —The future is unfettered! Oh, ah,
  ha-ha-ha . . .
  —The future is unfettered!

Preface 2

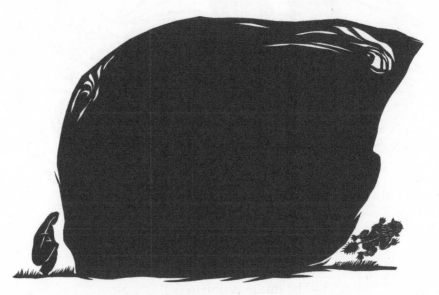

1. Where there is light, there is also darkness; and when there is joy, there is also sorrow. If Laozi shoulders this side of existence, then Guanyin needs to shoulder the other side. Guanyin's unknown future path is full of suffering and evil spirits, but because divine beasts are divine beasts, they have no choice but to leave her.

2. All alone, Guanyin begs for food as she walks along the dried riverbed and through the wilderness. Famished, she encounters an even more famished tigress who, although nearly dead from hunger, still wants to nurse her three cubs one last time. The tigress is so hungry that she can no longer produce any milk, so she cries out when her cubs bite her teats. She stands up and gazes at the sky and into the desolate wilderness, until finally her gaze comes to rest on her cubs.

The tigress decides that if she wants to live, she has no choice but to consume her own cubs.

Just as she is about to eat her cubs, however, she finds she is unable to continue, and instead spits them out.

She loses consciousness, as her cubs also pass out from hunger by her side.

3. Guanyin approaches and, after stopping in front of the tigress and her three cubs, decides to feed the tigress with her own flesh. She sits down and places her arm in the animal's mouth. The tigress slightly opens her mouth, but is so weak from hunger she doesn't even have the energy to bite down on the arm.

Seeing this, Guanyin pokes her arm with a thorn until it bleeds, then lets the blood drip directly into the tigress's mouth. As Guanyin does so, the tigress regains consciousness and begins to recover her strength, whereupon she proceeds to stare at Guanyin.

Guanyin closes her eyes and lies down beneath the tigress's mouth. The tigress begins to devour her, eventually spitting out one of the bones. Later, Guanyin awakens from the bone, her face covered in a glow as if from the rising sun. From the bone the tigress spits out, Guanyin attains a new life.

Preface 3

1

During the vacation, deities stopped hosting the Daoist Mingzheng, as did humans. During the first week of vacation, Beijing's air was so hazy that after taking ten steps you wouldn't be able to see anything at all. If you waved your hand through the air, it would become covered in countless tiny granules. In the street, apart from some people wearing masks, there was only the sound of dry coughing.

The city was as empty as a body without organs.

Unlike the other disciples, who had all either returned home or gone to their temples or churches for New Year, Mingzheng remained at the school's religion building, waiting to see his father. Nameless had repeatedly told him, "You should go find your father, and if he isn't already a minister or governor, he is probably a department director in that rich province in the south. It's even possible that he will soon be promoted to governor." After Yahui left Beijing with an urn containing her *shifu*'s ashes, Nameless visited Mingzheng three nights in a row, trying to convince him that after the remaining students left the school, he should go to the Beijing Hotel to meet a department director who might be his father.

After all the students returned home, the campus was left vacant, and the seventh floor of the religion building was as empty as a box.

No one was out in the streets, and whereas the city had previously resembled a parking lot filled with vehicles, it was now as empty as though a hurricane had just blown through. The few remaining cars resembled abandoned orphans squatting in a cemetery.

On this day, which happened to be a Sunday at the end of December, Mingzheng was planning to go to the Beijing Hotel to meet the department director, at which point father and son would hopefully be reunited. In preparation for the meeting, Mingzheng changed into a gray tunic and a brand-new pair of blue pants, in order to look more like a cadre at a government office. He emerged punctually from the religion building, then stopped and gazed at the empty campus, the sky, and the entranceway. He hailed a taxi, but as he rode down Chang'an Avenue, he realized he had left too early. He and the department director had agreed to meet in the Beijing Hotel reception hall at ten o'clock, but by eight-thirty Mingzheng had already reached Tiananmen Square, which was not far from the hotel.

Mingzheng got out of the taxi on the west side of the square. After gazing out at the solitude and emptiness of the hazy square, he headed toward Jinshui River. Upon seeing the enormous, God-like portrait hanging from the Tiananmen gate tower, he wondered whether the person in the portrait might one day become Laozi, Guanyin, Jesus, Buddha, or Muhammad. He wondered whether one day the image hanging from the gate tower might no longer be a portrait of that person, but rather a portrait of Mingzheng's own father. Mingzheng reflected that although the person he was about to see might not be a minister or governor, but merely the director of a minor department like a subchapter of the National Religion Association, he was nevertheless still a department director in China's richest province and was still on his way to becoming a governor. Mingzheng thought, *If he acknowledges me as his son today, I'll hoist a national flag at my temple in his honor after I return, and I'll remove the portrait of Laozi and replace it with a portrait of him.*

As Mingzheng was thinking this, he went to visit the Monument to the People's Heroes, the Great Hall of the People, and the Museum of Chinese History.

Finally, it was time for him to meet his father.

They had agreed to meet at ten o'clock in the easternmost reception room on the ninth floor of the Beijing Hotel. Mingzheng knew he should arrive at around 9:50, but he ended up arriving before 9:30. When he entered, he assumed someone would stop him and ask him some questions. In the end, however, the two security guards in the entranceway merely smiled and bowed as he passed. He hadn't expected that the hotel's lobby would be so large, and he now felt as though he were standing in the middle of Tiananmen Square. The ceiling was so high, it appeared to reach the clouds in the sky. As Mingzheng was passing through the lobby, he saw a waitress with some cups of tea. She had a smile like a red lotus, which reminded Mingzheng of Yahui on her way back to Xining carrying an urn filled with ashes. *Given that you were able to steel your heart and leave me, if today it turns out that my father is in fact that department director who is about to become governor of that southern province, will I still ask you to marry me? Would that be necessary?* Mingzheng thought, *In the end, you're still just a pretty nun who can make papercuts and recite the sutras. I might as well marry a college student.* To avoid having to speak to anyone, he headed directly to the elevator, from which another waitress emerged. She was also wearing a red dress and a red boat cap, and her smile also resembled a red lotus.

"Hello. What floor?"

He stared at her for a second, then replied, "The ninth floor."

So even the act of pressing the elevator button had been entrusted to someone else? This made Mingzheng wonder—if he was in fact the son of that department director who was about to become governor, would there also be someone to spoon-feed him when it was time to eat? Would a doctor immediately come running if he so much as coughed? The elevator was empty except for Mingzheng, and when, shaking back and forth, it finally reached the ninth floor, he found another waitress waiting for him. This third waitress closely resembled the first two—she was wearing the same outfit and had the same lotus-like smile. She solicitously asked Mingzheng a few questions, as he reached into his pocket and took out a note from the person he wanted to see. He showed the waitress the note, whereupon she stepped onto the red carpet in the hallway and led him to the reception hall on the east side of the ninth floor. There, she brought him a glass of water and asked him to sit for a while.

Then she left.

She quietly shut the door, as though closing a book she had grown tired of reading. It was only at this point that Mingzheng finally dared turn around and looked directly at the reception hall. The hall was not very large—roughly the size of three of the religion building's dormitory rooms—and there were yellow sofas against each of the four walls. On the back of each sofa there was a knitted white cloth, and in front there was a small table made from pearwood. In the east corner of the hall there was a purified-water dispenser, and in the other three corners there were evergreen lucky bean plants. Meanwhile, in the center of the hall there was a floral carpet thicker than the palm of your hand, on which were woven the words: *Fifty-six nationalities, fifty-six flowers*. Mingzheng stood on the carpet and, after testing its thickness and softness, headed toward the wall in front of him.

In this rather ordinary hall, Mingzheng noticed something unusual. On the walls there were more than a dozen identically sized glass frames, each of which contained a five-by-eight-inch photograph of a different famous figure. Some of the figures were sitting, some were standing, and some were chatting with foreigners. Positioned in the center, the most eye-catching photograph featured that person on the Tiananmen gate tower, and in this image that person was sitting on a sofa and smoking, with his belly slightly protruding and his right leg crossed over his left. The white ash at the end of his cigarette was at least a finger long, and he was smiling like a woman who has just discovered she is pregnant with a boy. Under the portrait there was a caption written in block characters, which read: "In 1951, Chairman Mao visited and rested here." The second portrait was of someone called Liu Shaoqi, who was shaking hands and speaking with someone who was the same height as himself and was wearing a colorful round hat. The caption read, "In 1952, Deputy Chairman Liu met here with an ethnic minority representative." The third photograph was of someone called Zhou Enlai, who was sitting on a sofa, speaking to an older man wearing a Chinese tunic suit and the sort of pointed-toe cloth shoes that only Buddhist priests and Daoist masters wear. The side of the shoe's opening was lined with a series of stitches. Mingzheng immediately recognized that these were the kind of shoes that only monks wear. He glanced down at the caption below the photograph, and it confirmed his assumption. It said, "On this location in 1952, Premier Zhou Enlai discussed some national religious matters with a religious master." Mingzheng stared at that short-haired, round-faced, septuagenarian figure, and wondered who this might be: the abbot of a Buddhist temple or the host of a Daoist temple? He wondered whether this image might be an anticipation of how in a few years he might become a religious master like this abbot or host, frequently summoned by national leaders to come shake hands, drink tea, and discuss the nation's religious matters. As Mingzheng was thinking this, a smile appeared on his face, and he quickly continued along this photograph-lined path. He looked at the fourth and fifth photographs, and continued until he reached the ninth one. These latter images included someone named Zhu De, who once took a nap in this reception hall, and someone called Ye Jianying, who once smoked a cigarette in this hall. There was also Deng Xiaoping, with whom Mingzheng was already very familiar, who once had a nice chat with the waitresses while waiting for someone in this hall. Finally, there was also that person known as Marshal He Long, who had once gotten angry and started lecturing people while waiting in this hall. Each of these visits was carefully documented in the captions below the photographs. Year after year, era after era, countless national leaders had, for some reason or other, come to this hotel and visited this reception hall.

To Mingzheng, all the figures in the photographs looked uncannily familiar, reminding him of the religious masters who appeared in his classroom photographs. He was surprised that this rather unremarkable hall had been visited by virtually all the nation's political leaders. He was convinced that his father was currently on a trajectory to ascend from department director to governor, and from there maybe even to a position in an office inside one of Beijing's red-walled buildings—because otherwise why would Mingzheng see himself in these photographs? Why else would he come here to find himself?

As Mingzheng was examining the photographs, he suddenly began to feel light-headed and his palms became clammy. For no apparent reason, he began to feel feverish. He gripped his waist with both hands, as though squeezing out sweat from between his fingers. It even seemed as though there was sweat dripping down onto the rug under his feet. He glanced down but didn't see any moisture on the rug or on the brick floor beyond it. This reassured him a bit, so he looked at his hands and wiped them on his pants. He unfastened his shirt's top button, lifted his collar, and shook it so that a cool breeze could blow down his back. Hearing footsteps outside the door, he quickly rebuttoned his shirt and sat back down on the sofa. Then he picked up his teacup from the table.

The door opened, and Mingzheng saw the waitress who had escorted him inside. He took a sip of tea, then put down his cup and stood up.

"The leader says he needs to go to Zhongnanhai to deal with an urgent matter, and suggests that he can see you the next time you come." The waitress said this rather apologetically, her smile less warm than before.

Mingzheng stared in shock and his vision blurred. Outside the window, the sky was as dark as though it were covered in a black cloth, and although the reception hall was well lit, he felt that the light in front of him was downright dazzling, as though there were countless stars floating through it like swarms of mosquitoes.

"The heater is turned up too high," he complained. The waitress smiled and, looking at the sofa and the photographs on the wall, remarked, "Deng Xiaoping once sat on that sofa."

Mingzheng looked down at the sofa and then at the photograph of the person called Deng Xiaoping. It seemed as though he were looking for something he had left on the sofa, and because he couldn't find it, he asked regretfully, "The leader . . . didn't say when I should return?"

"He didn't say. You should just go back and wait to be notified."

Mingzheng emerged from the reception hall. He took several steps forward, appearing as though he were about to collapse. He closed his eyes and supported himself by leaning against the walls of the hotel hallway.

2

That night, Mingzheng realized that this December was his personal hell. After emerging from the Beijing Hotel, he spent the entire day wandering through the city, and didn't return to the school until evening.

Dusk came early at that time of year, so by five o'clock it was already dark, and by seven the entire campus was as dark as a gallows in hell. It was only then that Mingzheng noticed that throughout the school's entire two-thousand-*mu* courtyard, all of the streetlamps seemed to be suspended in midair like demon eyes, and you couldn't even see them unless you stood directly underneath them. He could occasionally hear cars driving down the street, like ghosts chasing each other. All the school's buildings were hidden in darkness, as the literature, philosophy, journalism, and law institutes disappeared into the foggy night. Similarly, the school's institutes of Tang, Song, Ming, and Qing dynasty history were merely spots of light in the dark night. Mingzheng called his *shifu* at his temple, who said, "If you couldn't find your father, then why do you want to return to the temple? From now on, Daoism will rely on you and your father!" Mingzheng also called Yahui, but her phone's ringtone sounded as dead as the breath in her *shifu's* urn. After putting down his phone, Mingzheng felt as though he were being attacked by an unbearably heavy emptiness. On the surface, it appeared that this feeling was caused by people walking through the campus's solitude and fog, but really he did not know where this unimaginably heavy emptiness came from.

In his room on the third floor, the light was usually white, but on that particular night it had turned yellow. The light was tainted by the haze, such that all the lights resembled blocked conduits of belief. The air tasted like sand, and if you held out your hand, it wouldn't disappear into the haze as quickly as before. There was a table and a bed with an unfolded blanket and sheets. In the sink was a pile of socks and clothes that he had forgotten to wash, and lying in the corner was a copy of a yellow-covered textbook titled *Daoism and Marxist-Leninist Philosophical Perspectives*. Hidden behind the picture on the wall of Laozi emerging from the pass, there was a photograph of a female movie star. There was also a copy of the Daodejing and several additional annotated editions of the text, which were mixed in with popular magazines and a signed copy of *New Compilation of Chinese Religious Stories of Positive Energy*. There was also a volume of Japanese ukiyo-e paintings that Mingzheng had bought at a newsstand under the skywalk at the school entrance. The room was so messy that it resembled a set of Daoist scriptures annotated by someone with no understanding of Daoism, or Buddhist sutras that were so complex and baroque that they resembled parodies of themselves.

Fortunately, the room's heater was quite powerful, leaving the room so hot that as soon as Mingzheng entered he immediately undressed. He placed his clothes on the back of a chair and sat in the chair wearing only an undershirt and a pair of long underwear. As soon as his shoulder and back touched the chair, he was poked by his belt buckle, but was too lazy to move his pants from the back of the chair. His entire body felt stiff, but he wasn't sure whether he was exhausted from the attempted meeting at the Beijing Hotel or from wandering around the city all day. The belt buckle pressed against his right shoulder blade like an iron pin, producing a painful but also rather pleasurable feeling. To increase this sensation, he pressed back against the buckle while moving his shoulder back and forth, so that the prong would poke into his flesh. The prong pierced his shirt and his skin, whereupon a combination of searing pain and intense pleasure surged through his body. He trembled, then straightened his back and pressed backward again such that the prong would penetrate deeper into his shoulder. It hurt more, while also becoming even more pleasurable.

He felt warm blood dripping down his back, but as it dripped down, the blood's warmth dissipated. He tried to push the tip of the prong even deeper into his shoulder. Finally, he sat up, squared his shoulders and straightened his neck, then pushed the prong into the gap between his shoulder blades. By this point, a third of the prong had already penetrated his shoulder, and the resulting sensation was approximately three-tenths pain and six- or seven-tenths pleasure.

"Deeper, deeper," he muttered to himself, as he pushed his shoulder backward, while repeatedly muttering, "Press deeper, press deeper!" As he did so, tears of pleasure streamed down his face, and as he pressed back even more forcefully, he struggled to make sure that his upper body remained completely immobile to prevent the prong from slipping out of position. He could feel it impaling his shoulder like a nail drilled directly into a table. "Harder, harder . . ." Blood surged out like water from a mountain spring, staining the front and back of his shirt, and dripping down his back like red-bean soup. He felt as relaxed as though his body was about to float away. The feeling resembled the spasms of pleasure he experienced when he masturbated. The result was like an orgasm, and in that instant his entire body was in ecstasy. The light dimmed, the earth shook, and in front of him a black hole was spinning like a flywheel: it seemed as though his soul were dancing in front of him.

Suddenly, he heard a noise at the door as someone's shadow flickered in the entranceway. He stared at the figure who had just entered, but he didn't ask the visitor how he had gotten in, nor did he invite him to sit down or reproach him for barging in without knocking. Instead, Mingzheng simply asked himself, *Didn't I lock the door? Didn't I lock the door?* Now, however, this no longer mattered. The visitor entered and stood before him, and Mingzheng could see that the visitor's face was covered in sweat and his forehead was glowing like a piece of glass that had just been removed from a vat of water.

"What are you doing?"

Mingzheng realized that his visitor was the man known as Nameless, whom he had already encountered several times. Mingzheng didn't look at his visitor, and instead focused on pressing his shoulder against the back of the chair. The blood from his back dripped down to the ground, then flowed out in front of the chair, stretching toward the visitor's feet. Mingzheng looked down at the floor, and what he saw didn't resemble blood as much as blurry light. With regret, he pressed back even more forcefully, such that the blood would flow out even faster.

"I've come to notify you that there is a deputy department director who wants to see you tomorrow. He says you may be his son."

Mingzheng looked up and fixed his gaze on Nameless. He stared at the man's thin face and his clean and rustic clothing, as though staring at another religion's Jesus.

"What about the father from . . . the Beijing Hotel?"

"He has already gotten a job in Zhongnanhai, so I'm afraid that even if he really is your father, he won't acknowledge it now."

Nameless said this with an odd smile—but it wasn't clear whether he was smiling to himself, or smiling at the fact that Mingzheng hadn't been able to meet with his prospective father. As Nameless stood one step away, Mingzheng could now see him clearly—like a saint who hesitates upon seeing Moses rescuing people from hardship, unsure whether to continue following Moses on that path to the so-called land of milk and honey which might instead be a path of suffering. The room's yellow light became increasingly murky until it resembled a pool of black mud. Mingzheng stared at Nameless, and Nameless stared back at him, as the room became as still as the dead of night.

"Why don't you say something?" Nameless gently asked Mingzheng. "If you don't want to see the deputy department director, there's also an old professor who previously abandoned his son and is now searching for him. We could go see him instead."

Mingzheng wasn't sure whether he wanted to see the professor. Mingzheng first thought of Director Gong at the mention of the professor, but in his bones, he didn't have the slightest desire to see him—the same way someone might claim that Buddhism or Daoism is the only true religion, when in fact Daoists don't know anything about Buddhism, just as Buddhists don't know anything about Daoism. Mingzheng continued to stare at the person in front of him, as though hoping that Nameless would make the decision on his behalf. "There are also a couple of bureau heads in line behind him. Given that you are in your twenties, your father would probably be around fifty. However, if someone is around fifty and is still only a bureau or section head, he is probably already reaching the end of his career. I'm afraid that after we look around, we might discover that your father is someone like this."

Nameless continued standing there, as if the room's heat had no effect on him. He didn't even remove his jacket or unfasten his buttons. He had a kind and peaceful expression, like Jesus nailed to the cross or Laozi emerging from the pass and feeling desolate and famished, yet also relaxed and carefree.

"I recommend that you pick between the deputy department director and the professor, and then go meet one of them." As Nameless said this, he took a step back, then continued in a voice that was neither loud nor soft.

"After all, a deputy department director is still a department-level position. Meanwhile, a professor is an intellectual, and it is intellectuals who have the best understanding of Laozi, Zhuangzi, and Confucius. Just think, it wouldn't be bad at all if it turned out that you had this sort of father."

The blood on the floor reached Nameless's foot, and it seemed as though the entire world were red, sticky, and filled with the odor of blood. Nameless saw that Mingzheng's blood had reached his leather-soled shoe, which stopped the stream like a dam, forming a pool larger than a handkerchief and as thick as a flatcake. As the blood accumulated, it turned black, as though black ink had been poured into a bottle of red ink, and it formed a hard scab, like the scallion flatcakes that are sold in front of the school. Half of Nameless's left foot was submerged in the blood. He looked down and took a step back, then lifted his foot and shook it a few times. Finally, he looked up again at Mingzheng, and asked urgently, "Whom do you want to see first, the deputy department director or the professor?"

Without waiting for an answer, Nameless made a choice on Mingzheng's behalf, explaining, "If neither the deputy department director nor the professor is your father, I recommend that you might as well see the bureau head and section head. After all, it is better to have a father than not to have one at all."

He added, "At the very least, you should know why your father abandoned you shortly after you were born. You should go hear what he has to say for himself." Nameless shifted his blood-covered foot, and continued, "After all, don't you believers rely on stories for your gods? To tell the truth, religious faith is just a matter of believing stories. The world is governed by stories, and it is for the sake of stories that everyone lives on this earth."

As Nameless said this, he glanced to the left, and then, as if exhausted, looked away again. Sounding as if he had just made up his mind, he added, "I think that if either the deputy department director or the professor acknowledges you as his son, you should also acknowledge him in return. You definitely shouldn't drag this out to the point that you end up with a father who not only isn't a deputy department director, but isn't even a bureau head."

This entire time, Mingzheng's gaze did not stray from the thin and plain-dressed Nameless, as though observing Laozi emerging from the pass and proceeding west. Mingzheng saw that as Nameless was speaking, his mouth had a trace of a smile, as though he were smiling at how after learning the Dao and proceeding into the world, he did not obtain any proof of the Dao. Blood was still flowing down Mingzheng's back, but in order to focus on what Nameless was saying, Mingzheng had briefly stopped pressing against the back of the chair. To preserve that pleasurable sensation, he now pressed backward again, but within that sensation, a new feeling of pain emerged. Mingzheng's face flinched as he gasped, then he pressed back once again. He closed his eyes, opened them, and asked Nameless something he had long wanted to ask: "What about a businessman? Could you help me look among some businessmen?"

Nameless shook his head, as though he had already done this.

"I don't necessarily want my father to have a specific amount of money—it would be great if he had several hundred million yuan, but several tens of millions, or even just several million yuan, would be fine." As Mingzheng said this, his facial muscles twitched and his mouth twisted from the pain. But this time, as he clenched his teeth the pain coursing from his back to his face reminded him of something. He closed his eyes, and when he reopened them, he immediately corrected himself, saying, "This isn't about money, I'm simply trying to find my father."

Nameless glanced at Mingzheng's mouth, then said, "But what if your father turns out to be a bankrupt businessman?"

Mingzheng didn't reply.

"What if he is now penniless, and furthermore is carrying an enormous debt? What if, after you recognize him, he asks you to help him repay his debts?"

Mingzheng gave Nameless a death stare, and as he did so he remained perfectly motionless, as though his gaze were a pair of branches extending from his eyes directly to Nameless's face. At that moment, Mingzheng once again leaned back, so that the prong pushed even deeper into his shoulder blade, as though reaching the innermost regions of his shoulder. Even when the renewed pain overwhelmed the comfortable sensation, however, Mingzheng kept his gaze fixed on Nameless's face.

"Is that really possible?"

"Yes, it's certainly possible."

"Do you already know who my father is?"

". . ."

"Who is he?"

"It would be best if you didn't ask."

There was a dead silence, which made the room's warmth and light coagulate like the pool of blood on the floor. As if to break up that pool of congealed blood, Mingzheng raised his voice and demanded, "Tell me."

"I definitely can't tell you—because if I did, you would have to kill him!"

Mingzheng didn't ask again. It was almost as if he didn't care anymore. He glanced at Nameless in front of him, then suddenly pressed backward again until he felt as though a chopstick were penetrating into the innermost recesses of his shoulder, and the cry that emerged from his bone sounded as though his shoulder were being dislocated. This cry elevated him from his seat, whereupon he turned and grabbed the belt, letting that inch-long metal prong slide between his middle and index fingers, as though he were holding a nail. Then he turned and thrust the prong in Nameless's face.

At this point, Nameless disappeared like a gentle breeze. He closed Mingzheng's door and walked away without making a sound. Meanwhile, Mingzheng accidentally stepped into the pool of blood at his feet. He slipped and toppled over like an old tower, as a thunderous sound filled the religion building.

<h1 style="text-align:center">3</h1>

When Mingzheng woke up the next day, there was still a thick haze outside. The world had no light, and there were no deities present in the mortal realm. There were bloody shoeprints in the doorway, and his pants and belt had been tossed against the doorway's white wall. As Mingzheng stared at the belt, he suddenly noticed that someone had slid a note under the door.

Mingzheng went to pick up the belt and the note, and after tossing the belt onto the bed he examined the note. Upon reading it, Mingzheng was neither surprised nor happy, neither active nor silent. It was as though he had received something just by wanting it, but then realized that it wasn't what he had wanted after all. He lowered his hand, sat down on the edge of the bed, and proceeded to stare out the window.

The message read: *Your birth father, Gu Shengbao: 133 Daoliu Lane, 13th Alley, Eastern Quadrangle, Chaoyang District.*

Mingzheng immediately recognized Nameless's handwriting—a mass of black strokes, with every character resembling late-autumn foliage. The characters with many strokes resembled clumps of vegetation, while those with few strokes resembled solitary sprouts. But regardless of whether they were clumps of vegetation or individual plants, they were all grazed by the sun during the day and chilled by the autumn frost at night. It was as if the individual branches and leaves had been condensed, while still retaining a great clarity of lines and structure. After reading the note, Mingzheng was silent for a moment, then he tossed the paper onto the bed and began washing his face and brushing his teeth. After tidying up his room, he went outside to get some breakfast.

With deities up in heaven and humans down on earth, there is nothing in between. Like the day before, there were very few people at the school. Only a handful of religious masters and doctoral students remained on campus working on their theses and dissertations. Mingzheng emerged from the religion building, nodded to the white-haired, middled-aged man who worked as both doorman and dispatcher, then stood in the entranceway for a while. After eating a Tianjin bun in an off-campus alley, Mingzheng stood on a walkway over Zhongguancun Avenue. He noticed that the road under the bridge was like a dried-up riverbed, with barely any cars or people. He gazed at the blackness and emptiness of the dust overhead. He looked like he was pondering something, but in reality his mind was as empty as a patch of earth that had never seen a seedling. He had so much time on his hands that it felt almost unbearable. This reminded him of a temple's incense stick that smoked so vigorously that the deities couldn't even open their eyes.

After standing there for a while, he headed back down the walkway.

Under the bridge there was a taxi that seemed to be waiting for him, so he hailed it, opened the door, and showed the driver the note. Then, for forty-three yuan, the driver took him to the East Second Ring Road's 13th Alley. Daoliu Lane was at the western end of the alley. At the entrance to the alley there was an old willow tree that was so large, three people together wouldn't be able to wrap their arms around it, and nailed to the tree was a yellow sign with *Daoliu Lane* written in red characters that were covered in a thick layer of dust. Mingzheng proceeded to the lane, which was only six feet wide and was originally intended for rickshaws. The walls had been painted with lime several years earlier, and the tops of the walls were lined with yellow tiles. Many of the houses had numbers affixed to the brick column in the entranceway, with the odd-numbered doors on the left and even-numbered ones on the right. As Mingzheng proceeded down the alley, however, he noticed that several houses either didn't have numbers or else their signs had fallen off, as though the original obsession with designing the street had faded like a pot of boiling water that has gradually cooled off. The alley was empty except for a cat and a few winter leaves that had blown in from somewhere, together with some grass that had sprouted and dried up on some family's wall.

The area was so desolate, it was as though this weren't even Beijing. It was as though everyone had left and left the city empty.

As he proceeded forward, Mingzheng was stopped by a sense of loneliness and felt as though his breath was rushed. Suddenly, the sound of cars honking erupted, like some sort of mechanical rumbling. He looked up and saw house number 133. The house's courtyard wall was painted gray and the roof tiles were sulfuric yellow. The only difference from the nearby houses was that above the old wooden door there used to be a white sheet of paper on which there appeared a single, terrifying character: *Demolish!* Although the house's owner had ripped open the paper when he opened the door, he nevertheless left the disputes and confrontations from the preceding several years inscribed there.

After hesitating for a moment in the doorway, Mingzheng eventually knocked and entered. It turned out that all the houses on this side of the lane consisted of little more than rubble strewn about the inside of the Second Ring Road, like a square made up of dead cells. A dozen meters or so away, a broken beam was stuck in the ground, and the visible portion was jet-black, suggesting that the demolition had already been going on for years. Beside that broken beam, there was one house that had not yet been demolished, and it was obvious that this single-story residence had been one of the courtyard's wings—with brick walls, carved windows, and a closed door. In front of the door there was a brick floor that had already been cleaned up, together with a makeshift stove in the shed by the door. Mingzheng headed toward the house and saw that next to it there was another partially demolished residence. Sitting in the doorway of the latter structure was a fat man in his fifties or sixties who was drinking tea out of a jar. In a heavy Beijing accent, the man shouted, "Hey, are you a demolition cadre?"

Then, still holding his tea, the man walked over and added, "Show me the money! Don't think you can fucking rely simply on inspiration!"

As the man was cursing, he suddenly paused, took several gulps of tea, and in an even louder voice said, "I'm warning you, the old man is very sick, and if you let him die in that house, we'll take his corpse to Tiananmen Square and organize a demonstration!"

The man, who had already proceeded halfway to Mingzheng, suddenly stopped and turned around. Mingzheng saw that the man's wife was calling out to him from behind, as his feet dragged through the courtyard ruins like the paws of a lion trudging through a wasteland. Afterward, the vast ruins fell silent, and even the nearby sounds of traffic and construction work faded. Looking around, Mingzheng touched the wall and suddenly felt as though he were in the middle of a cemetery. Even though he had just heard the other person say that there was someone inside the residence up ahead, he was still unwilling to enter. He wanted his father to be someone very fortunate, not some sick old man. He wanted a father who lived in a villa with a doorman, not some commoner who was being evicted because his home was slated to be demolished. Mingzheng was standing next to a collapsed pillar and about to turn around, when he suddenly heard a voice saying, "Given that you're already here, why don't you come in?"

After hesitating for a moment, Mingzheng proceeded toward the entranceway. He pulled aside the curtain hanging in the doorway, and as soon as he stepped inside, he was so captivated by what he found that he was unable to leave. The room was more than twenty square meters, and even had electric lights. Everything was laid out exactly as it had been before the demolition, and it looked just like the Beijing homes that Mingzheng had previously seen—with a dark wooden bed, a gray brick floor covered with furniture, and a side wall so packed with clothing and utensils that it resembled a folklore museum exhibit. On the wall over the front door, there was a colorful painting the size of a tatami mat. The upper portion of the painting consisted of white clouds and blue sky, below which there was a terrifying image of a black coffin. At one end of the coffin, in the space between the white and black areas, there was an image of a smiling fat baby. The infant was wearing a red bib, and its auspicious expression made it appear as though laughter were raining down on the coffin and the entire room.

This image was from a heretical folk religion known as Vitality, which was popular in the north. Religious leaders told their disciples that if they followed this religion, they could add at least twenty years to their life. That way, those who originally would have lived to the age of sixty could instead reach eighty, and those who would have lived to eighty could instead reach a hundred. Of course, if you were willing to donate some of your assets to a religious leader, you might even be able to live to be a hundred and twenty. At the base of the mountain where Mingzheng's temple was located, most of the old villagers believed in this heretical religion, and they often took funds meant for their children and secretly donated them to this religion's leader instead. The government attacked this religion the way it would attack a traitor, and Mingzheng never expected he would find a follower of this heretical faith in Beijing, much less that this person would turn out to be Gu Shengbao.

The room was filled with the thick smell of smoke. Over the burning charcoal at the head of the bed was a kettle about to come to a boil, and the sound and warmth of the water filled the room. As Mingzheng stared at the painting, he heard a squeaking sound, like an old piece of furniture struggling to return to its springtime forest, after which there was the sound of wood cracking.

"Have you come again to deliver vegetables?"

Mingzheng turned around.

"Just leave them there. I'll get out of bed in a little bit."

Mingzheng walked in the direction of the voice. At the sound of Mingzheng's footsteps, the figure in the bed turned over, and Mingzheng saw that it was an old man. The man's bone structure resembled a wooden frame, with gray eyebrows, a high nose, and a sallow complexion that even his countless wrinkles couldn't conceal. He appeared to be seventy or eighty years old and was lying in the bed as though it were a coffin, his tangled hair resembling grass growing over a grave. Mingzheng recoiled in shock when he saw the man's face, because in it he glimpsed a premonition of his own future self. It was as though he saw his own soul flying away. He wanted to say something to the old man, but his body swayed and he averted his gaze, as though trying to avoid an image that reminded him of his ghost. Yet Mingzheng couldn't resist turning back—and although he was certain he didn't open his mouth, he nevertheless heard a voice coming from his throat: "Oh, you are . . . is your surname Gu?"

The old man turned and appeared surprised to discover that the person standing before him was not the vegetable deliveryman. He stared at Mingzheng's face and, after a slight pause, suddenly sat up like a young man. He had an eager expression, as though his eyes were on fire. Preparing to speak, the man swallowed, and Mingzheng saw the bedsheet slip off his shoulder, exposing an upper body that resembled a skeleton wrapped in dirty gauze. The light from the window, the lamp, and the burning charcoal lit up the room so that even a pair of chopsticks on the floor were clearly visible. As a result, the old man's trembling face was also fully illuminated.

"Your name isn't Gu Shengbao by any chance, is it?"

Staring at Gu Mingzheng, the old man nodded and replied, "Yes, I am Gu Shengbao."

Mingzheng felt as though his body and the entire room had been struck by an earthquake. He staggered and regained his balance, and the room became so quiet that you could even hear the sputtering of the flame and the squeaking of the water about to boil, as everything was shaking like the aftershocks of an earthquake. There was a fly trying to escape the winter chill. The insect flew up from the head of the bed and, after collecting some warmth on the stove, landed on the old man's quilt. Mingzheng's lips were extremely dry, and he desperately needed a drink of water. As the kettle came to a boil, the water that emerged through the kettle's neck and from under the lid splattered onto the stove. Mingzheng went over and picked up the kettle, whereupon the stove's flame illuminated the room. Even the curvature of the old man's shoulders was clearly visible. Mingzheng suddenly realized that not only could he see the old man, the man could also see him and even seemed to know who he was. It was as though it was precisely in order to wait for Mingzheng's arrival that the old man had remained holed up for years in this old house slated for demolition. Now that Mingzheng had finally arrived, the old man recognized him. The man's dusty complexion took on a red hue, like a dead willow tree coming back to life in the spring and about to sprout new buds. He suddenly reached out his hand, as though wanting to pull Mingzheng over, but Mingzheng merely placed the kettle on the edge of the stove and took a step back.

"I'm fine . . . I was simply passing by and stopped here out of curiosity," Mingzheng said. As though he had finally managed to untie some ropes that were binding him, he felt a sense of relief and his pace suddenly accelerated. But as he approached the door and was about to pull aside the curtain, the old man suddenly got out of bed and, wearing only a dirty pair of oversized underwear, proceeded to stand next to the door. With a single remark, he stopped Mingzheng in his tracks: "You're Mingzheng, right? I immediately recognized you! That's right, you're my son, Gu Mingzheng . . ."

As the old man said this, he took a step forward and, staggering slightly, immediately leaned on the bed for support. He bowed his head and muttered Mingzheng's birthday, then looked up again and asked, "Is that right? Isn't that your birthday?" When Mingzheng simply stood there without replying, the old man had no choice but to present his final piece of evidence. After clearing his throat, he quickly added, "I'm already seventy-eight years old and have no shame, so I'll come right out and say it—you can go someplace where no one can see you, pull down your pants, and take a look. You have a birthmark on the underside of your thing. When you were young, the mark resembled a dead mosquito. If it's still there, by now it should be about the size of a fingernail."

Still leaning against the bed, the old man stared at Mingzheng with a blazing hot gaze, as though waiting for him to confirm and sign the evidence he had just offered. Meanwhile, Mingzheng simply wanted to leave. His sweat-soaked shirt stuck to his back, and his forehead and face were similarly covered in beads of sweat. He wanted to leave but felt as though Gu Shengbao's gaze were binding him like a rope. If he wanted to leave, he would have to find a way to sever that rope. Somehow, he thought of money, and then—the same way that demolition and reparations are tightly bound together—he remembered the bank card he was carrying in his breast pocket, though he couldn't bear to part with it. Mingzheng heard another sound coming from the bed behind him, and thought that if the old man came and grabbed him, he would simply push the man away and run out. Otherwise, he would step aside, so that the old man would grab empty air and topple over, and it would be the man's fault, not his own. On the other hand, if Mingzheng didn't manage to get away in time, perhaps he might be forced to struggle with the other man? Perhaps he might find himself in a situation where he would need to break the old man's neck just to get away?

Mingzheng remembered that Nameless had told him the previous night that he couldn't tell Mingzheng who his father was, because if he did he would have to kill him. Mingzheng once again heard Nameless's voice, and the phrase *you would have to kill him* struck his head and body like a stick. His hands trembled as though he were desperately grabbing something. To prove that he wasn't the sort of murderer that Nameless had implied, Mingzheng quickly wiped his hands on his pants, then reached into his breast pocket and pulled out a black leather wallet, from which he extracted his green bank card. He glanced at the bed, then folded the card in half. He saw that in the middle of the card there were broken white lines. He placed the card on the corner of the table under the Vitality painting, then turned to the old man, who was still leaning against the bed, and said, "You are not my father, and I don't owe you anything. Everything I need to repay is contained in this card, as long as you can withdraw the funds. The PIN is my birthday, which you already know."

Then he glanced at the old man's sallow face and rushed out of the room. He went over to some ruins and stood there for a while.

The haze suddenly cleared and the sky became filled with yellow sunlight, but Mingzheng wasn't sure whether the haze had really lifted, or if his heart was just finally opening up. He noticed that inside the thick clouds in the eastern sky there was a white light that appeared as lively as Laozi standing on a cloud, with a strong head and round face, gray hair and a youthful expression, and a beard as thick as a bush. Every time he breathed through his garlic-shaped nostrils, the air would blow through his beard.

Mingzheng stood there in shock until he suddenly heard a thump behind him, as though the old man had fallen to the ground, but Mingzheng didn't even turn his head. This was the first time that he, as a Daoist, had observed an apparition of a divine ancestor in the sky. His *shifu* and his *shifu's* own *shifu* had all been very pious and would frequently look up at the sky, but even they had never seen an apparition of a divine ancestor. Meanwhile, Mingzheng had never really believed in divine ancestors, but now, upon finding his father, he finally saw one with his own eyes. As such, Mingzheng couldn't turn around to look at that figure who had fallen down behind him—whether it was his father or just a random old man. Nor could he allow the old man to make the divine ancestor disappear. Mingzheng's expression shifted from surprise to red-hot rage and his heart was pounding. He once again felt as though an earthquake were coursing through his body. Although Mingzheng didn't turn around, or even turn his head, his body nevertheless stiffened. In that moment of distraction, he looked up again and saw that the apparition of the divine ancestor had been devoured by the clouds, and all that was left was an elliptical white area above his head.

He didn't have a chance to hear the divine ancestor utter a single word, nor did he have a chance to say a word in return. Instead, the divine ancestor was replaced by the sound behind him, like darkness behind a light, as the secular world unfurled in front of and around him. Before Mingzheng had even had a chance to say anything, the man behind him got up, and Mingzheng heard him approaching as though a lame ghost were pursuing him.

When Mingzheng heard that sound, he silently cursed and, still without turning around, quickly ran out of the courtyard.

4

Mingzheng rushed over to a bank, where he took a number and stood in line. When it was his turn, he handed the teller his ID and explained that he had lost his bank card and wanted to declare it missing. The teller rummaged around for a while, then looked up and said that the money in his account had already been withdrawn—announcing this the same way she might tell him that he didn't need chopsticks or a spoon because his rice bowl was empty. Standing in front of the teller's window, Mingzheng's mind collapsed like a mountain. There was a buzzing noise as dust flew everywhere, and his legs became so limp that he thought he was going to fall.

"It's been withdrawn?"

"There are still a few dozen yuan left."

He stood there as though he had already died. Eventually another customer tapped him on the shoulder and asked him to get out of the way, and only then did he appear to come back to life. He walked out and stood in the middle of Chang'an Avenue. He looked up at the sky, where the dark clouds didn't have a trace of light, then looked down Chang'an Avenue, which was vast and empty, with few passersby and a handful of cars that resembled crazy people running around and screaming. Mingzheng suddenly thought of something and ran back to the bank. When he saw the security guard in the entranceway, he asked, "More than five hundred thousand yuan—how could someone withdraw all of that without an ID?!" The security guard stared at him, then smiled mysteriously and replied, "Give me a bank card and offer me a ten percent cut, and regardless of how much money might be in the account, I can withdraw it all." Mingzheng felt as though the sky had fallen and the earth had become desolate, as the entire world seemed to disappear without a trace. Without the world, humanity returned to a state of primal chaos, and Mingzheng walked through the river of humanity as though traversing an empty desert. He returned to the school's dormitory and fell into bed.

The extraordinary thing was that after such a consequential turn of events, Mingzheng simply went to sleep. A wave of exhaustion swept over him such that even his hair wanted to relax, and he slept as comfortably as though he had just seen a deity. He even had a dream within a dream, in which he hadn't found his father and lost his money, but rather was in bed with Yahui engaging in dreamlike activities of clouds and rain. This, in turn, reminded him of what his father had said about the birthmark on that thing between his legs. Dazed and confused, he got out of bed as though sleepwalking. After standing for a moment in the middle of the room, he went to the bathroom and flipped the light switch. He saw scattered towels, soap, and toothpaste, and in the sink he saw the bloodstained shirt and socks from the day before. A roll of toilet paper had fallen to the floor, and next to the bathtub there were a couple of scriptures and popular magazines to read while sitting on the toilet. One of the magazines was opened to a picture of a naked woman, who was staring at him with perky breasts. With his foot, he kicked the magazine closed. Standing in the middle of the bathroom, he momentarily forgot what he had originally wanted to do, but when he remembered, he closed the door and locked it. He tugged again at that freshly painted white door, confirming that it was securely locked and there wasn't anyone else in the room, in the religion building, or on the entire campus of the National Politics University who might walk in on him. He swayed for a moment under the light, then also turned on the light in front of the mirror, further illuminating the clutter as though it were an open-air garbage dump. Right in the middle of that dump, he removed his belt and pulled down his pants and underwear, then slowly flipped over that thing between his legs.

On the underside of his thing, just below the head, he did in fact find a fingernail-sized splotch that looked like it was formed by diluted blue ink. He was astounded that for twenty-three years this birthmark could have remained hidden in this area that he touched every day. Trying to peel the mark off, he pinched it with the fingernails of his thumb and index fingers and tugged, but only succeeded in lifting an inch of the foreskin. Feeling a sharp pain, he released his thing, and the mark returned to its former invisible location. Then he stood there staring at a shadow on the wall, as though he wanted to ask the shadow a question. He felt a pulse of energy surging toward his member, and when he looked down, he saw that it had become erect. He blushed and quickly glanced toward the door. Hearing the silence inside and outside the room, he was reminded of how, when Jueyu *shifu* was lying in her sickbed in Yonghe Hospital, this vulgar appendage had made him lunge toward Yahui. Upon being reminded of that person who brought him into this world, his father, Mingzheng stood there motionless, staring at his ugly vulgarity. He heard the light producing a squeaking sound as it illuminated his thing. He abruptly slapped at that sound, whereupon his thing bent a little and he squatted down on the floor in pain. After the pain subsided, he grabbed that thing as though grabbing an enemy by the neck. Gritting his teeth, he squeezed as hard as he could. Pain coursed through his body like an electric shock, as sweat droplets stuck to his forehead, face, and back like ice particles. After his vision started to blur, he saw Nameless standing in front of him.

"It would have been better if you hadn't gone to Daoliu Lane to look for him."

Mingzheng stared at Nameless.

"You can use a knife to cut off that birthmark, at which point you'll no longer have any connection to him."

Mingzheng loosened his grip on his member, then stood up and stared straight ahead while removing his pants and shoes. He tossed his pants into the sink and kicked his shoes against the wall. Then, he went into the kitchen to get a fruit knife. As heavy as a cleaver, the knife was one that he had originally purchased to peel fruit and slice vegetables, and it had a thick back and a sharp blade that was two fingers wide and several inches long. When he returned to the bathroom, he washed and dried the knife, then used a lighter to heat the blade and disinfect it. He smiled as though at Nameless, but as he did so, the person before him turned out to be not Nameless but rather Laozi. The divine ancestor was dressed completely in white, with a silver beard and a large forehead, and was as plump as a mountain bursting out of a plain. Mingzheng shuddered and just as he was about to kneel down, Laozi stopped him and said, "My child . . . come with me."

As Laozi was speaking, his lips came together and a cloud-like vapor passed before Mingzheng's eyes, engulfing the room in a heavy silence. There was no longer the slightest gap between this room and Mingzheng's inner heart. He had never experienced such a sense of calm and plentitude. The spirit before him appeared as real and substantial as an apple tree, a field of grain, a table, or a stool. Mingzheng put down his knife, knelt, and gazed up at the divine ancestor's ruddy face.

"Come with me . . ." the divine ancestor said again. Then he stepped forward and helped Mingzheng to his feet, while also picking up the knife from the floor and handing it to him. "You have already received the Way. The instant you grasped this knife, you were already one of Daoism's most loyal disciples."

Mingzheng accepted the knife Laozi handed him and examined it. The instant his gaze met the blade, Mingzheng had a glorious epiphany! The light in front of him was just like the light that he had seen emerging from the haze—it was bright red and so beautiful that once his gaze touched it, he was unable to turn away. His forehead once again became covered in sweat, and he grabbed a towel to wipe it. As though closing a city gate, he solemnly nodded to the divine ancestor. He placed his promise before Laozi as though making an offering, and to complete this offering he picked up an incense stick, lit it, and then bowed. Before placing the incense stick in front of the offering, he knelt and began reading from a sacred scripture.

Finally, he stepped out of the bathroom, picked up his phone and dialed 999, then shouted into the receiver, "Come quick! Someone has tried to commit suicide!!!"

After waiting for the voice on the other end of the line to respond, Mingzheng answered the urgent questions about the address, position, and street number of the religion building, then hung up. He stood there for a moment, then unlocked the door, went back into the bathroom, and placed a stool in the middle of the floor. After squatting down to compare the heights of the stool and his thing, he placed the knife on the stool, returned to his room, and filled a travel bag with the clothes and daily necessities he would need in the hospital. Finally, from the head of the bed he retrieved the copies of an Old Annotated Daodejing and a New Annotated Daodejing, which he rarely read, as well as a dictionary, and put them all in the bag as well. Then he stood behind the door until he heard ambulance sirens, the sound of squealing brakes, and feet rushing into the building. Only then did he return to the bathroom, grab the knife that was sitting on the stool, and slam it down. This was followed by a bloody scream that was louder than all the disciples cheering after seeing the deity, as a violent sound filled the religion building.

Preface 4

1. Guanyin appears in a backstreet of a small city, where she sees an
   old woman standing in the door of a brothel soliciting customers.
   Lying on the ground next to the woman is her daughter, who is
   sick and close to death. The old woman shouts, "Help me, help
   me!" But rich men merely approach, smile coldly, and continue on
   their way. At this point, Guanyin walks by, and when she sees this
   elderly woman soliciting customers, she asks, "You are already so
   advanced in age, why do you still need to do this sort of work?"
   The woman replies, "My daughter is sick and close to death, and I
   urgently need money to take her to see a doctor." Guanyin squats
   down and silently embraces the child for a long time. The child
   asks her, "Can you save me?" Guanyin replies, "Yes, I can." Then
   Guanyin goes to where the woman had been standing, and begins
   soliciting customers herself. She appears dignified and graceful,
   and soon is surrounded by a crowd of dignitaries and officials.

   Soon, Guanyin and one of the merchants enter the brothel
   hand in hand . . .

2. While Guanyin is in the brothel with her customer, many other men wait in line outside. Guanyin remembers how when she was young, she had wanted to marry "all the men in the world." A peaceful smile appears on her face, as an auspicious cloud appears in the sky. The men and the old woman all look up at the cloud, whereupon Guanyin emerges from the brothel and places several silver dollars in the old woman's hand. At this point, one of the men tugs at her, saying, "Come with me, and I'll give you twice as much." Guanyin replies, "No, thank you. This is already enough for the mother and daughter to see a doctor."

Guanyin leaves the brothel and continues forward, as the people behind her kneel down and shout, "Deity! Deity!" . . .

In this way, Guanyin saves nine sick children and nine mothers by working in brothels throughout the city. At the same time, she also rescues nine girls who would have been sent to work in brothels by their parents. As for Guanyin, for each child, old woman, and young girl she saves, she needs to enter a brothel herself . . .

3. Finally, Guanyin secures a second life from the brothel.

4. Afterward, the specter of death that covers the sky and earth presses down upon Guanyin. Korea's typhoid, Japan's cholera, and the Philippines' plague . . . Everywhere Guanyin goes, death follows her like a swarm of locusts. Therefore, in cholera and plague areas, she gives people medicine while running in the shadow of the specter of death . . .

5. People throw the children infected with the plague into
   the fire, while Guanyin pulls them right back out. Life is
   a series of lights, while death is the darkness that remains
   after those lights are extinguished. Guanyin is always
   walking into the light and emerging from the darkness . . .

6. Nation after nation, region after region, place after place,
   time after time—Guanyin repeatedly heads toward the
   specter of death, and repeatedly returns from the specter
   of death. Eventually, she succeeds in obtaining a third life.

7. After obtaining her third life, Guanyin becomes a deity of the masses.

8. She becomes the Bodhisattva Guanshiyin.

Preface 5

Thousands upon thousands of years ago, the Bodhisattva Guanyin, who succeeded the Buddha Shakyamuni, came over from the world of suffering.

Thousands upon thousands of years ago, Laozi left the Central Plains, and after leaving behind the five-thousand-character document in Hangu Pass, he emerged from the pass and headed west.

Laozi and Guanyin finally met up again at Crescent Moon Lake beneath Gansu's Mingsha Mountain. As they gazed at one another across the water, Laozi shouted to Guanyin, "The Dao is not the Dao."

Guanyin replied, "Sorrow is also sorrow."

Laozi said, "The Dao is everywhere."

Guanyin replied, "Sorrow is everywhere!"

Laozi said, "The Dao can cure the world."

Guanyin replied, "Love can cure the world."

Therefore, on opposite banks of Crescent Moon Lake, at the base of Mingsha Mountain, Laozi and Guanyin set aside worldly thoughts and bathed in the moonlit water. They discussed Buddhism and Daoism, and commented on matters relating to the East and West and to the world of suffering. They noticed that there were numerous points of convergence between Buddhism and Daoism, but also many points of divergence. When they discussed the points of convergence, Laozi's laughter rang out heartily and unfettered;

like an innocent child, his voice was as loud as though he had just achieved enlightenment, while Guanyin's smile was very faint and her face had an expression of unspeakable suffering. Meanwhile, at the mention of differences, Laozi would slap the ground, look up at the sky, and sigh, while Guanyin spoke softly, sadly, and sorrowfully. They talked and argued in this way until finally Laozi grabbed a handful of sand and went elsewhere to let it slowly flow through his fingers. He said, "Guanyin, you claim that existence is suffering and life is ephemeral, but why does this sand not feel any pain when it leaves its homeland and flows through my fingers?"

Guanyin replied, "What is flowing through your fingers is sand from the worldly desert, but what flows through my heart is human blood!"

Laozi said, "After the sand flows through my fingers, what is its relationship to you?"

Guanyin replied, "After it flows through your fingers, it also flows through my heart. Because I am watching, in the end it flows through my heart."

After nodding, Laozi smiled and said, "Given that it flows through your heart, why is it my hand that feels itchy?"

Guanyin said, "I am observing, and you are also observing. But when you observe, it is not your hand that has awareness, but rather your inner heart."

Then, Guanyin gazed at Laozi and sighed. Addressing him by name, she said, "Li Ran, you are no longer the Li Ran from before."

In this way, they both achieved divine understanding. Knowing that they had already forded the mortal river, they could once again coexist between heaven and earth, and in the same room. Therefore, they both began walking around the lake and toward one another, preparing to reenter the mortal world so they could embrace and hold hands. But when Laozi reached the spot on the shore of Crescent Moon Lake where Guanyin had been sitting, he discovered that, because Guanyin loved him, she had also headed toward where he had been sitting. Because both were proceeding in the same direction, when Laozi arrived where Guanyin had been, Guanyin arrived where Laozi had been. As a result, they once again found themselves separated by sand and water. They realized that even though their hearts could be united, their bodies could not, and they also realized the simplest truth: that they could only meet when facing one another.

As a result, Guanyin had no choice but to stand where Laozi had been, and ask him, "How does a Daoist view a woman who has worked as a prostitute?"

Laozi replied, "Can a Buddhist expect someone to live without eating?"

Guanyin asked, "Can you accompany me into the mortal world to distribute compassion?"

Laozi replied, "Unless you turn around and head in the opposite direction, I won't be able to accompany you."

Guanyin said, "We have our differences, but we also have our commonalities."

Across the water and on the opposite shore, Laozi reflected for a while, then he laughed and shouted, "I know! The earth is round—so neither of us needs to turn around. You can head west and I'll head east, and eventually we'll definitely meet up. When that day comes, we'll be able to enter the mortal world and embrace our love."

In that way, Laozi and Guanyin set off, with one heading west and the other heading east. They agreed to maintain a unified mind and not to deviate by a single inch from their respective trajectories. That way, when that special day finally arrived, they would meet in front of Jerusalem's Holy Sepulchre and get married. Guanyin then traveled though China, Japan, Vietnam, Thailand, Myanmar, Bengal, the Philippines, Nepal, Indonesia, and the Arabian Peninsula, while Laozi traversed the wild world of North America, ultimately reaching ancient Greece and Rome, proceeding to Spain, Portugal, France, England, Germany, and Hungary, and finally traveling from

Turkey to Jordan and Syria. On the day when they were scheduled to arrive in Jerusalem, Laozi couldn't find Guanyin there. He waited and waited—waiting not for Guanyin, but rather for a grand realization of the world. It turns out that the earth was not actually round, but oval, and therefore, although they headed due east and due west, respectively, and they didn't deviate by a single inch from their assigned trajectories, they still couldn't truly meet up, much less get married. When Laozi did not find Guanyin in Jerusalem on that day, he inscribed a stone with the Daoist phrase *The Way that cannot be Wayed is the true Way*. Then, having reached a new understanding of the world, he departed.

As for Guanyin, the reason she didn't reach Jerusalem on their prearranged day was that at that time humanity was enduring typhoid fever and the plague, and all the world's suffering had landed at her feet.

01 Director Gong

A few days before classes were scheduled to resume on the fifteenth day after the Lunar New Year, students began to return to school. The campus, which had been cold during the break, came back to life. The bare trees and the lanterns in the entranceway to each department were now animated and lively, and some students kicked the signs that read *In the interest of blue skies and public safety, firecrackers and fireworks are forbidden*. However, when the students saw the principal and professors walk by, they smiled innocently.

The principal and professors smiled back, as the city returned to its original state of liveliness.

The people who had rushed like a river out of the city and to their hometowns now came surging back. The bars and shops that had been closed for the holiday reopened their doors, and even the campus's canteens and stores began to have an endless stream of customers. Throughout the break, Director Gong had been at home working on his monograph, and even on New Year's Day he managed to write several thousand characters. The monograph's harvest season was just around the corner, and after he finished the final chapter and gave the press a subvention derived from the faith donations, the monograph would be printed and published. Soon the center might well be recognized as one of the university's institutes, given that the monograph would surely receive the nation's highest

award for a theoretician's scientific research. Thus, all the tensions
and conflicts over designations of bureau head or deputy department
director, expert or authority, professor or lecturer, would be resolved.

As Director Gong completed that final chapter of his monograph, he put down his pen with satisfaction and returned to the
school.

If the religious training center had money, it was also true that
Director Gong had money. A few years earlier he had bought himself
a BMW, and now he would always drive whenever he went to campus. Because of the religious training center's distinctive status, the
disciples had a slightly longer vacation than the other students, and
their first day of classes after the break was the Monday following
the fifteenth day of the Lunar New Year.

On the fifteenth, when the temperature was only three or four
degrees below zero, Director Gong parked his car in front of the
religion building's front gate and, wearing a down jacket and a long
scarf, came inside. A blast of hot air surged out, immediately warm-
ing his body. He saw that, apart from some dust and firecracker paper
that had blown into the auditorium, there wasn't a soul in the entire
building. Standing in the lobby, he removed his jacket, untied his
scarf, and began sweeping the floor like one of the center's disciples.
He even started to sing, and after he finished, he waved his broom
around like a martial arts actor on stage, before carefully leaning it
against the wall.

He continued singing as he went to his office and began wiping
his desk, at which point his door was pushed open. Standing in the
doorway was the nun Yahui, who had just returned from Xining's
Qinghai Lake. She stood there with a smile plastered on her face,
like a child who had been driven away from home and later returned
on her own. In her arms, she was cradling a large doll that was still
in the original box, and she was wearing a loose-fitting red sweater
and a pair of sharply creased grey pants that looked like they had
just been ironed. She had applied cold cream to some frostbite burns

on her face, such that it appeared as though her face were covered in a layer of yellow paper. Her hands and feet, also frostbitten, were wrapped in gauze, while her toes were sticking out of her sandals.

Director Gong stood next to his desk, the cloth he had been using to wipe it down frozen in midair. After examining Yahui with a shocked expression, he asked, "You, how did you return? Can Xining . . . possibly be so unbearably cold?"

Yahui replied, "Qinghai Lake was covered in two feet of snow all winter long, and Jing'an Temple collapsed under the weight. If I hadn't come back, I would surely have died there."

Director Gong stood motionless for a while, and then sat down on the stool, his face pale. He looked away from Yahui and stared out the door, then said, "But we agreed you wouldn't come back!"

Yahui replied, "The temple collapsed, so I didn't have anywhere else to go."

Director Gong thought for a while, and said, "Your *shifu's* funeral . . . has already been taken care of?"

"It was a Buddhist funeral . . . I erected a pagoda in the temple for her, as she had previously done for her own *shifu*."

Exasperated, Director Gong threw down the cloth he was using, then got up and headed to the door. After looking down the hallway, he closed the door, calmly tugged at Yahui's sweater, and pointed at the sofa, indicating for her to have a seat. Then he positioned his stool a comfortable distance away and sat silently for a while. Staring at her solemnly, he asked, "Did you return because you missed Mingzheng?"

Yahui's eyes widened. While watching Director Gong, she walked over and placed the doll she was holding on the desk in front of him. She stared at him and replied, "I returned for the Buddha and for my *shifu*. The Buddha and my *shifu* both wanted me to return, and someday I'll bring them to Beijing as well."

Director Gong gazed intently at her, and said, "You know that Mingzheng is living on campus?"

Yahui looked at him blankly.

"He had a boil on that area of his thigh." Director Gong offered an odd smile. "He had no choice but to have it operated on."

There was another silence, as though Yahui had encountered an unfathomable misfortune. She stared at Director Gong and wondered where exactly "that area on his thigh" was located.

Eventually Director Gong thought of something else, and in a measured tone he said, "If others ask you about your *shifu*, you know how you should respond, right?"

Yahui shifted her attention back and replied, "I'll say she is recuperating in Jing'an Temple."

Director Gong nodded, then was silent for a moment. "Given that you have returned . . . If I were to request it, could you collaborate with the center to do some . . . things?"

As Yahui silently gazed at Director Gong, he continued, "For instance . . . if we were to present you as a model student or something . . ."

Yahui blushed.

"I wouldn't ask you to leave the faith and join the Party." As Director Gong said this, he rocked back and forth. "Rather, you'd simply be expected to attend class and take notes. When the higher-ups come to see what we are doing, you would speak to them and say what you need to say."

Relieved, Yahui nodded.

Yahui and Director Gong fell silent. Director Gong had asked everything he needed to ask, and Yahui had said everything she needed to say. There was a sound in the building, and then a silence descended. Outside, students returning to campus glanced inside as they passed by the office window. Yahui felt she should leave, so she thanked Director Gong and headed to the door. However, as she passed, Director Gong suddenly stood up and caressed her head, like a father caressing his daughter.

"Your hair has grown out."

Director Gong then returned to his desk, and once he was a comfortable distance from Yahui, he picked up the blond doll she had bought for his daughter and turned it over, saying, "Ay—I'd say that if your Jing'an Temple collapsed . . . if it really did collapse, then you might as well buy an apartment in Beijing and live here."

As Yahui stood in the doorway listening to Director Gong, her heart warmed. With her hands clasped in front of her chest, she bowed deeply to him, and as she did so, Director Gong saw that her hair whorl was large and round, positioned like a coin in the center of her head. This reminded him of another matter, and he began plotting another scheme to raise more money.

02 Disciples

School resumed.

One joyful event followed another. First the frostbite on Yahui's face improved and was no longer as prominent and itchy as before. Then, on the day the disciples returned to campus, many of them did not perform religious rituals when they saw one another. The Buddhist disciples did not turn their prayer beads or make Buddhist mudras; instead, when they saw their classmates, they simply hugged them or shook their hands. Similarly, the Daoist disciples did not take care to first step forward with their left foot and clasp their hands to their chest, and instead, regardless of whether they were greeting a follower of Protestantism or Islam, they would laugh loudly, embrace them, and pat them on the shoulder.

"I missed you!"

"I missed you, too. Would you like to come to my room this evening and have a drink?"

Then they would look around, as though afraid someone might be watching. When they saw that there was no one else around, they would exclaim, "Why don't you come over to my room? Our religion has more investors than yours!"

These encounters resembled ones in which colleagues or siblings reunite after having been apart for several years. After greeting one another, the students would shout "Communism, Communism!"

and take some local products from their home region and distribute them to their classmates and fellow disciples. Muslim disciples from the northwest brought wolfberries and red dates, Buddhist disciples from Xinjiang and Tibet brought raisins, saffron, and caterpillar fungus, while Catholic and Protestant disciples from Jiangsu and Zhejiang brought pastries, *longjing* tea, and *pu'er* tea biscuits. The religion building resembled a local product expo, with Maotai-brand *baijiu* brought by disciples from Guizhou, butter cake brought by disciples from Inner Mongolia, jujube slices brought by disciples from Shaolin in the Central Plains region, and vacuum-packed seasonings and *suanjiang* noodles for pepper soup brought by disciples from the Henan cities of Kaifeng and Luoyang. There was also Taiyuan vinegar brought by monks from Taishan Mountain and sesame sauce for Hubei hot dry noodles brought by Daoists from Wudang.

Yahui received many excellent gifts. Imam Tian gave her a box of wolfberries, Pastor Wang gave her a box of *wulong* tea from Fujian Province's Wuyi Mountain, and Shuiyue *shifu* gave her a box of Belgian chocolates she said she had bought in Hong Kong. Even more remarkable were the rice noodles that an ethnic-minority priest had brought from Yunnan. He brought a table from his room, laid out more than a dozen single-use white plastic bowls, and placed a packet of rice noodles and seasoning in every bowl. Then he added boiling water and invited all the disciples to come and have a sample, filling the entire building with the pungent smell of Yunnan hot pepper.

The disciples also offered their teachers gifts, such that when the center's professors and instructors returned home, they each had a large bundle of packages. The faculty who drove had full trunks, while those who biked resembled people trying to move all their belongings because their homes had been slated for demolition. Associate Professor Huang received more gifts than he was able to eat or take home, so he invited colleagues and students from other departments and institutes to take what they wanted.

As a result, all the teachers and students from other departments and institutes were envious of the religious training center's extraordinary harmony and wealth.

Gu Mingzheng, however, was not among the classmates returning to school. Yahui searched the entire building but couldn't find any trace of him.

03 Tian Dongqing

It was time for class.

The first class of the new semester was on the significance of the Party Central Committee's remarks on the unity, integration, and stability of different ethnic groups and local religions. The class was held in the same first-floor classroom as the previous semester. Everything was the same as before, including the seats, curtains, stage, and propaganda posters on the walls, each of which featured a portrait of a Chinese political leader along with his observations about religion. There were also the same cracks in the classroom's cement floor. The cracks in the southern hallway formed a snakelike pattern, while the ones in the northern hallway were crosshatched like an array of crucifixes. Meanwhile, on the walls on either side of the stage, the painted depictions of the mosque and white caps of the disciples kneeling were the same as before. It even appeared that the dust was the same dust from the previous semester.

The scenery outside the window, the light in the sky, the invisible deities below the clouds, the tree branches and the birds flying back and forth over them—these birds were the same birds as before, just as the clouds were also the same clouds as before. It seemed as though nothing at all had changed. Even the bricks in the steps outside the classroom that had been yellow the previous year were still yellow this year, and very likely would still be the same shade of yellow next year. However, as the disciples and students returned to campus after more than a month of vacation at their respective churches, temples, mosques, and homes where they lived with their children, they felt everything had changed and nothing was the same. The disciples felt that the air and light were purer than before, and that all the trees were newly planted. It even seemed as though over the break someone had rearranged the beds in the dormitories.

Freshness always brings joy, and as the disciples went to class, they sang a variety of songs like birds singing in the morning. Some were singing hymns, some were listening to the Sanskrit "Great Compassion Mantra" on their cell phones, and others were singing popular tunes like "My Beloved Deskmate" and "Grandma at Penghu Bay." By eight-thirty the classroom was nearly filled with students arriving early for their nine o'clock class. Seeing that everyone had arrived early, Director Gong arrived in person to distribute the grade reports from the preceding semester. Everyone received a single sheet, on which was printed the disciple's secular name, religious name, title, and denomination, together with their final exam scores in each course. Each sheet, accordingly, listed the student's required courses "Socialist Characteristics of Chinese Religion" and "Tutorials on Marxist-Leninist Religion," as well as their electives, followed by their individual subject exam scores and their average scores for all subjects.

After everyone received their test score reports, they looked them over and beamed. Even the septuagenarian and octogenarian religious masters appeared as delighted as children.

"Director Gong, you're the best!" one disciple shouted while holding up his scores.

"Director Gong, you're the deity we should be venerating!" shouted another.

The classroom was filled with interminable applause, and the entire building shook until it seemed like it was about to collapse.

It turned out that no student received a grade below a ninety in any single subject, and every student's average grade for all subjects was between a ninety-two and a ninety-five. The elective course "On the Relationship Between This Religion and Political Leaders" included the exam question, "The Party directs everything—does this also extend to directing one's religious belief?" If a student replied "yes," they would have to explain why, and if they replied "no," it would be even more necessary for them to explain why not. This question was so incisive that if it were to strike a wall, it would surely knock a hole in it. For this reason, many disciples chose not to take this course at all, or if they did take it, they would deliberately avoid answering this question on the final exam. Yet there were still some disciples who did take this course and who did answer this question on the final, and regardless of their answer, Director Gong simply gave everyone full credit.

Full credit—how could this not invite thunderous applause? How could it not invite applause so loud that it would kick up the dust on the classroom floor? Yet at that moment, Imam Tian, who had been sitting on the western side of the classroom the entire time, stood up despondently. He appeared pale and humiliated, and after staring at the grade report for a while, he approached Director Gong and pulled him over to a corner of the classroom. Then, noticing that the other disciples were watching them, he led Director Gong outside and they ended up standing next to the bamboo pond, where the bottle of sulfuric acid had been found the previous semester.

"Director Gong," Tian Dongqing said softly, then paused. "In this class, there isn't anyone who studies as well as I do, nor is there anyone who is more diligent. Had I wanted to, I could have correctly answered every question on every exam. However, in each examination booklet there were some questions that I deliberately either left blank or else answered incorrectly. I knew that my score on each exam would not exceed sixty-five, but I was equally certain that I had done well enough to pass. Why, then, did you still give me scores between ninety and ninety-five on every exam?"

"If you are afraid of receiving a high score, you shouldn't attend this religious training center!" Director Gong turned pale. He pursed his lips, gazed off into the distance, then looked back at Tian Dongqing. "Everyone who enrolls here must receive an average score of ninety or above. If anyone's average score falls below ninety, the institute will not be certified by the National Religion Association and the United Front Work Department as a first-rank class for training religious masters. And if the institute cannot be certified as a first-rank class for training religious masters, then the quota for the class's hundred or more students to be promoted to religious master would drop, which would impact everyone's salary, housing, and medical coverage! Maybe those of you of the Islamic faith don't need to worry about these gradations of religious rank, but do you think that members of other religions who have a more finely calibrated hierarchy of religious masters won't care about these scores? Do you really have it in your heart to make them all miss out simply for your sake?"

Director Gong continued, "Everyone here is a disciple, but they are also social beings. Everyone needs to consider issues of promotion, title, and treatment, and if they didn't care about these things, they would be deities, not humans. But isn't it even more incumbent on deities to look out for humans? After all, if deities don't look out for humans, why do we need them in the first place?" He once again glanced to the side, then looked up at the sky, as though he wanted to pull over a deity and ask it directly. Given that there weren't any deities beside him and there wasn't a trace of clouds in the sky, Director Gong turned back to Tian Dongqing and asked quietly, "What do you think?"

When he saw that Tian Dongqing wasn't answering, Director Gong patted him on the shoulder. "Go to class. I know you are a true disciple, and a true disciple should think on behalf of others who are not. If no one thought on behalf of others, then this world would have no disciples or deities, or it might have deities but no real disciples."

With this, Director Gong headed back to the classroom, where he saw that the professor he had invited from the National Religious Study Institute had already entered through another door. Meanwhile, Imam Tian remained frozen in place as he watched Director Gong depart. It was as though someone had walked away with his brain, leaving his skull as disordered as a city that has been locked up for a thousand years. By the time he had come up with a response to Director Gong's theory about humans and deities, a bell marked the beginning of class. It sounded just like the bell at the mosque, signaling that all thoughts and questions should be wiped clean, leaving the imam's mind as pure as a white cloth held by an evangelist. Imam Tian took the score sheet he was holding and tore it to shreds, and then tossed the ripped-up paper onto the sulfuric acid bottle behind the bamboo. Only then did he return to the classroom.

04 Director Gong, Yahui, and Mingzheng

A week after classes resumed, Yahui had not yet seen Gu Mingzheng. By the end of the second week, their class had already met three times, but Mingzheng still had not returned to campus.

Yahui was becoming impatient, and Friday afternoon before class she once again knocked on Mingzheng's door, but there was only dead silence inside the room, even as uproarious laughter could be heard coming from several Daoist masters in the adjacent dormitory. Yahui felt that Daoism's attitude toward the world was one of uproar—uproariously eating, uproariously laughing, and uproariously watching the heavens, the earth, and people. She stood for a while in that laughter, then went downstairs. When she reached the bottom of the stairwell, she ran into Director Gong, who was heading outside. Director Gong was carrying a printed copy of his manuscript as well as the tens of thousands of yuan that he would need to give the publisher as a fee for publication. When he reached Yahui, he suddenly came to a halt.

"Yahui, the center has decided that you will work as an assistant in Mingzheng's stead beginning next week."

Yahui stood very still in the corner of the stairwell.

"Me . . . How could I do that? What about Mingzheng?"

"You know as well as anyone that Mingzheng is extremely ill, and if he asks to be let go, we'll let him go." As Director Gong said this, he turned and headed out, as though he were hurrying to an exam.

Yahui followed him and shouted, "Director Gong . . ."

"Don't you want to advance?!" Holding his car keys, Director Gong stood next to his white BMW in a parking lot by the side of the road, simultaneously encouraging and scolding her. Then he got into the car and drove away, leaving Yahui looking like someone who has gone to harvest some fruit but found that someone else has already left the tree bare. She was astonished that such a major development could have been handled so expeditiously—without a formal discussion and explanation, and without even asking her opinion. She stood in the entranceway, watching as Director Gong's sedan disappeared into the crowd of people on campus. Then, dazed, she returned to the classroom.

After several more days, the novelty of attending class began to wear off and everything reverted to its earlier routine. When the morning bell rang, everyone emerged from their dormitories holding cups of tea, and when the bell didn't ring, they remained in their dormitories, either praying, chanting, and meditating, or else watching television, eating melon seeds, and playing chess. Attending class was no longer perceived as a divine activity, but merely part of the center's regular business. Students rarely showed up to class early with their wolfberry, safflower, and cordyceps tea anymore, and some had even gone to the center and asked, "Why are there no more tug-of-war competitions? Of all the religion classes, the best one is still the athletics class."

That day, Yahui entered the classroom and saw someone sitting in the middle of the first row of seats. His head was buried in his chest as if he were reading something, and his shoulders resembled a pair of withered pumpkins suspended in midair. After staring at the person's grayish-black shoulders for a while, Yahui went up to him and said, "Gu Mingzheng."

Mingzheng glanced up, as a look of surprise flashed across his face. He was much thinner than before, to the point that even his cheekbones protruded. When he attempted to stand up, there was an acute pain between his legs and he immediately turned pale. He slowly lowered his body back into the seat and then gazed at Yahui's sweater. Without a word, he laughed bitterly, then looked again at the book he was holding in his lap.

Yahui asked with surprise, "What's wrong with you? Why have you lost so much weight?"

Mingzheng looked up again and his eyes widened.

"I'm not sick. I'm perfectly fine."

"Even if you won't tell me, I know what illness it is." Yahui sat down next to him, and in a formal but joking tone, said, "When my *shifu* was still alive, she told me about this illness. Buddhists call it retribution illness, and Daoists call it divine punishment illness."

They both fell silent. They looked at one another, their gazes making a rattling sound as they collided in midair. Outside the classroom, the sky was dimly lit, as though the sun wanted to emerge but couldn't. The bird that alighted on the tree outside the window seemed to be not a bird but rather a bird's nest resting on a branch. Fortunately, the bird flew away, leaving the branch bare, and in this way the bird became a bird, and the branch became a branch.

After the bird flew away, Yahui finally turned and said quietly, "I'll tell you something, but you mustn't tell anyone else. I want to return to secular life. I want to buy an apartment and live in Beijing."

Mingzheng stared at Yahui without moving. He looked at the last remaining frostbite mark, which was faint and sunk into her face like a pea. Yahui touched it with her hand, then added with a smile, "I hadn't expected it would be so cold in Xining this year. The main hall of Jing'an Temple collapsed under the weight of the snow." She scratched the frostbite mark, then brought her fingers up to her nose and smelled them. Half consciously, her gaze came to rest on the crotch area of Mingzheng's robe, as Mingzheng turned pale and a trace of humiliation flickered across his face. He didn't say anything, but his expression became a twisted grin. He was silent for a while, until he heard footsteps outside the classroom, whereupon he put down his copy of the New Exegesis on the Daodejing, stood up by leaning against a table, and slowly walked out of the classroom.

Mingzheng took an elevator to the third floor, and Yahui took the next one. In the third-floor hallway, Mingzheng didn't encounter any other disciples, and he went into room 309 as though entering the wrong room by mistake. Meanwhile, Yahui stood in the doorway, unable to believe that this used to be Mingzheng's room. With the monthlong winter break and the first two weeks of the new semester, more than forty days had passed. It no longer appeared to be the same room as before, just as Mingzheng no longer appeared to be the same Mingzheng. Yahui was astounded at how orderly the room was. The basin, bucket, and mop that had been hanging from the wall were gone, while the clothes hook that previously had been latched to the wall had now returned. The room now resembled that of a female disciple obsessed with cleanliness. A portrait of Laozi was hanging over the bed, and an incense burner was placed in a wall panel below the portrait. The yellow desk in front of the bed was so polished that it seemed it could even reflect the locations of the deities up in the sky. Meanwhile, on the corner of the desk, there were some Daoist scriptures and interpretations, as well as all of Mingzheng's textbooks. On the desk there was also a notebook, two ballpoint pens, and a dictionary. After observing the room, looking at Mingzheng, and glancing down at the floor, which had just been scrubbed with clear water, Yahui eventually fixed her gaze on Mingzheng's face and body.

"Did you really . . . have an operation there?"

Mingzheng looked at her, and almost seemed to nod.

"It was Director Gong who told me." After a pause, Yahui once again glanced outside, then returned her gaze to Mingzheng. She asked, "Was it really on account of the illness that Director Gong mentioned?" Upon seeing Mingzheng's mouth start to open, then close again, as the shadow of a smile appeared in the corner of his mouth, Yahui clasped her hands in front of her chest and exclaimed, "*Amitābha*—you have truly converted, and I, Yahui, have some merits I can grant you."

At this point, there was the sound of footsteps in the hallway, and Yahui and Mingzheng both looked out the half-open door. After waiting for the footsteps to recede, Mingzheng lifted his shoulder and then lowered it slightly. With his gaze fixed on Yahui's face and body, he asked solemnly, "Do you really intend to return to secular life?"

Yahui forced herself to smile, and said, "I never anticipated that, after leaving Beijing, I would find myself missing the city so much. But if I hadn't returned after the blizzard, what could I have done?"

Mingzheng was silent for a moment, then asked, "Is there anything else?"

"What do you mean, anything else? Is it my *shifu* who would be buying the apartment, or me?"

Mingzheng didn't say anything else, as though he regretted asking the question. He was as depressed as though on the other side of a wall there was a deity who was unwilling to come over to this side, while the disciples on this side of the wall knew the deity was there but were unable to cross over to the other side. Yahui glanced outside, then laughed.

"Gu Mingzheng, I want to buy an apartment in Beijing. Can you lend me some money?"

Mingzheng reflected for a moment, then said, "How much do you need?"

"The more the better. I'll take however much you can lend me!"

"What if I don't have very much?"

"How much do you have?"

"I currently have only a few thousand yuan. It's not the several hundreds of thousands that we previously discussed."

Yahui stared in shock and didn't reply. The corners of her mouth tilted upward and she once again clasped her hands in front of her chest. She looked away from Mingzheng and stood there silently for a while. Then she performed a departure ritual and, without a word, headed for the door. When she reached the entranceway, she suddenly stopped and turned around. Staring at Mingzheng, she said, "Tell the truth: if we were to get married, would you give me your savings?"

Mingzheng hesitated. He opened his mouth, then shut it again. They stared at one another for a second or two, for ten days or half a month, or even for a year or two—each waiting until the other got tired. Eventually Mingzheng turned to look at the portrait of Laozi on the wall, then looked at the stool below the portrait, and finally shifted his gaze from the stool to the bed. The bed's quilt was folded and aligned with the wall, and in middle of the quilt there were medical case histories, photographs, and medical records he had brought back from the hospital. He seemed to want to pick up those documents and show them to Yahui, but then he saw that she had already noticed them. He waited for her to go pick them up herself, hoping that she would ask him about his illness. However, when Yahui saw the medical records, she made the sort of sneering smile of someone who has encountered many things in life.

She looked away from the bed and muttered: "I really thought that you Daoists had no room in your hearts for money or objects, or anything other than heaven, earth, and nature."

Upon saying this, she walked away, as though turning the page of a book she had just finished.

05 Yahui, Director Gong, and the Real Estate Agent

1

Yahui went to work for the center, replacing Mingzheng as Director Gong's assistant. Day after day, week after week, she answered the phone, delivered newspapers, wiped tables, and served tea in Director Gong's office, and slipped letters under the doors of other professors and lecturers whom she rarely saw in person. She learned to type in no time. When she went to the finance department to deliver signed documents on behalf of the center, she was reimbursed. If she wanted to attend any of the center's courses, she could, but if she didn't want to, she wasn't obligated. The other students initially complained about her skipping class, but these complaints faded away before they even reached her ears.

In the end, gossip was less important than class, prayer, incense, and worship.

Day after day, time passed like clouds floating by. By early spring Yahui was as familiar with her office tasks as she was with the ritual of clasping her hands in front of her chest and chanting *Amitābha*, at which point her thoughts returned to her plan to purchase an apartment in Beijing. Whenever she had a chance, she would leave the school and visit nearby real estate agencies with names like Rye

Field and Happy Nest. She would check out old apartments that were being resold, and would also go even farther away to see new ones being built.

It was at this point that she finally understood why Beijing is Beijing. It turns out that the cost of a large apartment in Xining is only enough to purchase a small kitchen or bathroom in Beijing. She initially thought that a hundred thousand yuan was a vast sum, and in the suburbs of Xining it would probably be enough to purchase two entire floors. If the same sum were donated to the temple, it would be sufficient for a stele erected in the donor's honor. In Beijing, however, this sum would only be enough to purchase a sleeping space the size of one mat or just half a mat, or a piece of land only large enough for a coffin.

Nevertheless, Yahui was determined to buy an apartment. Jueyu *shifu* and Jingshui Convent had left her more than two hundred thousand yuan, and she herself had saved up several tens of thousands more, bringing her total savings to around three hundred thousand yuan. In purchasing an apartment, she was interested not so much in the apartment itself but rather in its neighborhood: Yujian Street in front of the school. This was a pedestrian street about one or two *li* long, and both sides of the street were lined with old tile-roofed buildings. Every shop had a door curtain and a small room, and the shops included eateries, clothing stores, barber shops, makeup rooms, ice cream parlors, and video arcades. It seemed as though every door was either a shop or a supermarket, and the windows of every establishment were adorned with cartoon figures and English-language text. The pedestrians in the street were more numerous than the stones in Xining's Gobi Desert, and Yahui thought living on that street would be like living in heaven.

Because Yahui was so fond of this street, she took particular interest in a small apartment on the twenty-second floor of a building in the Yujian residential quarter on the eastern end of the street. It was fifty square meters and had one bedroom and one living room. After considerable discussion, the real estate agent said the apartment would cost more than two million yuan, or four million for the entire floor. Yahui was shocked when she heard the price, but the agent was several years older than she, was taller and larger, and had a wild expression as though she had experienced many adventures, and she took Yahui by the hand to patiently help her with the calculations like an elder sister. She said that if Yahui could make a down payment of four hundred thousand yuan, the agent could offer her a 1.6-million-yuan mortgage. The agent asked, "How much do you earn a month?" Yahui told her how much the municipal religion association gave her every month, and added that whenever she ran into a fellow Buddhist, she could receive some additional money in the form of alms.

The agent's tone brightened. "That's great. Your monthly salary is just enough to pay the interest on this mortgage."

"But then what would I eat?"

"In Beijing, you can always do odds and ends and make enough to support yourself, particularly given that your alms will flow in like water. In Beijing, street sweepers and garbage collectors can earn eighteen thousand yuan a month, and given that you are as pretty as a fairy, who would be able to resist giving you alms?"

Then the agent invited Yahui to join her for a meal on Yujian Street. While they were eating, she mysteriously told Yahui, "You mustn't believe people when they claim that Yujian Street used to be called Jianyu Street, meaning 'prison street,' or that the Yujian residential quarter used to be a prison district for criminals who had been condemned to death. This is the new society, and real estate prices are rising crazily. If you buy this house today, in another six months the per-square-meter price will increase by ten thousand yuan, and you'll be able to make five hundred thousand yuan in profit off your investment. In a year or two, the per-square-meter price will have increased to sixty thousand. Before you know it, you'll have earned a million yuan."

Yahui was so excited by the agent's words that she stopped thinking about the significance of the inverted terms *yujian* and *jianyu*, and instead was swept away by thoughts of money and its accumulation. She calculated that if the National Religion Association didn't know that Jueyu *shifu* had died, and kept issuing her *shifu's* monthly salary, it wouldn't be difficult for Yahui to quickly repay the mortgage and interest. So, at ten o'clock on a Monday morning in the middle of March, Yahui accompanied the agent to the Yujian residential quarter to check out the apartment. The apartment had a window, living room, and kitchen, and the bathroom even had a new toilet. It was hard to say how good the apartment itself was, but from the window Yahui could see the Yujian pedestrian street, which made her feel that the apartment was definitely desirable. Meanwhile, if you stood on the balcony outside the window and looked up, you could touch the clouds in the sky and the light above the clouds—as though the balcony were steps leading to heaven. This made Yahui feel that the apartment was unbelievably wonderful. She pictured herself descending from the clouds, enveloped in auspicious mist while holding light, and entering a mortal street, where she could see and eat whatever she wanted—as though she had suddenly arrived at a heavenly supermarket.

Standing at the window, Yahui finally looked away from the street. As her gaze came to rest on the agent, she mumbled, "I'll buy it . . ."

"Then I'll wait three days," the agent replied. "If by that point you haven't yet paid your deposit, I'll sell the apartment to someone else."

A shadow passed over Yahui's face.

"Actually, you wouldn't necessarily need to use your own money. I once knew a girl who wasn't nearly as pretty as you, and she wanted to buy a house but didn't have a cent to her name. However, within three days of when I showed her an apartment, she returned with a man who was willing to pay her full down payment."

Bewildered, Yahui stared at the agent.

"That is the advantage of big cities like Beijing and Shanghai," the agent explained. "As long as someone is young and pretty, and particularly if they have never been with a man before, there are always men who are willing to buy them a house or a car, and who would even give them tens of thousands of yuan a month in spending money."

Yahui understood the agent's insinuation. She clasped her hands to her chest, closed her eyes, pursed her lips, and silently chanted *Amitābha*. After a silence, she said, "But . . . you forget I'm a jade nun!"

The agent replied brightly, "What if some people actually *prefer* jade nuns?"

Yahui shifted her clasped hands from her chest to her lower jaw, then closed her eyes and chanted *Amitābha*. She opened her eyes and gazed resentfully at the agent, after which she headed toward the door. The agent froze for a second, then followed after her, repeatedly exclaiming, "I'm sorry" and "I should die." She grabbed Yahui's hand and said, "I'm simply trying to think of ways for you to buy this apartment. If you really want to buy it but can't come up with sufficient funds, I can pay your initial down payment myself." The agent took Yahui's palm and placed it over her own chest, then used it to cover her face. Yahui forgot her earlier resentment and opened her heart. She pulled her hand back from the agent's face, and her earlier enthusiasm returned.

"Please give me a week," Yahui said. "Three days is not enough."

"I can put down an advance and hold the apartment for up to ten days," the agent said. "I said some evil things just now, and therefore I should put up the advance in order to expiate that evil."

After this, everything brightened. The clouds parted and the sun shone through. They took the elevator down and, after crossing the street of this heavenly neighborhood, they parted. As Yahui was leaving, she offered the agent a Buddhist mudra, and the latter reciprocated with a hug. The agent leaned over to Yahui and whispered, "My mother is also a Buddhist."

Yahui walked for a while, then took the skywalk to cross the street and return to the school. This process of purchasing an apartment made her as excited and anxious as though she were about to have her period, but also left her feeling empty and unbalanced. The scene at the school was the same as before, and the religion building was the same as before. However, Yahui was no longer the same person as before. She worried that someone else would purchase the apartment before she could, but she also felt delighted, as though the apartment were already hers. As she entered the religion building, she lifted her feet very high with each step, and when she saw the middle-aged man stationed in the guard room, she shouted to him through the window, "It's such a nice day, why don't you come out and enjoy the sun?"

Not knowing whom she was addressing, the man gazed blankly out the window. Meanwhile, Yahui simply smiled and proceeded inside. When she saw a cleaner mopping the floor and wiping the walls, Yahui went up behind her and said, "I have a nice piece of clothing I'd like to give you."

The cleaner looked around to see who Yahui was addressing, but didn't see anyone else nearby, so she stood there and stared at Yahui in confusion. Eventually she gave an embarrassed laugh and said, "Look at how big I am, how could I possibly wear your clothes?!" It was only then that Yahui noticed that the other woman was in fact rather overweight, with a waist that was as wide as her shoulders. So, she laughed as well, remarked that the floor wasn't dirty at all, and suggested that the cleaner rest for a while before finishing the remainder of the room. Then Yahui continued down the hall.

2

Yahui arrived at the office and sat down, whereupon there was another incident. Director Gong emerged from his office and handed her a draft of a letter to type up as quickly as possible. Then he smiled and gave her a brotherly pat on the head.

"You mustn't tell any of the other disciples about this."

After Director Gong left, Yahui quickly looked down at the text that he had scrawled on the sheet of paper. It read:

Esteemed alumni, masters, and disciples at religion centers throughout the country:

As spring approaches and everything comes back to life, I, on behalf of the teaching staff and related individuals at National Politics University's religious training center, offer you my greetings. Regardless of whether you are in a boisterous area of the city or an isolated area in the mountains, as long as we were classmates for even a single day, we'll be bound together forever. Regardless of whether you are a Catholic, Protestant, or Muslim, or a Daoist or Buddhist, we all belong to the same people in the great family that is our nation—we are all children of the Party and people of the deities. And, regardless of how long you study and train here, our religious training center will—along with your churches, mosques, and temples—serve as another spiritual home and homeland.

Therefore, to make this alternate spiritual home better and happier, and to help make the lives of every religious master and disciple here at the center more comfortable, our center proposes a nationwide fundraising event. Based on the results of this fundraising campaign, we will pursue several objectives. First, we will improve and promote the culture and educational life of our students and disciples. Second, we will establish a divine religious library and document collection center, for the purpose of researching the origins, development, and future of our nation's religions. Third, once our donations reach a certain threshold, we will replace the center's air-conditioning, reconfigure the computers, and redecorate all the rooms in the religion building, such that National Politics University's religious training center will truly become the higher education institution and spiritual home of religious masters and disciples from all five of China's major religions.

Our center's Party committee has researched the issue and decided to invite those of you who have money to donate money, and those of you who have labor to donate labor. In this way, we will initiate a completely voluntary fundraising initiative to establish a high-level institute and spiritual home for religious figures. We hope that all of you—including every disciple who has previously studied at National Politics University's religious training center, as well as those who plan to come study here in the future so that they may advance to the status of religious master—will donate voluntarily and generously.

Our center's professors, experts, and workers and I all look to you with hope and respect, and eagerly wait for you to return to this soul habitat for inspections, reconstructions, lectures, and sermons.

This text concluded with the center's name, bank account number, and the date, followed by three exclamation marks.

Yahui initially stared in shock before a wave of happiness swept over her, as though this call for donations had already started bringing in money, which belonged not merely to the center but also to her. She quickly opened her computer to type up this text. The announcement was only a single page, totaling about eight hundred Chinese characters, but in her attempt to type it quickly, she ended up making mistakes in almost every line. Her hands trembled as she typed, as though she were seeing a real deity and were unable to light an incense stick. She took a deep breath, followed by another, and in this way she was eventually able to calm down enough to finish typing and print it out.

Yahui went to give Director Gong the document, and when she reached the door of his office, she paused for a moment and took a deep breath before knocking.

Director Gong was sitting at his desk proofreading his *Synthetic Treatise on Tug-of-War and the Contradictions Between Religions*. The window faced southeast, and the sunlight that poured in made the office look as though it were bathed in divine light. When Yahui saw Director Gong bathed in this light her palms became so sweaty that it was as though she had just dipped them in a pool of water. She wiped her hands on her pants and waited for Director Gong to read over the document. He corrected several typos, and when he handed the document back to her, he gazed at her like a brother or father. Yahui responded with a comforting smile, asking, "Will the funds be raised?"

"We can raise the requisite amount," Director Gong responded with a laugh. "If the organization needs it, everyone will inevitably respond with great compassion." When he said this, he emphasized the word *organization*. But when he finished speaking, he seemed to remember something, and looked at Yahui inquisitively. Yahui hesitated, then told him about her plans to purchase an apartment. She said that after hearing what Director Gong said, she had decided not to return to Qinghai, and instead had gone to a real estate agency. She said that she had found a small apartment, but still needed another hundred thousand yuan for the down payment. Again, she wiped her hands on her pants. The room fell so silent that you could even hear dust particles floating through the rays of sunlight. Yahui noticed that Director Gong was looking at her like a teacher examining a student who has given a very peculiar answer on a homework assignment.

After a while, he turned in his chair, as though suddenly understanding a problem, and said, "Such an important matter—and all you need is to borrow a hundred thousand yuan?" Then he straightened his waist and shook his shoulders, as though trying to shake off the preceding silence. "*Buy!* You should definitely buy! When it comes to Beijing real estate, if you can buy something, you should—regardless of where and how large it might be. If we don't raise enough money this time around, I can even lend you some of my own."

With this, Director Gong stood up and promptly asked Yahui when she needed the money, adding that if the matter was urgent, he could go to the bank and withdraw a hundred thousand yuan from his own account today.

Blushing, Yahui asked, "Really?"

Director Gong replied even more loudly, "Yes, really!"

"And what if I can't repay you for a year or two?"

"What does it matter if you don't repay me?" Director Gong asked in return. "Will I starve to death without an additional hundred thousand yuan? If I, as center director, decide to lend a student or disciple a hundred thousand yuan, do you think I should worry every day whether that student or disciple will repay me?!"

The room developed a certain warmth and dryness, as though the sound of the light flying through the air had just gotten louder. In that sound, Director Gong stared at Yahui with an odd expression. Breathing rapidly, Yahui let him examine her, even as her face turned red and became covered in a thin layer of sweat. After a moment's silence, Yahui seemed to suddenly understand something. She quickly clasped her hands to her chest and said, "Thank you, Director Gong." Then she took the call for donations and headed out of the office. But when she reached the doorway, she seemed to have an epiphany. She hesitated, then slowly turned and once again stared at that person who was still watching her.

"Director Gong, you agreed so quickly to lend me the money . . . It's not because you want me . . . to leave Buddhism and join the Party, is it?"

Director Gong shook his head. "This has nothing to do with that."

Yahui blushed and asked, "Then do you want . . ."

Director Gong stared at her for a while, then asked, "Do you think that if I lend you money . . . I necessarily have to have an ulterior motive?"

Yahui's gaze remained fixed on him. "Even people who voluntarily donate to a Buddhist temple always have their own motives."

Director Gong laughed coldly. "And if I don't lend you the money?"

Yahui didn't know how to respond to this. She looked away from Director Gong's face, and reflected for a moment as her face turned bright red. Then she uttered another astounding statement.

"That is to say, if you don't have any objectives . . . then you must be thinking that I'm a . . . jade nun?"

Director Gong stared at Yahui's red face, and replied, "So what if you're a jade nun?"

Yahui replied, "By my count . . . from the beginning of this semester up to now, you've already caressed my head five times."

Now it was Director Gong's turn to blush. He abruptly turned away, but after a while he turned back and examined Yahui's face with an odd expression, as though hoping to find some clear meaning there. In the end, however, he looked away again. When he turned back to her, he said in a rather formal tone, "So, if I were to want to be with you . . . would you . . . agree?"

Yahui didn't reply, and instead she clasped her hands to her chest and bowed her head. The room became so quiet that they could hear each other breathing. Director Gong was the first to break the silence. He laughed, pulled himself out of the stillness, and once again gazed at Yahui's face and body.

"Isn't it true that if you and I were to get together, then you wouldn't need to repay the money?"

"Repay . . ." Yahui looked up with a hard and formal expression. "The Bodhisattva says, 'Repay with kindness, not with lasciviousness.' I'm not a high monk, a host, or a religious master. I'm simply a nun from Qinghai. If you want to lend me money for nothing, I don't know what sort of kindness I should use to repay you."

At this point, not only was the room very still, but in the stillness there was a hint of an impending explosion. Yahui stood behind the door, as Director Gong walked toward her. When he reached her, he paused and, with a sheen of sweat on his brow, said, "Do you not care that I'm more than twenty years older than you?"

"You are the organization," Yahui replied. "This has nothing to do with age."

Director Gong stood there frozen, as a pale shadow flickered over his face. He silently bit his lip like a child, then said in a strange voice, "Did you know? Like you, I'm an orphan—I was also adopted and raised by foster parents. If I were the real son of my foster father, and not an orphan, I would immediately get together with you." As he said this, he took a step forward and grabbed Yahui's head, pulling her to his chest. Then he released his grip, opened the door, and asked her to print out at least a hundred copies of the call for donations.

06 Shuiyue *shifu*

"You want to purchase a Beijing apartment?" Shuiyue *shifu* asked as she blocked Yahui's path. "And I hear you've already paid a deposit?"

"..."

"Is your Jueyu *shifu* alive or dead?! If she were still alive, would you buy an apartment in Beijing?"

"..."

"You don't need to answer, I already know everything. *Amitābha*—your *shifu* treated you like a daughter, yet you view her dead body like an encumbrance to be tossed into the Qinghai Sea."

Shuiyue *shifu* said this at midday on a Tuesday, when the midspring greenery was the color of water, and the entire campus was filled with the scent of vegetation. The weather was excellent. There was sunlight below the clouds, and the clouds were moving between the rays of sunlight. After eating, the students emerged from the canteen and into the sunlight, feeling full and energetic. Some of them kicked at rocks in the road while walking along, while others would abruptly start running for no reason. Yahui had just finished her lunch and emerged from the canteen when she saw Shuiyue *shifu* waiting for her under a tree in the entranceway. Shuiyue *shifu* stopped Yahui in the middle of the street and began pelting her with questions.

"Are you and Mingzheng still seeing each other?

"You can return to secular life, but you mustn't be an embarrassment to Buddhism. Don't let members of other faiths speak negatively about our Bodhisattva.

"Yahui, tell me the truth. For better or worse, your Jueyu *shifu* and I spent more than ten years together in the convent of Baima Temple, and although we may not be sisters, at least we shared the same Buddhist master. Now that Jueyu *shifu* has passed away, I am your new *shifu*. So, tell me the truth, did Jueyu *shifu* really pass away in Qinghai?"

A group of students approached, and after glancing at Yahui and Shuiyue *shifu,* they continued on their way. As the students passed, Yahui collected the sunlight from their bodies, then gazed at Shuiyue *shifu's* face. She replied that Jueyu really had returned to Qinghai and died from illness, and that she did not pass away in Beijing. Shuiyue *shifu* gazed up at a white cloud overhead, as though seeing something in it. Eventually she turned back to Yahui and asked in a tender voice, "What kind of funeral did she have?"

"It was a Buddhist tower funeral. I paid for it and sent out the invitations."

The two of them stood silently in the middle of the road, then Shuiyue *shifu* pulled up her robe so that her navy-blue clothing would hang over her body more comfortably, and with both hands she rotated her prayer beads one after another. After she had rotated each bead more than ten times, she sighed and reached out to Yahui's bowed head and lifted her chin to examine her face as though reading a sutra. It was unclear what text she saw in Yahui's face, but she sighed again and said something that laid the sutra's secrets out in the sunlit dust: "If you really want to return to secular life, then go ahead. You can become a Beijing resident. That way, whenever I come to the capital, I'll have a place to stay and eat."

With this, Shuiyue *shifu* walked away, holding her out-of-season blue robe and counting her prayer beads as though counting the trees she passed.

07 Tian Dongqing

"Is it true that Jueyu *shifu* is no longer with us?"

Yahui nodded.

"Did she really have a heart attack induced by the tug-of-war competitions?"

Yahui gazed at Imam Tian for a moment, then nodded again.

"In that case, they should notify the school, or the National Religion Association and the United Front Work Department. Not only must the center pause its religion classes, but Director Gong might also be punished. Because of this incident, this religious training center might even have to close down altogether."

Yahui gave Tian Dongqing a pleading look, like a baby begging her elder brother for something. She continued like this for a while, and then for a beat longer, until eventually Tian Dongqing's tone softened.

"So, you really want to leave Xining?"

Yahui grunted in assent.

"Then come join us here." As soon as Tian Dongqing said this, he clarified, "I don't mean for you to convert to Islam. Rather, I just mean for you to join us here, where you would be with others. Allah would treat you very well."

Moved, Yahui nonetheless shook her head. "I want to buy an apartment in Beijing. I'll invite my new *shifu* and the Bodhisattva to come from Qinghai Lake and live in Beijing."

Tian Dongqing asked, "Do you still believe in Buddhism?"

"I want to become a layperson."

They were both silent for a while, until Tian Dongqing repeated the same thing that Shuiyue *shifu* had said: "That's fine. If you buy an apartment in Beijing, then I'll always have somewhere to stay when I come to visit."

08 Wang Changping

Just south of the philosophy institute's administrative building there was a turn in the road, and when Yahui went around the turn she found Pastor Wang standing there. He smiled and walked beside her, like Jesus accompanying one of his disciples.

"Did you really borrow a hundred thousand yuan from Director Gong?" the pastor asked Yahui. "Why didn't you ask me for help? Why didn't you ask us Protestants?"

"I wasn't borrowing from Director Gong," Yahui replied. "I was borrowing from the organization."

"You are truly naive. The director and the organization are one and the same. The director is the organization, and the organization is the director. Don't you realize that?" As Wang Changping said this, he slowed down and looked at Yahui. "You need to find an excuse to return the money to Director Gong and to the organization. I'll give you a hundred thousand yuan, and you can treat it as though it came from Jesus and from God. Then it'll be up to you whether or not you pay it back."

Yahui came to a stop and gazed at Wang Changping. There was warm afternoon sunlight everywhere, and the air was filled with energy. It was mid-March, and everyone felt impulsive and powerful. As Pastor Wang spoke, he stared intently at Yahui, trying to use his gaze to force her own gaze back into her eyes. As a result, his gaze become rough and warm, like a father using his hand to caress his daughter's head.

"When Buddhist monks and nuns borrow money from the temple, it is like when farmers go to their own land and harvest it early. Meanwhile, when Protestant and Catholic believers borrow money from the church, they do so because they have faith in the Lord. For believers, it is the Lord's favor that, if you want to borrow a hundred yuan, He will give you a thousand; and if you want to borrow a thousand, He will give you ten thousand. But what is it called when you, a nun, borrow money from Director Gong and the organization? Is this called a disciple lacking faith in religion and in the deity? It's called faith being unable to favor its own believers, and the deities being unable to favor their own children."

"It's not that," Yahui protested, looking away.

"Then what is it? Are you going to find anyone who understands this better than me?"

Without responding, Yahui turned and saw that the pagoda tree by the side of the road had spring buds that were producing a golden glow in the sunlight, and sap was surging through the tree's leaves. There were a couple of sparrows on one of the branches, which made the leaves sway as if to some classic tune.

"There is an athletics class this weekend, but as soon as the bank opens tomorrow, I'll go withdraw some money and repay Director Gong for you." As Wang Changping said this, he began to move forward, and when the two sparrows in the tree saw him leave, they also flew away, leaving behind a trembling branch. But after the sparrows flew away, Wang Changping stopped, then he turned and asked Yahui, "Is one hundred thousand enough? If not, I can give you two hundred."

Yahui gazed gratefully at Pastor Wang like a disciple gazing at a deity.

"One or two hundred thousand—just tell me how much you need. But remember what I told you: we disciples are our own collection box, unlike infidels who don't believe in God."

Wang Changping again started walking, and proceeded to the corner of the large field in front of him. The midspring sun bathed the field in red light, as though it were a lake of blood. Among the students practicing athletics in the field, there was a young monk and a young imam playing basketball—like a pair of rabbits that have been hibernating all winter and then dash out of their burrow at the first sight of sunlight. Wang Changping headed toward the field, but after taking several steps he quickly returned. He went back up to Yahui and exhorted her, saying, "You should return to the religion building. But I need to keep active, because if I don't, I'm afraid that later I might not have the chance." Then he smiled and added mysteriously, "I know how much you borrowed to buy an apartment in Beijing. Take a look in a few days, and perhaps you'll find that a deity has already repaid your entire loan."

Wang Changping didn't wait for Yahui to respond, and instead he ran over to the field like a middle-aged winter deer bounding toward spring. However, Yahui stood awkwardly on the edge of the field. It occurred to her that today was the day for Director Gong's athletics class, so she returned to the center to prepare the equipment.

09 Yahui, Director Gong, and the Disciples

Yet another tug-of-war competition began.

There were also other events. Director Gong's monograph needed other examples of athletic competitions between China's five religions, so he organized a comprehensive athletics class featuring a variety of different sports. By the time Yahui and the center's cleaning staff took the tug-of-war ropes, jump ropes, and badminton shuttlecocks down to the main athletic field at two o'clock on Friday afternoon, most of the disciples had already arrived. When Yahui returned with paper cups and a thermos of hot water, the field was already overflowing with people. The weather was perfect, and if people didn't spend time outside moving around, they would truly be letting the weather down. Therefore, at the mere mention of the athletics class, everyone surged down to the field as though participating in a pilgrimage.

The field was still the same field, the chain-link fence was still the same chain-link fence, and the rubber ground still had the same texture as before. The only difference was that now the tug-of-war ropes sitting on the ping-pong table were thinner than the previous year, and there were more of them. In addition, while in previous years they had used domestic Double Happiness badminton rackets, this year they were using imported ones from Malaysia.

This is how things were at the religious training center that spring.

Yahui, meanwhile, would be able to immediately sign the contract with the real estate agent and the landlord after first paying a down payment. This process had unfolded much faster than she had expected. Even after eighteen years of burning incense, kowtowing countless times to the Bodhisattva, and wearing out innumerable lotus cushions while kneeling to pray, Yahui had never heard the Bodhisattva utter a single word to her, and she had never even glimpsed the Bodhisattva in her dreams. However, this process of purchasing the apartment had proceeded very smoothly, and it seemed as though all she had to do was hand over the money, and the seller would immediately give her the goods.

Three days after Yahui mailed off Director Gong's call for donations, a high monk called the center's office. He reached Director Gong's cell phone, and soon several tens of thousands of yuan appeared in Director Gong's bank account. The next day Director Gong told Yahui to check her own account and see if a priest named Tianming had deposited a hundred thousand yuan. Yahui quickly ran over to the local branch of the Industrial and Commercial Bank of China across the street from the university. She took a number and stood in line, and when she checked the account linked to the card in her breast pocket, she found that it didn't have three hundred twenty thousand yuan, as it had before, but rather it now had four hundred twenty thousand. She immediately transferred four hundred thousand yuan to the property owner's account. As soon as the transfer was complete, she returned to the bank with the agent and the property owner to sign the sales contract. Several days later, after Yahui submitted the special talent certificate that Director Gong had issued her on behalf of the National Religion Association, the apartment could finally be transferred to her name.

In this way, Yahui would soon become a Beijing resident, and would no longer be a nun at Jing'an Temple on the shore of Xining's

Qinghai Lake. Who could have anticipated that the world held not only darkness and chaos, as the deities had said, but also good fortune? The purchase proceeded as smoothly as a pilgrim burning an incense stick on the first day of the New Year. Yahui was in such a good mood that she wanted to jump for joy, particularly after Pastor Wang Changping told her that the next day, he would give her one or two hundred thousand yuan. He asked her to return the funds she had received from the organization, and instead accept the money from him—money that, like a gift from God, she could repay or not, as she wished. Furthermore, if she later needed more money, she and Jing'an Temple could view him, Wang Changping, as a merit box. It was truly as though the deities had come down to earth and were looking after her. It was such a wonderful development, like someone walking through the desert and seeing the ground covered in pearls. Such a beautiful sky, with sun and clouds that resemble the smiling face of the Bodhisattva.

As Yahui was taking the paper cups down to the athletic field in her state of bliss, she heard Director Gong shouting at the disciples, saying, "We finally received a substantial donation from the higher organization, which will be enough to cover this semester's culture and sports fees, as well as everyone's expenses and prizes for each competition. To express our appreciation for the organization's care and support, and in order to welcome the school officials who will come today to observe and participate in our center's spring athletics festival, I have decided that, regardless of whether you are participating in a tug-of-war competition or individual ping-pong or badminton matches, and regardless of your religion, gender, and age, every winner will receive a thousand yuan and every loser will receive two hundred." Director Gong gazed excitedly at the disciples in front of him and shouted, "What do you think of that?!"

There was a wave of laughter and cheers. Before the laughter had begun to die down, people started to grab ping-pong paddles and badminton rackets. However, Wang Changping, Tian Dongqing, and Shuiyue *shifu* gathered around Director Gong, contending that the prize system was inherently unfair, since a victorious two-person ping-pong and badminton team would receive a thousand yuan, while six-, eight-, and even ten-person tug-of-war teams would have to split the same amount among them. They argued that the tug-of-war prizes should be increased to several thousand yuan. Additionally, Shuiyue *shifu* took Director Gong's hand, and said that the prizes given to Buddhist and Daoist nuns and other female disciples should also be larger, because only in this way could they express the Party's and the nation's love and support for female disciples.

The group debated this issue while laughing happily, and their corner of the field came to resemble a theatrical venue. When Director Gong noticed that they didn't have enough equipment for the scheduled competitions, he asked Yahui to go to the center and fetch the remaining tug-of-war ropes, as well as the badminton rackets and shuttlecocks. The field was soon transformed into the center's athletic field, with many disciples playing ping-pong, badminton, and tug-of-war, and female Muslims and Protestants jumping rope and kicking shuttlecocks. The sounds of knocking, whistling, and shouting by each competition's interim referees overflowed to the point that even the cloudy sky was filled with the Buddha's light rays. Yahui brought a carton of badminton rackets up from the center, as well as three boxes of whistles. She also brought several cases of water and *wulong* tea, which she pushed out to the field on a cart. She made one trip after another, and on her fourth trip, as sweat was filling her shoes, she saw the school's principal and vice principal heading toward the field. On her fifth trip, she saw the two principals standing in a corner of the field. They had called over Director Gong and were saying something to him. As Yahui pushed her cart past them, Director Gong and the two principals turned and looked at her, whereupon she noticed that all three of them had very serious expressions, as though their discussion had escalated into a dispute.

When they saw her, silence immediately enveloped them like an umbrella.

Yahui pushed her cart into the field, which was still as animated as a spring breeze. The people playing ball were still playing ball, those kicking shuttlecocks were still kicking shuttlecocks, and even disciples who had previously said that they would never participate in tug-of-war competitions for money had removed their shirts in the hot sun and joined the competition between the Islamic and Catholic teams. Only Pastor Wang Changping was standing next to the table where an eminent monk and a senior bishop were playing chess, and he was gazing past the various athletic competitions at Director Gong and the two principals on the edge of the field, as though he himself were a piece in a giant chess set.

The world seemed to have been arranged by a chess player. The competitors were summoned by the promise of money, and Yahui had been summoned by the promise of excitement. Each time she unloaded her cart, she pushed it back to the center for additional supplies. On her final trip, she loaded the cart with scoreboards for various types of competitions and hauled them over. But as she once again passed Director Gong and the two principals, a chill cut through the tumult. A police car drove over from the entranceway and stopped under the two poplars in front of the philosophy building, as though concealing some sort of danger. Then, a couple of plainclothes policemen passed Yahui and headed to where Director Gong and the two principals were standing. There, the group of people stood and discussed something.

A chill struck Yahui. Her inch-long hair had been drenched in sweat from the midspring heat, but now the sweat evaporated as the breeze blew through her hair. It seemed something momentous was about to happen, though she didn't know exactly what. So, she stood by the side of the road, watching. Then, she pushed the cart into the center's lobby, loaded it with four more scoreboards, and pushed it back out. The entire process took less than fifteen minutes, and when she reemerged it was still warm midspring weather outside. However, some of the people who had previously been enjoying this spring weather now found themselves transported back into winter. Wang Changping, his face as calm as a poplar leaf, was now leaving the athletic field with Director Gong. When they passed the corner of the field Director Gong said something to the people standing there, after which the two principals remained in their original location while the two plainclothes policemen escorted Wang Changping to the police car parked under the two poplar trees in front of the philosophy institute.

It was as though philosophy itself were taking him away, like hailing a car. The group formed a single-file line, with Director Gong bringing up the rear. Director Gong didn't look particularly surprised by these developments, nor did he appear particularly agitated. Instead, it was as though something had happened as predicted, and he had already prepared his response. Director Gong watched the plainclothes policemen escorting Wang Changping out, and when they reached the poplar trees in front of the philosophy institute, Wang Changping came to a stop in front of the car, as did the two policemen. They all turned to look at Director Gong, who was standing not far from the police car.

Wang Changping nodded to Director Gong.

Director Gong nodded back.

As Pastor Wang was being pushed into the car by one of the policemen, he saw Yahui standing on the side of the road with a stunned expression. Her face was as white as a sheet of paper, sweat dripping down from her head, and her lips trembling as though she wanted to say something but couldn't get the words out. In the distance, the athletic field was still a hub of activity with multiple different athletic contests underway, and Wang Changping's departure was as if one member of a ping-pong or badminton doubles team had disappeared, in that it had virtually no effect on the overall liveliness of the field. Closer by, students headed to their three o'clock classes were moving in bunches back and forth. Even closer, Yahui, Director Gong, and Pastor Wang were standing quietly like trees waiting for a rain shower. Eventually, the policeman quietly said to Wang Changping: "Get in."

Only then did Wang Changping smile at Yahui, and say, "I'm sorry, I didn't have time to withdraw that money for you. If you want to blame someone, then blame me. Don't blame my Master!"

Then he was pushed into the car.

Director Gong stood next to the car, looking helpless. Without saying a word, he waved feebly at the car.

The police car started up and the engine sounded just like that of other cars, the same way that the green of one tree is no different from that of others. At this moment one of the car windows opened and Wang Changping's face appeared. With a wan smile, he slowly waved, then shouted to Yahui and Director Gong: "You, the students, and the disciples may say I am being punished for my sins. However, ever since I first entered the faith, I have never done anything to let down God or my fellow believers." Someone else rolled up the car window while he continued to wave through the glass—but even as he did so, they could see a white hand grab his wrist.

The police car drove away, like the sun setting behind the mountains and darkness falling.

"Let's go . . ." Director Gong said to Yahui. "When we return to the athletic field, you mustn't tell anyone that Pastor Wang was taken away." He saw Yahui gazing at the police car as it headed toward the main gate. She seemed not to have heard what he had said. Director Gong came over and took the cart she had been pushing and repositioned the scoreboards that were about to fall off. Then he offered, "Or you could just return to the dormitory."

Yahui still stood there motionless.

Director Gong pushed the cart toward the athletic field, and as he was walking away, he turned around and said, "Make sure you keep your mouth shut. This is a matter pertaining to the organization, and it isn't something you believers can hide from God."

Then he picked up his pace, leaving Yahui staring at the school's main gate. She stared so long that one of the clouds fell out of the sky. However, she still didn't see Pastor Wang's revered Jesus, Mary, or God coming to rescue her. She didn't see Shakyamuni, the Bodhisattva, or any other Buddhist deity. Finally, she proceeded quietly to the religion building.

10 Ruan Zhisu

Without speaking or even moving, Yahui remained in her room from afternoon until after dinner. Finally, when she began to feel truly lonely, she got up to polish the porcelain Bodhisattva statue on the table, and when she felt even lonelier, she lit an incense stick in front of the statue. Eventually she lay down and went to sleep. When she woke up, she became curious what crime Wang Changping had committed, so she went downstairs to ask Director Gong. It was only after she reached the first floor that she noticed it was already dark outside, though the lights in the lobby were so bright that it seemed like midday. The door to Director Gong's office was so tightly locked that not even air could pass through. Classmates and disciples had all gone to the canteen to eat, leaving the religion building empty like an old temple without any humans or deities. Yahui stood for a while in the lobby, then went back upstairs to her dormitory. She prepared a packet of instant noodles, and just as she was about to eat, Tian Dongqing arrived.

He stood silently in the doorway for a while, holding a thick wad of bills wrapped in a newspaper. He placed the bills on her bed, then looked at her and said, "This is the prize money the center issued for the competitions this afternoon. There was ninety-eight thousand yuan in all, and I added another two thousand to make it an even hundred thousand. You can use this to repay Director Gong.

We disciples can owe each other money, and we can owe the deities money, but we definitely mustn't owe money to the organization."

Holding her bowl of noodles, Yahui stood frozen next to the bed. The red-pepper soup appeared yellow in the lamplight. Yahui gazed at Tian Dongqing's face as though trying to solve a riddle. However, his face didn't contain a riddle, nor the solution to a riddle—it just had a normal expression. She wanted to ask him, "Did you know that Pastor Wang was taken away?" However, when she remembered what Director Gong had told her, she offered Tian Dongqing her bowl of noodles instead.

"It's clean. I haven't touched it."

Tian Dongqing shook his head, and said, "Do you know why Wang Changping was taken away?"

Yahui's eyes widened with surprise as she shook her head.

"Didn't Director Gong tell you?"

Yahui again shook her head.

"Do you know who ratted on him?"

"No, I don't."

"You really don't know?"

"I really don't!"

After standing there quietly for a moment, Tian Dongqing eventually said, "Eat your food," and walked out, leaving her alone in her solitude. She ate her noodles, then sat down and tried to make some papercuts. But every cut was in the wrong place, and eventually she threw the scissors onto her bed in frustration, while also balling up several sheets of paper and tossing them onto the desk next to the sutras and textbooks. Then she got up and went to walk around the building. She saw that the disciples who should be praying were praying in the hallway and in their rooms, while those who should be drinking tea and playing chess were drinking tea and playing chess in an empty area near the entrance to the stairwell. An imam was in his room playing the *qin* and *erhu* and singing Qin opera lyrics, his tone as sorrowful as sand blowing in the wind:

I let out a mighty cry—here I stand outside!
Brave warriors all about cheer in great delight
I, Shan, alone astride my horse, trampling the Tang camps in a
*   single stride*
Wreaking death and destruction until grown men cry
Wreaking death and destruction until rivers of blood flow to the sea
*   and nigh*
Wreaking death and destruction until mountains of corpses pile
*   high*
Those piddling Tang troops, cowering in terror from my might
My horses have trampled and conquered all five battalions—who
*   still dares to challenge my might?*
When Jingde captured me, that was as fate would have it
But I do resent that the hearts of all the braves were his to buy
Thinking back to how we sealed our brotherhood with blood, and
*   all bonded as one,*
Yet now, one after another we bend to the Tang—should that be right?

. . .

Yahui didn't know which northwestern Muslim was singing this rendition of *The Decapitation of General Shan*. It almost seemed as though the tune was playing itself. At the end of the song there was also a dance performance, followed by the sound of disciples clapping their hands and stamping their feet. The imam's room became filled with people, to the point that they couldn't fit anymore, whereupon they poured out of the room and into the hallway.

Yahui listened in the hallway for a while, then proceeded down the stairs of the religion building and through the campus. As she walked along, she thought about many things, but it also felt as though she wasn't thinking of anything at all. Even if she wasn't thinking anything, however, her brain was still so full of thoughts that there wasn't any empty space left. At ten o'clock that night, the moon appeared in the sky, and by eleven o'clock the entire campus was bathed in light. She walked and sat in this light, and eventually returned to her dormitory and went to bed.

Yahui was depressed and anxious from exhaustion, and quickly fell asleep. She slept until almost eight the next morning. It was a Saturday, and it occurred to her that Director Gong would come to campus, because recently he had been coming every Saturday and Sunday to polish his monograph. After he paid his fee, the press accepted the manuscript, and merely requested that he increase all the scores mentioned in the study, and also increase the number of anecdotes. This way, after the book was published, he could submit it for a National Humanities and Social Sciences Research Award and would surely win the nation's top prize.

Therefore, Yahui got up and washed her face, then from behind the Bodhisattva portrait she removed the hundred thousand yuan that Tian Dongqing had given her, and after placing the money in a blue cloth bag, she headed out. She intended to return the hundred thousand yuan to Director Gong and the organization as Wang Changping and Tian Dongqing had recommended. However, as soon as she left her room, she stopped in front of the stairwell. She saw that in an empty area in the entranceway someone had painted a new white line, lying across which there was a tug-of-war rope—as though Jesus's cross had fallen to earth.

Tian Dongqing's wife Ruan Zhisu and two other female imams were standing at the other end of this cross, waiting for Yahui to get out of bed as though waiting for a thief that they could catch. The women stood there with an odd smile and a hard expression, looking like they were hatching a plan. Ruan Zhisu, her arms crossed and leaning to the side, said, "Have you gotten up yet, Yahui? We saw Director Gong go to work and knew that you needed to return his money, so we came here to wait for you." As she said this, she stared at the cloth bag Yahui was holding. The smile in the corner of her lips mirrored the hard words that were emerging from her mouth.

"That ninety-eight thousand yuan is everyone's prize money—so wouldn't you feel ashamed if you took it? Is it because your Buddhism is really a religion of money? Is it true that you aren't interested in anything other than money?"

Yahui was stunned and for a moment didn't know how to respond. The seventh floor was as still as an abandoned ruin, without even a trace of movement. The light at the entrance to the stairway was gray, as though it were overcast outside and there were fog inside the fog and clouds above the clouds. There was a smell of moisture in the air, and through this moisture Yahui stared at the light and air in the entranceway. While gazing at Ruan Zhisu, she instinctively held out the bag she was holding. She said, "Sister Zhisu, it was your husband, Imam Tian, who told me to borrow everyone's money. If you don't want to lend me any, however, I can return you the money." Then Yahui took two steps forward and handed Ruan Zhisu the bag. Seeing that Ruan Zhisu made no move to accept it, Yahui placed the bag next to Ruan Zhisu's feet, then headed back to her room. However, after she had taken only two steps, Ruan Zhisu called out to her. Ruan Zhisu opened the bag and looked inside, then came over and placed the bag back at Yahui's feet. With a faint smile that was quickly replaced with a hard expression, she solemnly declared, "Allah has never used His strength to bully anyone. Allah's soul is absolutely fair. I, Ruan Zhisu, did not want you to give me back the money, but rather I want to *win* it back."

Yahui stopped, attempting to read Ruan Zhisu's face as though it were a sutra.

"You want to use this money to buy an apartment in Beijing, while I want to use it to repair a mosque back home." Ruan Zhisu resembled the text of a scripture. In a measured tone, she continued, "This is money our classmates won in competition, and if you want to use it, you'll need to win it." She looked down at the tug-of-war rope, then looked up again and added, "I know that you can't do anything other than burn incense and make papercuts. Some even say you are merely a papercut artist. However, there is no disciple who can't compete in a tug-of-war. Come, let's have one match for ten thousand yuan. There's nothing fairer than this."

At this point, the other two female imams—one of whom was somewhat older than Ruan Zhisu, while the other was a few years younger—picked up the rope and handed one end to Ruan Zhisu and the other end to Yahui.

Yahui didn't take the rope. Instead, she picked up the wad of bills and once again placed it at Ruan Zhisu's feet. "I don't do tug-of-war, and neither do I need this money."

Yahui turned to leave, but found her way blocked by the older of the two imams.

"In acting this way, you are disrespecting Islam."

Yahui came to a halt.

The younger of the two imams came over and once again placed the rope in Yahui's hand, and then the two of them stood still, as though frozen in the middle of the hallway in the dead of winter. Time became like a drop of water suspended from the eaves. There was the sound of footsteps downstairs heading toward a lower floor. It was already after eight, and the female disciples should have already gotten up, washed their faces, and begun to get on with their day, but there still wasn't any hint of movement. Yahui held one end of the tug-of-war rope, like someone holding a hoe when they had never farmed before. She didn't know whether she should pull or not, and instead she merely stared at Ruan Zhisu, who was significantly thinner than she. Yahui resembled someone who had been pushed to the edge of a cliff and had no choice but to jump.

"Let's begin."

Yahui repeated, "Do we have to do this? I really don't want the money."

"Does Buddhism kneel down to accept favors from other religions?" Ruan Zhisu once again produced an odd laugh. "Allah would not let us accept favors from the government or money from other religions."

So they had no alternative but to proceed.

Yahui hesitated for a moment, squeezing the finger-thick rope and trying to find the best place to grip. Here, there wasn't the soft rubber ground they had out in the athletic field, nor was the area as spacious and bright as the main lobby. However, the hallway was just long enough for a competition. Similarly, the entrance to the stairs was bright and open enough for the other two imams serving as referee and scorekeeper to stand and observe the match. Yahui was on the west side of the hallway, while Ruan Zhisu was on the east. There was no referee's whistle or hand signals, and instead, as soon as Yahui grabbed the rope, Ruan Zhisu said, "If you are not pure of heart, then Allah will spit in your face." Yahui turned pale and, biting her lip, she gripped the rope, as Ruan Zhisu pulled even more vigorously.

The rope was pulled taut and the tassel swung back and forth several times before finally stabilizing over the center line—like a deity appearing before an imam has even had a chance to kneel. Seeing the rope pulled taut, the older imam ran to the other side of the center line. In this way, four individuals—including the two imams—quietly began the competition. In more than a hundred tug-of-war competitions spanning more than a semester, the center had never had one between two female disciples, yet here were two women from different religions awkwardly competing with one another. When Yahui leaned over, she felt a hot pain shoot from her hand to her wrist, arm, and body. Yet just as she was starting to worry about the pain that was surging through her body, she saw that the pair of legs across from her were not angled backward, but rather were standing straight, which reassured her that the other woman didn't have any more tug-of-war experience than she did. Even though Ruan Zhisu was more than a decade older than Yahui and was very thin, neither competitor appeared to have any tug-of-war experience, and therefore Yahui would be hard-pressed to come up with an excuse not to compete. Accordingly, she decided to let the outcome be determined by the deities and by the contestants' respective strength, and viewing things this way, she found herself at ease, with more strength in her hands and arms as she looked over at Ruan Zhisu. Yahui didn't know what kind of expression she herself had, but she saw that the face across from her, which was not particularly attractive to begin with, had turned red and purple as the blood beneath the skin welled up to the surface.

Meanwhile, the two female imams on either side of the rope had originally been standing straight as rods, but they seemed to have received instructions from the deities and were now putting their entire bodies into observing the competition, bending at the waist and staring intently at the tassel as it swung back and forth. When they saw the tassel swing over to their side of the center line, they made fists and cheered Ruan Zhisu on, shouting, "Allah! Allah! Allah!" On the other hand, when they saw the tassel being pulled back toward the center line, they bit their lips and shook their fists at the rope—as though they weren't acting on behalf of Allah or Ruan Zhisu, but rather were threatening the rope and tassel themselves. Meanwhile, Yahui didn't have any nuns cheering her on, nor did she have anyone shouting "Buddha! Buddha!" or "Go! Go!" on her behalf. Nevertheless, Yahui hoped that she would win this match, because that way she would win ten thousand yuan, and even if she wasn't doing it for the money, she should at least do it for the sake of this competition between Buddhism and Islam, between Shakyamuni and Muhammad. Yahui would have preferred that the two imams stationed on either side of the rope stand farther away, not sway back and forth directly in her line of sight. However, she was afraid that if she said anything it might break her concentration and the tassel might drift to the other side of the line.

Sweat poured down her forehead and into her eyes, and as a result the scene in front of her became enveloped in white fog. She very much wanted to check on Ruan Zhisu's posture and expression, but all she could make out was a shadowy figure. Behind her, she seemed to hear footsteps in some room, followed by a toilet flushing and then silence. The tassel was pulled back and forth. Whenever it came to her side, at most it only crossed the center line by a few inches or perhaps a foot, but just as she was about to reposition her feet, it would slip back to the other side. It was cold that morning and the robe she was wearing kept blocking her knees, as though there were a rope underfoot that kept tripping her up. She regretted that she hadn't thought to take off the robe and wished she had worn a shirt, pants, and flexible sneakers like her opponent. It occurred to her that she should have worn that red athletic suit that she had recently bought. It occurred to her that it would have been better if, instead of her pointed-toe cloth shoes, she had instead worn the kind of flexible athletic sneakers where you can tie the shoelaces across the instep. She wondered, *How many times has the tassel crossed the center line? And how long has this competition been going on? For five minutes? Eight minutes? Maybe ten minutes? Sister Zhisu, are you not in pain? After having experienced almost unendurable agony giving birth to three children, how is that you can now hold out for so long? How is it that every time the tassel comes over to my side, you can immediately pull it back?*

Yahui's legs became sore and her ears began to pound as though she had tinnitus. Time passed as slowly as an interminable sutra, with every second stretched out like a sentence uttered without pausing for breath. However, no matter what, she had to focus in order to endure the progression from one second to the next. There was a sparrow perched outside the window, and although Yahui couldn't hear the bird clearly, she could see its mouth opening and closing. Then, another sparrow flew over and similarly began opening and closing its mouth. Each time the birds opened their mouths, Yahui could hear the female imams' shouts of "Allah! Allah!" exploding in the entranceway and in her ears. She pulled with her knees, hands, and arms, until she felt the rope slowly inching toward her side. She finally managed to shift her left leg, which had been bent in front of her, back a step, and to place her right leg in front. At this point, she saw Ruan Zhisu's rear leg inexorably move forward, as her flushed face became even more red than before. Yahui took advantage of the opportunity and shifted her front leg back and leaned backward at an even sharper angle. She glanced down and saw the tassel swaying back and forth on her side of the center line, as though it were about to fall off. She knew that if she was going to win this match, she needed to exert herself just a bit more. If she could hold out for just a few more seconds, she would be able to claim victory. After winning the first match, she'd also be able to win the second and third. After she won the entire competition, this ninety-eight-thousand-yuan pot—really, a full hundred thousand yuan—would be rightfully hers, and she wouldn't need to borrow from her classmates via Tian Dongqing. The two female imams kept shouting "Allah! Allah!" and it was as though the chirping of the sparrows in the window had suddenly become the cawing of a crow. Becoming increasingly annoyed by the imams' cawing, Yahui glared at them and saw that their faces were covered in sweat, like stones scattered in the sands of the Gobi Desert, while the stairwell railing and the white wall behind them resembled cliffs and ravines. Yahui thought how nice it would be if one of them were to fall into a ravine and the other were to hit her head on the cliff wall.

The shouts of "Caw! Caw!" and "Allah! Allah!" made Yahui feel as though her head were about to explode. She needed to make the imams close their mouths, but the only way she could do so would be to win this match as quickly as possible by pulling the rope toward her side like water in a sluice. She seized on this thought, and it was as though the Bodhisattva were hovering in front of her—as though the white walls were lotus clouds, and the Bodhisattva were sitting on a lotus cloud gazing down at her. The Buddha also arrived and stood behind the Bodhisattva, enveloped in a golden glow. His steady gaze was fixed on Yahui, which granted her considerable hope and perseverance. Yahui no longer felt the pain in her hands nor the fatigue in her legs, and she no longer felt as though her arms were about to be ripped out of their sockets. Instead, she felt as though the shouts of "Allah! Allah!" were urging her on, as were the imams' sighs of hopelessness after their calls to heaven fell on deaf ears.

One of Ruan Zhisu's feet was already at the center line, and Yahui just needed to pull her a little more so that more than half of Ruan Zhisu's foot was over the line. By this point, the two imams were panicked, and their hoarse shouts resembled the squawking of chickens and ducks facing certain death under the eye of an eagle.

As far as the eye could see, there was prayed-for hope and Buddha light.

As far as the eye could see, there were the joyful smiles of the Buddha, the Bodhisattva, and their disciples. Now Yahui could clearly see Ruan Zhisu's face, which was as wrinkled as a wet shirt that someone from Xining is wringing out after having just forded a river. Ruan Zhisu's complexion had shifted from blood red to yellowish white, and her face was as sweaty as Jueyu *shifu's* had been when she first managed to get up from her sickbed. If Yahui could pull just a little harder, adding an increment of force equivalent to a bean or a grain of sand, she would be able to pull Ruan Zhisu over to her side of the line. Yahui had already received this additional strength from the deity, and simply needed to transfer it to her legs and to her big toe that was pressing through the sole of her shoe and into the concrete floor. But suddenly Yahui's shoes seemed to become one or two sizes smaller and no longer fit her size thirty-six feet. It was as though her feet had become so swollen that her shoes would burst open. It was as though this were no longer a battle between Yahui and Ruan Zhisu, but rather between Yahui's shoes and her own feet. Because of the force she was exerting, her feet became swollen as though they were full of blood and were determined to burst out of their shoes. In particular, her right foot, which was in front of her, became as swollen as a water bag, but the shoe dammed up the water and prevented it from flowing out.

Yahui could feel her right shoelace pressing against the top of her foot, like a rope tied tightly around a water bag filled with blood. She prayed the shoelace would bind her foot and prevent the bag from rupturing and letting the blood flow out. She prayed that the Bodhisattva and the Buddha would protect her shoelace. She made a wish that she would win the match and the money, so that after buying a house she could immediately place the Bodhisattva and the Buddha over the head of the bed, thereby transforming her entire apartment into a Buddhist temple and giving the Buddha and the Bodhisattva another home in Beijing. Maybe if she hadn't gotten distracted thinking about her shoe and her shoelaces, she could have won the match. But she did think about them, and remembered how, when she had been washing her shoes a week earlier, she had noticed that the thread connecting the laces to the top of the shoe was a bit loose. At the time, she had wanted to sit down and resew the thread, but because she was in the process of making a papercut image of Guanyin and Laozi talking and drinking tea, she didn't have a chance to fix it.

Now, however, the situation had come to a head, like an entire dam collapsing because of a tiny ant hole. As soon as she remembered the loose thread at the base of the shoelace, the thread did in fact snap at that very location. There was a loud explosion, as though a stone had fallen from the top of a tall building. Yahui felt the ground trembling beneath her feet, and before she knew what was happening, she felt her right foot weakening, as her toes, which had been digging into the ground, started to slide forward. At this point, Ruan Zhisu quickly took several steps back, as though her entire body were being pulled backward by Allah, and Yahui's feet were dragged over the center line.

The hallway immediately fell silent. The sound of wind blowing suddenly congealed, pressing down onto their heads and their chests. Unable to believe what had happened, Ruan Zhisu stood in the entranceway to the stairwell, appearing not particularly happy and excited, but rather staring, with a taut expression, at Yahui's shoelace, which had fallen to the ground. After a while, she said, "It was God who didn't want you to win, and who broke your shoelace. Now I've won ten thousand yuan." Her gaze shifted to the wad of bills, as though she wanted to immediately take back the money. However, she appeared to remember something, and said, "Just put it anywhere. Allah has already decided that I've won this money."

Yahui didn't say a word. Instead, she merely stared at that dark-blue shoelace and that fat wad of bills.

"Allah gave me strength, while neither the Bodhisattva nor the Buddha offered you any assistance." As Ruan Zhisu said this, she looked around, then suddenly bent down and removed her own shoes. She also took off her socks, stuffed them into her shoes, and placed the shoes against a wall. Then she returned and said to Yahui, "Of all the gods, Allah is the fairest. Given that your shoelace broke, we will therefore both go barefoot."

Yahui looked at that pair of black, ugly, duck-like feet that appeared as though they hadn't been washed in several days. She could see mud between the toes and smell the stench of the feet. Yahui stared for a moment, then looked away. She slowly removed her own shoes and put them aside. At this point, several female disciples opened their doors and emerged, including the Protestant disciple Lin Xiaojing and the Catholic disciple Sister Daxue. Missing, however, were the Buddhist nun Bikhuni and the Daoist nun Zai. Everyone was staring at the scene in the hallway, including the two pairs of feet. Initially no one said a word, but then they started shouting, "What is missing from Director Gong's book is an account of this sort of tug-of-war competition! But wouldn't that be like putting lipstick on a pig, or a deity's face on a human's butt?" Upon seeing that Ruan Zhisu, Yahui, and the two female imams were not responding, the other women laughed and simply stepped aside to serve as spectators. The women watching stopped urging them not to participate in the competition so as not to promote conflict and resentment between different religions. Instead, they came to have a glow of excitement, as though they were being illuminated by the miraculous scene in front of them.

Ruan Zhisu once again placed the rope in Yahui's hands.

Upon accepting the rope, Yahui glanced down at her feet. She noticed that next to Ruan Zhisu's, her own feet resembled a pair of white doves next to a pair of black crows. The concrete floor was freezing cold, making Yahui feel as though there were a painful thorn in her foot. In response to the pain and the hardness of this concrete floor, Yahui arched her toes, and only then did she look over at the end of the rope.

Her opponent had already bent down and grabbed the rope, her feet resembling a pair of eagles with their wings spread. The second match began and Yahui bent over, pulled hard, and struggled to hold on. With the ground cutting into her bare feet like a knife, Yahui lost the second match in less than three minutes.

For the third match, Yahui put her socks back on, but as she and her opponent pulled each other back and forth, the sandstone floor rubbed holes in the bottoms of her socks and she felt an excruciating pain in the soles of her feet. As Yahui was attempting to endure this agony, she felt pieces of gravel being drilled into her feet, and eventually she gave up again.

For the fourth match, Yahui picked up the rope after removing two pieces of gravel embedded in the sole of her right foot. She had rubbed a hole in her right sock, and her big toe was poking out. At this point, Ruan Zhisu also stared at her snowy-white toe, then smiled and said, "The Bodhisattva's feet were cultivated in the clouds, and your nun's feet were cultivated in a mountain spring. As for us imams, our feet developed in yellow earth, desert, and rocky ground. In our tug-of-war competition today, the winner will be not the strongest, but rather the one who is most able to endure hardship."

After saying this, she looked at the female disciples who had gathered around. They had all finally emerged from their dormitories after sleeping in, and were in the hallway watching the match. There were several Buddhist nuns in the group, and they were chatting with each other, remarking that "Gu Mingzheng's heart is true, while Yahui's has strayed." After saying this, the nuns dried their recently washed faces and applied some skin cream. Yahui looked at the group and saw that there were also several male disciples who had come upstairs and were standing on the outside of the cluster, craning their necks as though watching a comedy. Laughing uproariously, the disciples pointed at Yahui and Ruan Zhisu, but Yahui couldn't make out what they were saying. She once again looked down at her right foot and saw that she now had three toes sticking out of her sock. She then saw that her left sock also had a hole, from which a toe with an overgrown nail was sticking out. Yahui hesitated a moment, as though she would have to admit defeat, then she did in fact go over to Ruan Zhisu and said quietly, "Sister Zhisu, I concede. You can keep the money."

Ruan Zhisu reflected for a moment, and replied, "Allah doesn't permit us to accept money from people belonging to other faiths. For each match I win, I can only take the ten thousand yuan that corresponds to me."

"What if it's not me who is giving you the money, but rather the Buddha?"

"I can't take the Buddha's money either. Other than Allah, we don't recognize any other deities, including the Buddha, the Bodhisattva, Jesus, or the Virgin Mary. If I were to accept the Buddha's money, I would effectively be acknowledging that other deities exist." Ruan Zhisu glared at Yahui and continued, "Let's begin. Other than the Buddha and the Bodhisattva, everyone must bow down before Allah."

Yahui stood there as Ruan Zhisu picked up one end of the rope and took two steps back. At that moment, Shuiyue *shifu* suddenly appeared out of nowhere. She was holding a pair of new white athletic shoes, and after making her way through the crowd, she placed the shoes in front of Yahui and whispered, "One can lose to a person, but one cannot lose to the Buddha!" Immediately afterward, several more Buddhist and Daoist nuns jostled in, and they all started shouting, "Yahui, can't you defeat her? You're not even twenty years old, while she has already had children of her own." Afterward, they laughed while chanting *Amitābha*, and said, "Don't be an embarrassment for us Buddhists! Don't let them speak ill of our Bodhisattva!" Then they were pushed back by other classmates who had just arrived, and their voices were drowned out by other people's laughter.

The entire hallway became filled with people.

The entrances to the stairwell and the elevator became filled with male disciples from different religions, and even an eighty-two-year-old priest was in the crowd, supported by other disciples so that he could watch the excitement. Through the window they could see that the blue sky was perfectly still, except for a few clouds drifting by. The sky was cheerful, but some of the clouds were still sorrowful. An imam brought Ruan Zhisu her own shoes and placed them in front of her, indicating for her to put them on before continuing. However, Ruan Zhisu glanced at the shoes and kicked them aside, then looked contemptuously at Yahui, who was putting on the new pair of shoes, and at Shuiyue *shifu*, who was helping her tie them. Yahui saw Ruan Zhisu kick away her shoes and, after a brief hesitation, removed hers again and stuffed them into Shuiyue *shifu*'s hands. Then she stood up, took off her socks, and tossed them aside as well.

The fifth tug-of-war match began, and what followed was a repetition of what had come before. Yahui dug her toes into the ground and felt that this time the strength in her feet and body would surely be enough for her to win. Ruan Zhisu was in fact pulled part of the way over, but then she regained her balance and planted her feet. Ruan Zhisu had figured out the secret to winning: she bent her knees, angled her back, lowered her head, and stared straight ahead while biting her lower lip, holding her breath, and exerting all her strength. She would then manage to find a foothold as her toes dug into the ground, and Yahui's own feet and legs would seem to rise up from the ground.

The raucous crowd briefly fell silent, then again started shouting, "Go! Go!" The Buddhist and Daoist disciples stood on Yahui's side, while the Muslim disciples stood on Ruan Zhisu's side. Meanwhile, some of the Catholic and Protestant disciples cheered for Yahui, others cheered for Ruan Zhisu, and others simply cheered for whichever side appeared to be losing, as God was always on the side of the weak. Shouts flooded the hallway as the tassel clearly edged over to Yahui's side of the center line, although in the end it always ended up on Ruan Zhisu's side. The results of the fifth and sixth matches were the same as the preceding ones. Finally, Yahui couldn't stand it anymore. Her face drenched in sweat, she stood in the spacious entrance to the stairwell, and after a brief hesitation she went to pick up the bag at the base of the wall and handed it to Ruan Zhisu. With trembling lips, she said, "Sister Zhisu, it is not I who am giving your Islam money, nor is it the Buddha. Instead, it is Allah who has directed that I give it to you, so that you can then return and renovate that mosque."

Everyone's shouts of encouragement immediately subsided. Their gazes became as still as moonlight, neither bright nor pitch black, such that everything appeared murky but could still be seen. Apart from the sound of the disciples holding their breath, there was also the whirring of the elevator. At this point, Ruan Zhisu stood still. She knew she had won this competition, but from the look in everyone's eyes, she seemed to recognize that the Buddha was the real winner and Allah was the loser. Therefore, Ruan Zhisu didn't take the money, nor did she say another word, and instead she simply pushed away the bag Yahui was handing her.

"Allah doesn't let me accept this!"

After a brief hesitation, Yahui took another step forward and suddenly reached out to Ruan Zhisu. At this point, all the disciples saw that Yahui's palm was covered in blisters, one of which had burst open and covered her palm in blood. No one said a word. The deities also stopped walking through the crowd and down the hallway. Everyone stared at Ruan Zhisu, as though she were a sinner or a criminal.

However, Ruan Zhisu appeared perfectly calm, and as she looked at Yahui she simultaneously scanned the crowd of disciples and calmly asked, "Are you able to declare, in front of these disciples, that Buddha lost to Allah?"

Yahui shook her head. "No, I cannot!"

"Then can you declare that Buddhism is really not as powerful as Islam?"

Yahui replied, "It was not Buddha who lost to you, but rather it was I, Yahui—who does not even deserve to be called a Buddhist."

Ruan Zhisu picked up the bloody rope and handed it to Yahui, saying, "Take this."

As she said this, she turned to the female imam who was serving as scorekeeper, and said, "Take out your knife; I said that Allah is the fairest of all deities." Seeing that the imam wasn't responding, Ruan Zhisu shouted to her, "Take it out, and don't forget that we are all the daughters of Allah!" The imam finally picked up the small bag next to her and removed a copy of the Quran. From beneath the Quran, she took the stationery box she used for class, and from the box she selected a small pocketknife and calmly handed it to Ruan Zhisu. She said quietly, "Sister Zhisu."

Ruan Zhisu did not respond. Instead, she took the knife and opened it. With one hand she passed the knife with the inch-long blade to Yahui, while simultaneously holding out her other hand.

"Are you going to do it, or should I? You tell me how deep to slice, and how many cuts to make."

Yahui turned pale.

Shuiyue *shifu* and the other monks and nuns watched in alarm. The male disciples standing behind the female disciples all turned pale and didn't dare speak or even breathe loudly. The entire floor once again became as still as an abandoned tomb. It was as though before any of the disciples had seen God, the Buddha, the Bodhisattva, or Laozi in the flesh, Ruan Zhisu had brought forth Allah's real body and real voice, positioning this sacred Allah in front of these disciples from other religions. All the disciples' palms were bathed in sweat, and everyone's eyes appeared ice cold. Yahui stood in the middle of the crowd, her body like an old tree that Ruan Zhisu had dug up. She felt so light that it seemed as though she were about to float away at any moment. She stared at the knife and at Ruan Zhisu's hands in front of her, and saw that those hands' calluses resembled rocks protruding from the northeastern soil. Yahui finally understood that the reason she had been unable to defeat her opponent was because she had been raised by the Buddha, while Ruan Zhisu had not only raised herself but furthermore was a true disciple of hardship and of Muhammad. Yahui didn't know what she should do or what she should say. Her forehead was beaded with sweat. It seemed that she had not perspired very much while competing, but now, upon seeing that knife, her entire back became completely soaked. A chill ran up her spine.

At this point, there was a loud commotion. Everyone turned toward the elevator, where someone emerged through a gap in the crowd.

It was Gu Mingzheng!

Like the other disciples, Mingzheng had slept late this weekend, and upon hearing that some female disciples on the seventh floor were having a tug-of-war competition, he returned to his room, poured himself half a glass of water, took several sips, and then sat for a while. In the end, however, he couldn't resist taking the elevator up to the seventh floor. He suspected Yahui might be competing against someone, and immediately realized what was happening as he watched from the edge of the crowd. In this pivotal moment, he appeared before them, almost as if he had done so without even thinking. It was almost as though the reason he had had so few interactions with Yahui this semester was precisely because he had been waiting for this very moment to approach her. Neither fast nor slow, neither rushed nor panicked, he removed his gray robe as he walked forward, revealing a white shirt tied at the waist. Then he tossed his robe into the crowd, pulled his shirt out of his pants, tightened his belt, and rubbed his hands. After passing in front of everyone, Mingzheng went up to Yahui like Jesus walking up to a prostitute who was about to be stoned to death. He pushed her aside, then stood in her place, picked up the bloodstained rope, and examined it. Holding the rope, he said gently to Ruan Zhisu, "Buddhism and Daoism have always been part of the same family. I'll compete against you."

Ruan Zhisu scornfully asked him, "Are you a woman?"

"Yes!" Mingzheng said. "Would you like to see?"

Mingzheng turned and surveyed all of the disciples and classmates who were assembled around him and then, standing face-to-face with Ruan Zhisu, placed both hands on his waist and said, in a voice so loud it sounded as though he had a microphone in front of him, "I'm a female disciple. I've already been operated on! If any of you won't take my word for it, I'd be happy to remove my pants in front of everyone and show you." With this, he again looked around and saw that everyone was mesmerized by what he had said—as though a rumor had suddenly become reality.

It was Ruan Zhisu's turn to turn pale. It appeared as though a layer of frost had appeared on her wrinkled yellow face. She didn't know whether she should let Mingzheng remove his pants to prove that he was in fact a female disciple. Ruan Zhisu glanced at the female disciples behind her, and saw their look of confusion as they sank back into the crowd. In the end, she said rather comedically, "Priest Gu, go right ahead—if you dare to show your ugly regions in public, I'll be happy to compete with you."

Even more surprising was that Mingzheng did, in fact, remove his pants. With his hands on his waist, he hesitated a few seconds, then began unfastening his belt. This was the same shiny black Lacoste plastic belt that he had previously used to poke himself, and the stainless-steel square buckle was still just as dazzling. The belt prong that previously penetrated his shoulder blade was still in the middle of the buckle. He unfastened the belt, and the entire floor seemed to be filled with the buckle's clatter. As he pulled his pants down, the hallway became as quiet as a mountain about to suffer a landslide. Then, when his red underwear was revealed, the sound of the landslide drowned out all other sounds. He wasn't wearing the sort of homespun underwear that other Daoist monks usually wear, but rather the dark-red briefs that people wear each anniversary of their zodiac birth year—and that resemble the swimsuits that people in movies wear at the beach.

It was already after nine in the morning, and from somewhere on campus there was the sound of a bell summoning students to their weekend classes, like the sound of cicadas outside the religion building in summer. Although the rest of the world was the same as before, Mingzheng was no longer the same Mingzheng. He was no longer the same shallow and impetuous Daoist disciple as before. Instead, he appeared to have achieved enlightenment. He seemed to have matured into a Daoist master, and had a steady, introspective demeanor. He inserted both hands into his pants and pulled down his underwear, and when his white skin appeared in the opening between his shirt and his underwear, it was as though the sun were rising in the middle of the night. Some of the Daoist nuns, Buddhist nuns, and female imams closest to him muttered as they pushed their way to the back of the crowd, others screamed as they covered their faces with their hands, and others simply stood there waiting to see what horror might unfold next.

However, the next step would not come from Mingzheng, but rather from Tian Dongqing and Director Gong. No one saw them arrive, and it was unclear whether they had come up the stairs or taken the elevator, but as Tian Dongqing swept through like a tornado, he glimpsed his wife through the opening in the crowd, and also saw Mingzheng, who by this point had already pulled down his underwear. Tian Dongqing rushed forward and gave Mingzheng a slap that was neither particularly strong nor particularly light. Mingzheng stopped pulling down his underwear and instead used his hands to cover his crotch.

Tian Dongqing roared, "Are you even human? I'm ashamed and humiliated on behalf of all you Daoists!"

Without waiting for the other disciples to come to their senses, or for Mingzheng to respond, Tian Dongqing spun around and slapped his wife with all his strength. The slap was more than twice as loud as when he had slapped Gu Mingzheng. As Ruan Zhisu held her cheek and was about to cry out, he roared again, "This isn't Allah striking you, it's your husband!"

Ruan Zhisu stared at Tian Dongqing, and then glanced at Yahui and Mingzheng. Then, through her clenched teeth, she asked Tian Dongqing, "Whose husband are you?"

Tian Dongqing replied, "I'm *your* husband!"

Ruan Zhisu was silent for a moment, then said, "Do you dare publicly declare, in front of these disciples, that you will remain my husband for as long as you live?"

"I'll be your husband for two lifetimes!"

"Will you swear to this in front of these disciples and in front of Allah?"

Tian Dongqing turned halfway and looked at the students and disciples gathered around him, then he looked up at the white ceiling overhead. Finally, in a loud, solemn voice, he announced, "To Allah up above and to the disciples assembled before us, I swear that, for this life and the next, I will remain Ruan Zhisu's husband, and will also remain Allah's son, grandson, and great-grandson!"

In this way, the situation rushed to a conclusion, like a strong wind blowing a tree's yellow leaves to the ground. Upon hearing Tian Dongqing's oath, Ruan Zhisu didn't look at her husband, nor did she say anything to the crowd. Instead, she picked up the bag in which Yahui had put the money, then reached past Gu Mingzheng and handed it to Yahui, who was still standing there motionless. Ruan Zhisu shouted brightly, "Go buy your apartment—Allah has agreed to give you the money." Then she turned and, upon seeing Director Gong through an opening in the crowd, said, "Now your monograph will have an example of every form of competition. It is sure to be a great work!"

As everyone watched her leave, Yahui proceeded toward her dormitory at the other end of the hall. Then the crowd dispersed, whereupon Yahui took the hundred thousand yuan that Ruan Zhisu had given her and handed it to Director Gong. In this way, this incident involving humans, deities, and money reached its conclusion.

11 Yahui, Mingzheng, and the Real Estate Agent

In fact, this incident involving deities, humans, and money had not yet fully concluded, and was still waiting for Yahui to do more. After handing Director Gong the wad of bills, Yahui returned to her room and sat there for a while. Then she went to the bathroom to wash her hands and blow on her blistered palms. When she emerged, she glanced at the Bodhisattva on the table, took two steps toward the door, then went back to sit on the bed again. She only sat there for two seconds, but during those two seconds she was suddenly transformed into a mature woman—leaving no trace of that eighteen-year-old jade nun who had grown up in Jingshui Convent. When she got up from bed the second time, she found she harbored Ruan Zhisu no resentment, and even felt rather grateful to her. Ruan Zhisu had helped transform her from a jade nun into a mature nun and helped her understand that being eighteen years old is significant, as this is the age at which a person becomes an adult. It is the age at which those living in the secular world can get married and have a family. If she were still in that village in the outskirts of Xining, by this point she possibly would already be a wife who herded sheep while carrying her child during the day and then hurried home to cook dinner.

Yahui once again emerged from her room and passed an old Daoist nun in the hallway. The nun turned to her, and Yahui nodded to the nun and headed to the elevator.

Yahui took the elevator down, and as she was emerging from the religion building, she continued to nod to everyone she saw—without saying a word or even making a Buddhist mudra. She walked quickly, as though there were something that she absolutely had to do on time. Her loan was about to be approved, and once it was, she would simply need to go to the bank, give them a copy of her ID, and fill out some paperwork, and then she'd be able to go to the Fourth Ring Road's real estate transfer center to get a relocation certificate.

All of a sudden, she desperately wanted to be able to hold the deed to the apartment, and to begin the process of painting, redecorating, and moving in. She wanted to be able to show Ruan Zhisu, Tian Dongqing, Shuiyue *shifu*, Director Gong, and all her classmates that she had really bought an apartment in Beijing.

She would not be returning to Jingshui Convent in Xining.

Instead, she wanted to bring the entire convent to Beijing. She wanted to bring her *shifu*, the Bodhisattva, and Tathagata to Beijing to visit her.

A little after ten that morning, she went to the bank to inquire about the loan, and at eleven she proceeded to the real estate transfer center to fill out some additional paperwork. That afternoon, she went to a furniture store to check out beds, tables, and sofas. The next morning, she hired a contractor to paint the apartment, and by afternoon she was sitting by the side of the road drinking water and eating some fried flatcakes and grilled sausages she had bought from a stall. As she did so, she watched the passersby and looked up at the sky, as though afraid that the passersby had noticed that she, a jade nun, was breaking her dietary prohibitions and eating meat.

Yahui was still the same Yahui as before, but she also wasn't. As she sat on the side of the road wolfing down her food, Mingzheng, who had come with her, was standing anxiously by her side.

"Would you like some?" Yahui offered Mingzheng a grilled sausage.

Mingzheng hesitated before accepting it. Then he wrapped the sausage in a piece of paper and said, "I'll take it back to the school to eat it."

"If you aren't going to eat it now, then give it back to me." Yahui accepted the sausage from Mingzheng, and added, "I'm going to eat it here. I'm waiting for the Bodhisattva and Tathagata to show up and slap me, spit in my face, and kick me out of the pure realm." As she ate, she spoke as though she were angry at the Buddha and the Bodhisattva, as though they were her enemies. She seemed to be waiting for them to appear and fight her.

Mingzheng felt that ever since Yahui had participated in that competition with Ruan Zhisu, she was no longer the same Yahui as before. It was as though a gentle paulownia tree had suddenly sprouted thorns overnight. He stared at her in surprise, then walked up and used his body to block the heretical sight of her eating. At that point, the sun was in the lower part of the sky. It was three or four in the afternoon, and the air was comfortably warm.

When Yahui finished, she wiped her hands, then threw the tissue to the ground. She stood up and stared at Mingzheng for a while, then said, "I want to ask you something—when we return, will you show me that place between your legs, where you had the operation?"

Mingzheng stared at her in shock and reflexively took a step backward as he protectively placed his hands between his legs. He looked at her and was about to ask her to repeat the question, as though he had not heard her clearly.

"If it had been last semester that I had this sort of experience with Ruan Zhisu, I would have immediately agreed to return to secular life and marry you. Even if my *shifu* had reprimanded me and the Bodhisattva had cursed me, I would have still wanted to be with you." After saying this in a voice that was neither loud nor soft, she glanced at Mingzheng's eyes and then walked past him, heading back to the school. She left him behind as though he were her shadow.

In this way, Yahui and Mingzheng reconciled and were able to express themselves freely. It was as though Yahui had suddenly matured and realized that the mortal world was like the tug-of-war competition between herself and Ruan Zhisu, and that all worldly events are controlled by deities, humans, and money. She came to understand that the world originally had no deities, and all worldly events simply followed one after another, like her tug-of-war competition with Ruan Zhisu. At the same time, however, it was also as if she didn't understand anything at all, and instead simply knew that having already turned eighteen, she was now headed toward nineteen. In Xining, when girls reach nineteen or twenty, they need to work hard to find a family to marry into, and once they get married they will need to work hard for a living. Yahui, meanwhile, felt that she now had to rush around trying to purchase an apartment, to secure her own future livelihood. She waited one day, and another, and another—until finally, the following Tuesday, she was notified that her loan had been approved. She returned to the bank at ten in the morning to fill out and sign some forms, and at eleven she went back to the real estate agency on Beijing's Fourth Ring Road.

The real estate transfer center was in a glass-walled office building. With her certification letter, power of attorney letter, transfer receipt, and bank card in hand, Yahui arrived at the third-floor lobby, where everyone was standing in line. She took a "transfer flow chart" from the counter and, following the instructions, lined up at window number two on the west side of the floor while tightly gripping her bank card. She calculated that after paying the down payment and other fees, she had about thirty-five thousand yuan left on her card. However, the property tax was 1.5 percent, meaning that for a two-million-yuan apartment, she would have to pay thirty thousand yuan in taxes. There were also printing fees and administrative fees, so finally, after everything was fully accounted for, her card should still have about a thousand yuan on it. After receiving the property deed, she wanted to use the remaining money to invite the real estate agent out to dinner that evening, and then take Mingzheng out for drinks.

But as she was standing in line, her plans began to change.

Half an hour later it was finally her turn, and as she passed her documents through the window, she saw a pair of hands transfer them from one pile to another, then take several documents from yet another pile and insert them into a folder. Then, the woman behind the counter tapped the documents on the table and began to examine them one after another, giving particular attention to every item with an official seal. Finally, in a pleasant voice, the woman said, "No problem. Will this be cash or credit? The total is one hundred three thousand and eight hundred yuan."

Yahui stared in shock.

"There must be some mistake. Shouldn't the tax be thirty thousand yuan?"

"The tax rate increased at midnight last night, from 1.5 to 3.5 percent. Didn't you hear the news this morning? Didn't you see the announcement posted in the entranceway?"

Yahui stood frozen in front of the window.

The woman behind the counter leaned back in her seat. It appeared she had already had this discussion countless times today, to the point that she was no longer annoyed by it. She took a sip of water without looking at Yahui's shocked reaction, and after the water moistened her throat, she put down her cup and said in a loud voice, "Are you going to pay or not? If not, I'll take the next person in line!"

It was as though the woman knew that Yahui didn't have enough money in her account, and as she shouted at Yahui, she pushed the documents out through the window.

Yahui had no idea how she managed to collect her documents or make her way through the crowd of people waiting in line. There was a loud buzzing in her head, as though the words she received at the window had struck her like an avalanche. Her reaction was not at all like that of a typical Buddhist or Daoist who takes something as nothing, and nothing as emptiness, and for whom all principles and teachings are positioned at the margins of presence and absence. Instead, she stood in shock in the lobby before slowly proceeding downstairs. For what seemed like an eternity, she stood by the Fourth Ring Road looking at the passersby, buildings, and cars. She remembered how, several days earlier, her palm had started bleeding after her tug-of-war competition with Ruan Zhisu, and she looked down at her bandaged right hand. She remembered how she had originally planned to come pay the taxes later that same day, but since she still had not received the loan approval, she had instead gone to the furniture store. Then when she received the notification of the loan's approval, she dropped everything and rushed over to the transfer center, but by that point the tax rate had already increased by two percentage points. Three point five percent of two million is seventy thousand. Seventy thousand yuan—if this were paid in ten-thousand-yuan installments, it would require seven installments, and if it were in cash, it would be half a brick of bills.

She felt as though her head had been beaten with a club. She should have burst into tears, but the instant the club struck her, she felt no pain. Instead, her head was as empty as though nothing had happened, or as if she didn't know what had happened yet. She stood by the side of the road, staring blankly at the street, the pedestrians, and the sky. The weather was crisp, with only a few clouds, and the sky was the color of water. It was almost midday, and the clouds overhead were as white as the funerary clothing traditionally worn by the people of Xining. Yahui stared at one of the white clouds. She knew that the Bodhisattva definitely wouldn't emerge from behind that cloud, yet she still continued to stare at it, thinking how wonderful it would be if the Bodhisattva were to suddenly appear. If she could see the Bodhisattva appear over that cloud, she would rush across the intersection up ahead and kneel down, even at the risk of being run over by a car. Conversely, if the Bodhisattva didn't emerge but the cloud itself took a human form that bore any resemblance to the Bodhisattva, she would leap over the railing and kneel down in the middle of the road, even if there were vehicles approaching and threatening to grind her body into the ground.

She held out her hand again and looked at it, while silently shouting to herself, "Ah, deities! Ah, humans! Ah, home!"

She had no idea why she suddenly thought this, it just naturally came to her. As she shouted this she felt carefree, and once again began to feel a peculiar sense of gratitude to Ruan Zhisu.

It was Ruan Zhisu who helped her transition from being a jade nun to a mature nun.

It was Ruan Zhisu who had helped her realize what she needed to do next. She did not regret at all having returned those hundred thousand yuan to Director Gong several days earlier, nor did she regret the fact that, because she was a day late, she now had to pay an extra seventy thousand yuan in real estate taxes. She had heard Pastor Wang mention that in the Bible there is a figure called Job, who endured an almost unimaginable amount of suffering. However, when Job's entire family was killed in a conflagration, he didn't shed a single tear, because he knew that God was simply testing his loyalty and bravery. So, who's to say that this wasn't the Buddha trying to test her? Who's to say that this wasn't the Bodhisattva deliberately transforming her from a jade nun into a mature nun? She observed as a steady string of cars drove by and footsteps landed in front of and behind her like raindrops. She once again stared at that cloud that resembled a large sports field. The cloud was neither round nor square, and it had ragged edges. Around it, there wasn't any hint of movement, much less any trace of the Bodhisattva emerging from behind it.

Yahui suddenly wanted to laugh at herself. Although she knew that the Bodhisattva wouldn't emerge from behind the cloud, she had still looked up and waited. This reminded her of what Imam Tian had told everyone three days earlier. He said that before Pastor Wang was taken away, he had given Imam Tian a letter and asked that, if some day he were to run into trouble, Imam Tian mail the letter off on his behalf.

Shortly afterward, Wang Changping did in fact encounter a setback.

As instructed, Imam Tian put postage on the envelope and placed it in a campus mailbox. The next morning he waited next to the mailbox, and watched as the mailman emptied the contents and took them away. Imam Tian had assumed that everything would be fine. Just as a sail rises with the arrival of a wind and flowers bloom with the arrival of spring, he had assumed that that letter would take care of Wang Changping's life and fate. He had assumed that when the addressee received the letter, Wang Changping would be released and permitted to return to the religion building and to his former position between deities and disciples. Second by second, minute by minute, Tian Dongqing waited—waiting for the moment when Wang Changping would suddenly appear in the entranceway to the religion building or in one of the classrooms. But after he had waited minutes and days, the letter was eventually returned to him with a note attached, on which was printed a single sentence: *Postal rates have increased. Please add more postage.*

Three days earlier, when Tian Dongqing told everyone this, he laughed as he squatted down while covering his face in his hands, even as everyone could see tears seeping out from between his fingers. Everyone stood in shock, waiting for him to stop laughing. When he finally stood up and wiped the tears from his face, a disciple asked him, "What was the letter's destination?"

Imam Tian looked at that disciple, and replied, "Somewhere far away, to the west."

Another disciple asked, "Who was the intended recipient?"

Imam Tian looked at the disciple and replied, "Jesus and the Virgin Mary."

Then he stopped laughing and fell silent.

Everyone looked at Tian Dongqing and the twilight sky—as though Pastor Wang were in the western sky gazing down at everyone. Postal rates had increased, and the urgent letter sent to Jesus and the Virgin Mary had been returned: a ludicrous situation. Now, remembering this incident, Yahui stared at the cloud overhead and said to herself, *Shakyamuni, if you don't emerge from behind that cloud, then regardless of whether it is Guanyin, Manjusri, Samantabhadra, or Ksitigarbha, as long as one of you reveals yourself, I'll accept my fate and not purchase the apartment, even if that means that I'll have to return to desolate Qinghai. However, if you don't reveal yourselves, then no one can stop me from leaving Jingshui Convent, and I'll buy this apartment in Beijing even if it kills me.*

Still staring up at the cloud, she continued, *I'll count to three, and then see if you emerge from behind that cloud. If you show yourselves, I won't buy the apartment and will instead return to Jingshui Convent, but if you don't, I'll buy the apartment and stay here in Beijing.*

Like a child, or like someone who wants to steal something but also wants to blame someone else for telling them to do it, Yahui gazed up at the cloud and quietly counted out loud, "One, two, three . . ." Then she looked again at the cloud, and saw that it was still a cloud, and that the sky was still the sky. She laughed coldly, looked away, and bowed her head. She abruptly walked away from the railing at the base of the transfer building and headed toward Zhongguancun Avenue.

"If you don't reveal yourselves, don't blame me for what I might do. Don't blame me for who I go see, for violating my religion, or for rebelling!"

With this thought, she angrily headed west. She strode so fast that before her front foot had even landed, her rear foot had already left the ground, as though someone were pushing her from behind. Even other passersby looked at her strangely.

She wanted to have the agent take her to see that man whom the agent had said could lend her some money. She thought, *Since the bodhisattvas were not willing to come out from behind the cloud, and since for the past eighteen years no deity has ever had a face-to-face exchange with me or said a single word to me, I have no choice but to do something heretical, just like Mingzheng last semester.*

She really did want to go see that man and agree to the proposal that the agent had repeatedly mentioned.

The people heading in the other direction passed her like a breeze, but no one also heading west was able to pass her. She was walking extremely fast—crazily fast. She didn't even know why she was walking so quickly. She felt as though there were a force in her chest and abdomen that was spinning like a hurricane, pressing against her breast and belly, and moving downward through her body. An indescribable sense of energy and comfort was surging down from her upper body to her calves, lifting her feet into the air and pushing her body forward. The faster she walked, the more she felt as though the vortex in her breasts and abdomen were spinning wildly. This, in turn, made her legs feel strangely relaxed, as though she were about to have an orgasm.

She began walking even faster. When she turned and passed a red light, she quickly hailed a taxi. But after getting into the taxi, she felt as if it weren't she who had hailed the taxi, and instead the taxi had suddenly stopped in front of her on its own accord—as if a roommate had sent it to pick her up. After ten minutes or so, the taxi delivered her from the North Fourth Ring Road to the entrance to National Politics University. Although she had definitely given the driver more than ten yuan, she felt as though he had driven away without taking the money. By the time it occurred to her to ask the driver whether he had taken her money, the taxi had already disappeared into the flow of traffic.

Yahui suddenly experienced a wave of happiness, as though the world were about to end and the final thing that she needed to do had suddenly become as clear as a wooden stake protruding from the water. When she descended from the skywalk, she crossed the street and proceeded directly to a nearby open area in front of the Happy Nest real estate office. Yahui needed to find the agent, who was in the doorway flirting with another young man looking for an apartment. The young man reached out and pinched the agent's butt, as she smiled and kicked him in the shins. At this point, Yahui approached and they both suddenly fell quiet.

"Have you completed the transfer?" the agent asked, blushing slightly.

When Yahui told her how she had learned at the transfer center that property taxes had increased, the agent acted as though she already knew, and might have even had something to do with it. The agent stared at Yahui, then took a napkin from her pocket and handed it to her so she could wipe her brow. The agent looked at something in the street, glanced to the side, and saw that the young man who had been flirting with her was walking away from the real estate agency, leaving her standing alone with Yahui under a flowering magnolia tree. She quietly asked Yahui, "What are you going to do? Perhaps you could sell the apartment to someone else?"

Yahui stared at the agent.

The agent said, "You could sell it for more than two million, and that way I could also earn an additional commission."

Yahui still didn't respond as she shifted her gaze from the agent's face to her chest.

"To tell the truth . . ." The agent stared at Yahui's face. "It would be inauspicious for you to live here. Not only was this previously the site of a prison and execution grounds, for a period it was even a dedicated prison and labor camp that the government had set up for you disciples."

Yahui remained silent with a disaffected smile.

Seeing something in that smile, the agent bowed her head and said gently, "Or you could borrow some more. I know that all of your religion's ghosts and deities have plenty of money."

Yahui shifted her gaze from the agent's chest to her lips, which glistened when she spoke, and replied, "No need." In a voice that was neither loud nor soft, she added, "I want to go see the person you mentioned."

The agent again stared at Yahui with a stunned expression.

"Will you regret it? If you do, don't blame me."

Yahui bit her lower lip and looked away. Then, in a quiet yet firm voice, she said, "I won't regret it. If the bodhisattvas and the deities won't protect me, then I have no choice but to look out for myself."

The agent reflected for a moment. "OK, then. If you've made up your mind, I'll make the necessary arrangements." She paused and said slowly, "If you had spoken sooner, not only could this have covered the seventy thousand yuan in property taxes, it might even have covered the full two-million-yuan cost of the apartment."

Yahui blushed. She reflexively lifted her clasped hands to her chest, and as they were passing in front of her chest they paused for half a second, then continued upward—such that she ended up with her thumb pressed against her chest and her other fingers extended outward. Holding this mudra, she said solemnly, "Please make the appointment. I want to see him now."

"But it's the middle of the day . . ." The agent hesitated. She looked up at the sky, then glanced at Yahui's body and face.

"Don't you want to go home first to change and bathe?"

Yahui shook her head firmly, as she stood there like an unmovable tree. At this point, the young man from before reemerged and stood in the doorway, shouting for the agent to do something. The agent took Yahui's hand and led her to the lobby—as though if they didn't leave, someone might see them, and Yahui might suddenly change her mind.

12 A New Nameless

The man Yahui was going to see was Nameless.

They were going to meet in the Shangri-La Hotel on the north-west corner of the Third Ring Road. The hotel consisted of two tall buildings that resembled a celestial ladder, next to which there were numerous twisted overpasses like a bowl of overcooked noodles. It was just after lunchtime, as Yahui was preparing two packets of instant noodles at the real estate agency, that the real estate agent called Nameless. As Yahui poured boiling water into the bowl of instant noodles, the agent smiled and winked at her, then took her cell phone and went outside. Just when Yahui decided her noodles were ready and was about to start eating, the agent returned. She closed the door, looked outside, and whispered, "It's been arranged— he's at a meeting at the Shangri-La."

Yahui didn't know where the Shangri-La was, or whether this was the name of a place, a village, or a hotel. She stared for a moment at the agent's blushing face and knew that within an hour she would have the extra seventy thousand yuan she needed to pay the property taxes. Then, either later that day or the next, she would be able to transfer the property deed to her name. As for the fact that, from that point on, she would no longer be a jade nun and instead would become a mature "lady," she tried to avoid thinking about this, as though she had just seen something that she was pretending she hadn't.

"Is it true that if I just keep him company for a while, he'll pay me seventy thousand yuan?"

"That depends on whether the two of you are fated to be together."

As they broached the topic of fate, Yahui and the agent agreed that it was something they wouldn't know until it happened. Yahui didn't ask anything else, and instead merely wondered who the man might be. How old was he? Was he attractive? Would he get along with her, as Mingzheng did, or would he simply stare at her face and her breasts, stripping her naked with his gaze? At this thought, Yahui looked down at her open-necked shirt and the light-blue knitted skirt she often wore at that time of year. She tightened her belt and glanced down again at her shoes and clothing. She knew her clothing was rather plain and the color of her shoes made her appear older than she was. However, given that she was a jade nun who had recently turned eighteen, she decided it was probably a good thing that she was wearing this old-looking clothing, since it would reveal her status as a jade nun more effectively. This was particularly true of her shoes, which were the low-heeled, square-toed shoes that women in Xining like to wear. Even though the shoes were rustic, they made her feel as though her entire body were simple and elegant.

Yahui bowed her head and began to eat the noodles she had just prepared. After she finished half the bowl, a taxi pulled into the entranceway and began honking, whereupon the agent came and took her hand, gave her a napkin, and led her out of the real estate agency. Yahui and the agent got into the taxi, and fifteen minutes later they arrived at the Shangri-La Hotel, located under the Northwest Third Ring Road's Zizhu Bridge. They got out of the taxi, paid their fare, and entered the building. The lobby was spacious with high ceilings, which reminded her of gazing up at the sky while at Qinghai Lake. The elevator was as quiet as the first time Yahui attended a scripture class with her *shifu*. The walls were covered in yellow wallpaper, and each time the elevator stopped at a different floor, foreigners wearing suits entered or left. These people smiled when they saw waitresses wearing dark-red cashmere uniforms. Yahui knew that this was one of those five-star—or even five-star-plus—hotels that people often talked about. Now she knew what the Beijing Hotel Mingzheng was always telling her about was like.

This was particularly true when she reached the twenty-second floor. The moment she emerged from the elevator and stepped onto the soft carpet, she was reminded of the sense of surprise and panic that Mingzheng described having felt when, over winter break, he had gone to the Beijing Hotel to search for his father. Not only were her palms covered in sweat, but her heart was beating so quickly that it was as though it were about to escape through a crack in her chest. The agent accompanied her the entire way, as though she were Yahui's sister. She took Yahui by the hand, and as they walked forward, she kept telling Yahui how the Shangri-La wasn't far from National Politics University—less than ten *li* as the crow flies. She told Yahui that as long as she had a key to the Shangri-La, the room would be like her own home—it would become her private property, and no one else would be allowed to enter. The agent observed that Yahui had not had much for lunch, and suggested that in the room she could eat or drink whatever she wanted. She noted that the man was somewhat older than Yahui—adding that if he weren't, then why would he be willing to pay seventy thousand yuan to simply sit and chat with her? In fact, if he were younger, he probably wouldn't be willing to pay seven thousand yuan, or even seven hundred.

Yahui and the agent found wall plaques indicating the floor's various room-number ranges. When they reached the plaque for the range 2201–2210, the agent pointed and said, "Room 2210 is at the end of the hall." She repeated this, hugged Yahui, and added, "You really should take a bath. You stink, even if you can't smell it." Then she indicated for Yahui to proceed alone.

Yahui, however, merely stood there motionless. She was silent for a moment, then asked, "Is he really a Buddhist?"

"Go ahead," the agent said. "When you see him, you'll know."

Yahui continued standing there, gazing at the agent.

The agent waved to her and began to head back. After taking several steps, the agent turned and shouted, "Later, after you have a benefactor, don't forget the sister who helped you cross this bridge." Her voice was like the wind, and she turned around and disappeared into the elevator. Yahui was left all alone. Next to each door in the hallway, there was a pink lamp, and the numbers on the doors gleamed in the lamplight. The glass of the windows opposite the doors didn't have a trace of dust. When it occurred to Yahui that this was the hotel's twenty-second floor and the apartment she wanted to purchase was also on the twenty-second floor, she began to feel less alarmed, as though she had returned home. She looked out the window, gazing toward northern Beijing. All the buildings in her line of sight appeared messy and disorganized, as though a powerful wind had just swept through. However, the sky above this disorder was bright blue, and the clouds were a moist white. The spring sunlight shone brightly in the sky, giving the clouds a golden tint. Yahui once again saw the same sports field–sized cloud she had seen when emerging from the lobby of the real estate transfer building. That's right, it really was the same cloud she had watched while waiting for the Buddha to reveal himself. Seeing this cloud through the window now, she could clearly discern the softness at its center, and every tangled thread along the edge. Some strands ran clockwise, while others ran counterclockwise.

Through a crack in the window, Yahui seemed to smell a warm cloud scent. She stood at the window and gazed at the cloud and thought, *Bodhisattva, if you emerge from behind that cloud right now, I'll immediately go back without saying a word. However, if you don't reveal yourself, I'll have no choice but to proceed to that farthest room.* Then she said out loud, "I'll count to three—let's see if you show yourself or not." In a soft voice, she counted, "One, two, three." She stared at the cloud, then counted again, "One, two, three." After counting to three out loud three times in a row, she saw that the cloud had not changed in the least, and there wasn't even a trace of the Bodhisattva. She therefore had no choice but to head toward the room at the end of the hall. As she was looking away from the cloud outside the window, she continued muttering, "*Shifu!*" She didn't know whether she wanted to tell her *shifu* that there were really no spirits in the world or she wanted to say that if spirits don't exist then her *shifu* didn't exist, the same way that she had no choice but to continue forward to the room up ahead.

She was no longer flustered nor surprised, yet in addition to feeling that her legs and body were weak, she also had an urge to hide. She went up to room 2210, and after a brief hesitation, she knocked on the door.

The door quietly opened.

When the door opened, Yahui should have initially looked up to confirm the other person's age, appearance, and attire. However, when she heard the door opening, she first looked down at her low-collared shirt and the fist-sized patch of skin and cleavage that only she could see. She instinctively raised her hands and positioned them over the opening of her shirt, while at the same time chanting *Amitābha*. She didn't know whether it was to chant the sutra that she had positioned her hands in front of her chest, or whether she was trying to cover her exposed chest. Afterward, she quietly stood with her head bowed. She saw that inside the room there was a gray carpet with a red grid pattern. Between two of the gridlines, there was a pair of large feet wearing hotel slippers. The light shining in through the window happened to land on that pair of feet.

She was quiet for a while. It seemed as though the other person was staring at her in surprise. At first, the other person seemed about to push her out, but then, as if out of politeness, he said, "Come in!"

The voice was somewhat hoarse, and sounded a bit impatient. Yahui had no choice but to look up. She took a step inside and slowly raised her head, whereupon she saw a hand in a thick sleeve reaching out to shut the door. The hand quickly turned a small lock below the knob. When the person lowered his hand, she was finally able to see him clearly, just as he was able to see her clearly. She saw that he was, in fact, an older man. He was thin, tall, and ruddy, and stood there like a tree. In fact, he was standing even straighter than a tree. He had just bathed and was wearing one of the hotel's red silk robes, which on his body resembled a flag on a bamboo pole. Between his slippers and the lower hem of his robe, she could see his ankles and calves, which were light red and as thin as sticks—resembling pieces of smoked bacon she had once seen somewhere. From the lower hem of his robe, her gaze slowly moved upward until she saw his thin neck. Loose skin was hanging over two protruding tendons, and there was a layer of deep wrinkles over his Adam's apple. Like his body, his face was long and thin, and the bladelike ridge of his nose gave his face a quality of perseverance and uprightness. Over his gray eyelashes he had a pair of two-inch-long "longevity brows," which extended to the outer edges of his eyes. He had large eyes, a broad forehead, and hair that was gray but lush, as though he had never lost a single strand of hair his entire life.

"Have a seat," he said dispassionately, as he went to pull the window curtains. The room immediately became dark and warm. This was a sitting room outside of the bedroom, with a red sofa and a mahogany tea table. Against the wall there was a television on a cabinet, and between the two windows there was a large painting of a white birch forest. There was also an odd fragrance and the smell of bathwater. Yahui stood in the doorway like a child, while the other man gazed at her like a grandfather. After looking at her for a moment, he prepared her a cup of tea, then from a cabinet he took a pair of slippers like the ones he was wearing and placed them in front of her. He sat on the sofa and gestured for her to change her footwear and take a seat in a chair across from him. The large tea table stood between them, like a bed connecting them.

Although the air-conditioning kept the room at a comfortable temperature, Yahui nevertheless felt rather warm. After putting on the slippers, she placed her own square-toed cloth shoes by the door. Then she peeked into the bedroom and saw the man's clothes on the bed and his belt hanging over the edge. As soon as Yahui saw his pants and belt on the bed, everything changed. The blurry calmness she had felt before entering the room was shattered. Her heart began to pound, and she immediately began to worry that the man would rush at her and press his body down onto hers. Her breasts began to shudder, and it was unclear whether they wanted to hide or run away.

After waiting for her to sit down, the man pushed the cup of tea toward her.

"The agent told me to come and chat with you," she said in a trembling voice while staring at the teacup, "just to talk and have some tea."

He looked up with raised eyebrows.

"Did you really just turn eighteen?"

Startled, she nodded.

"From the way you are dressed, you look like you're in your twenties." As he said this, he turned to look at the shoes she had left in the entranceway.

This remark helped reassure Yahui, as she blushed and looked down.

"But your short hair makes you look like a child," he continued.

Upon hearing this, Yahui looked up. Although she didn't say anything, her panic began to abate and her courage began to grow. She examined the man's expression and tone of voice as he continued to stare at her, as though trying to undress her with his eyes.

"Are you really a jade nun who grew up in a convent?"

She didn't detect any lascivious intent in the man's expression, and instead she merely saw him watching her with a combination of curiosity and skepticism, as though he didn't believe what the agent had told him. She gave him a slight nod, whereupon the room fell silent. He appeared as though he still wanted to ask her something, but felt as though he shouldn't. He hesitated, then grabbed the cup on the tea table and took a couple of sips. He put the cup down, turned to one side, and looked back at her. Then he smiled and said, "I'm rather old and not particularly respectable. Have you really not been friends with monks or other men?"

With a shock, Yahui felt humiliated. She stared at his face, which appeared completely calm. She wanted to put on her shoes and leave, but she remembered that she had come to talk to him so that he would give her seventy thousand yuan. If she didn't talk to him, why would he give her the money? So she continued sitting there without moving. With a steely gaze and a red face, she clasped her hands in front of her chest, as though trying to use a Buddhist mudra to conceal her humiliation. Meanwhile, Nameless wasn't paying attention to her Buddhist mudra, nor was he thinking about the significance of her steely gaze. Instead, he simply continued staring at her, as though trying to determine whether she was in fact a jade nun. One second passed, then another, and another—until finally Yahui lowered her hands and asked, "What if I am a jade nun? And what if I'm not?"

"If you are, I promise to help you resolve this seventy-thousand-yuan tax obligation."

Then Nameless paused, and once again gazed at Yahui's face. Meanwhile, Yahui was waiting for him to say what would happen if she wasn't a jade nun. After a long time, he still hadn't said anything, so she looked up and her gaze met his. It was only then that she saw he was smiling. She saw that the old man's kindness had disappeared, and instead he now had the expression of a young thief forcing a homeowner to reveal how many valuables his family had and where they were hidden. With this, time froze, and Yahui looked away and began to move toward the sofa. Her tone became soft as she asked, "And if I told you that I slept with a Buddhist monk when

I was fourteen and a Daoist master when I was sixteen, would you believe it?"

"Yes!" Nameless suddenly stood up, as his voice became rough and sonorous. "Do you think that I don't know what goes on in your Buddhist and Daoist temples? Did you think I really believed what your agent told me?" He laughed coldly, then impatiently turned and looked at something before turning back around. It was as if he had been tricked by the question of whether she was a jade nun, and he now had a disdainful and resentful expression. He stood for a while with his mouth closed, then quickly went around the tea table and, like Shuiyue *shifu*, grasped her chin and gazed down at her. He ruffled her inch-long hair to see if her scalp had any ringworm scars, then took a step backward and crossed his arms.

"It isn't particularly important to me whether or not you are a jade nun. What is important is that you tell people the truth. You should burn incense for the Bodhisattva, while acting like a young woman in society as soon as you leave the Bodhisattva."

He gazed at Yahui, and after his resentment subsided, he asked her, "So, you'd like to resolve the seventy-thousand-yuan tax debt that you need to pay in order to purchase your apartment?"

"Yes." Yahui looked up and gazed at his face.

"Where is the apartment?"

"It's in the Yujian residential quarter across from the school."

"The Yujian residential quarter!" Startled, Nameless suddenly raised his voice. "Is that the Yujian residential quarter on Yujian Street? Heavens . . . Not only was there a prison and execution grounds there, but for a while there was also a labor camp specifically for you disciples. Once, during the Republican period—when the government united in its attempt to abolish religion—the military police killed more than a hundred pastors and monks. They also tied countless pastors, monks, and nuns to posts and invited the deities to come and rescue them—and if the deities came, they too would be detained, forced to labor, and executed. In the end, needless to say, the principal deities did not come. Jesus, Mary, Guanyin, Shakyamuni—none of them came. But then all Beijingers knew Yujian Street had been a prison for both deities and disciples, where deities were lured so that they could then be detained. How could you consider buying an apartment there? Don't you find that site cursed? Aren't you concerned that if you bring deities with you, they too will be detained and executed?" As Nameless asked this, he stared at Yahui's face, which was pale and covered in sweat. Then he laughed and added, "Don't be afraid. I'm just mentioning it to you. In any event, you aren't a real disciple, and therefore you wouldn't be able to lure deities there."

Nameless moved to stroke Yahui's head, like a father or grandfather caressing a child. Then, as if to make amends for having frightened her, he went to the inner room, where he picked up the phone. She didn't know who he was calling, but he spoke loudly with the other party, asking them to give his greetings to someone in their same residential quarter. Then he explained that a nun from Qinghai named Yahui wanted to buy an apartment, and asked them to back-date the transfer document by a few days to before the tax increase, so that she could pay the property tax at the old rate. He hung up the phone, then came out and stood in front of Yahui, and said with a smile, "You can leave now. As long as you aren't afraid that the deities will be detained, tomorrow you can return to the transfer center."

Yahui stood there bewildered.

She couldn't believe that deities would follow her wherever she chose to live, nor that the issue of the seventy-thousand-yuan tax could be resolved with a simple phone call, the same way that a deity's word could change the world. The same way that if the deity says let there be light, there will be light, and if the deity says let there be water, there will be water. Day and night were separated. The sea and the earth were separated. Her hands were now empty. Not only did she not have the brick-like seventy-thousand-yuan pile of bills that she desperately desired, she didn't even have seven cents.

All she had were a pair of empty fists and the blood blisters from her tug-of-war competition with Ruan Zhisu. She reflexively raised her hands to look at them, then quickly clasped them to her chest while chanting *Namo Amitābha*. She wanted to offer a few words of gratitude and ask whether it was true that she no longer needed to pay the seventy-thousand-yuan tax. Could a single phone call really resolve this problem? However, before these words had even left her mouth, she heard the other voice say, "Don't believe that Yujian Street is a site for detaining deities. You know better than anyone whether or not deities exist."

As Nameless said this, he smiled at Yahui, then walked over and kicked the shoes in the doorway toward her. As she was putting her shoes on, he suddenly asked her, "Ay . . . do you really not know who I am?"

Yahui was about to put on her right shoe, but pulled back her foot and looked up at the man's face, then shook her head in embarrassment.

"Maybe it's better if you don't know. If you did, you would view me as a celestial deity capable of overseeing the other deities."

Upon hearing the words *celestial deity*, Yahui almost dropped the shoe in her hand. She grasped the shoe, straightened her waist, and opened her mouth, then stared at Nameless intently. At this point, the room became as quiet as if it were the middle of the night. It must have been around three in the afternoon, and while at first the light shining in through the curtain was soft yellowish red, after Yahui stared at it for a while, it became blindingly bright. The air conditioner was making a whirring sound as it emitted cold air, as though there were some people watching and commenting as she and Nameless spoke. Yahui no longer doubted that the man's phone call could resolve her seventy-thousand-yuan tax debt, and she even believed that with another phone call he could easily resolve anything. She cautiously raised another matter.

"Pastor Wang from our class was detained and taken away."

The old man replied, "Yes, so I heard."

"Is it true that you secretly believe in Buddhism?" Yahui asked. "The agent said that sometimes you even enter a temple to burn incense."

The old man paused, then laughed.

"I've fought nine battles for this country, and still have shrapnel embedded in my body. Do you think I could believe in Buddhism? I burn incense in order to pray that I may *become* a true omnipotent deity, not because I believe in your deities."

Yahui gazed at his face with clear eyes.

"But didn't you say that you were already an omnipotent deity? If that is true, you could certainly rescue Pastor Wang."

The old man reflected for a moment, then replied, "That isn't something that can be resolved with a phone call."

Yahui also reflected for a moment, and then, in a soft voice she said something very strange: "As far as you are concerned, I am in fact a jade nun."

She didn't know why she said this, nor did she know what the result of this statement would be. She simply felt she should say it, so she did. She kept her head lifted and directed at Nameless, waiting for him to respond. She didn't observe any trace of surprise in his expression. Instead, he merely paused, then smiled and turned away. Then he quickly turned back and said something that Yahui found equally mysterious: "How many days has it been since you last bathed?"

Yahui replied, "This morning I was sweaty after I went for a walk."

Nameless was quiet for a while, then said, "Then let's do this. You can go to the bathroom and wash up, and use some extra bodywash. Meanwhile, I'll see what I can do for Pastor Wang."

They stared at one another for a while, whereupon Yahui did in fact go to the bathroom between the sitting room and the bedroom, and Nameless returned to his seat and prepared himself a cup of tea.

13 Yahui and Nameless

The situation changed so quickly, it was as though the deities themselves had arranged it. It was as if Yahui had come to room 2210 precisely for this result. She didn't feel that her tattered body was particularly remarkable, nor did she grant it much importance, the way nuns from Jueyu *shifu* and Shuiyue *shifu*'s generation had done. She was almost nineteen years old, and it seemed as though from the day she first started having her period, she had been waiting for this day. It seemed she had grown up just for this day, and that she had fallen in love with Mingzheng and saved her body precisely for the sake of this day. Only, this day should not have been with a person like Nameless.

Nevertheless, the day had now arrived, and the person before her was in fact Nameless. He claimed he could get Pastor Wang released from wherever he was being detained. He said he burned incense precisely to become an omnipotent deity capable of overseeing all other deities. Yahui had an inchoate sense of remorse, but at the same time she also felt a taut sense of anticipation.

She entered the bathroom, closed the door, and turned the lock. After confirming that the door was locked and the person outside wouldn't be able to enter if she didn't unlock it, she stood in front of the mirror, placed her hand on her open-collared shirt, and unfastened the first button. At this point, she felt that things had fundamentally changed. It was as though her heartbeat was no longer a heartbeat, and instead was a crazed bull trying to break out of its pen, producing an intense pounding sound in her chest, like a door repeatedly slamming shut. She placed her hand on her chest, and after waiting for the pounding to die down she suddenly felt a tightness in her inner thighs, as though her muscles were contracting spasmodically. Her body began to tremble so violently that she felt she was about to collapse.

It was only by grabbing the sink in front of the mirror that she managed to remain upright. Her face was covered in sweat, but her body felt so cold that it was as if she had typhoid fever. She originally wanted to unfasten her buttons one by one while standing in front of the mirror, so that she could carefully examine her breasts and belly, as well as that most mysterious area between her legs that had never seen the light of day. But after her trembling fingers unfastened the first button to reveal her small, round breasts, she suddenly felt that there wasn't enough time. She was so dizzy that when she looked at the mirror in front of her, it was as though she were looking at a curtain or bedsheet that was unable to produce a reflection. Her body was pulled down by her trembling hands and arms. She attempted to use her legs to stabilize herself, the way that she had dug her toes into the ground during the tug-of-war competition with Ruan Zhisu, but this time when she dug in her toes, her ankles felt so weak that it was as though they possessed no bones or muscles. Her lips were very dry, and she desperately wanted to drink some water. The bathroom's toilet, sink, and glass shower door, as well as the piles of bath towels and hand cloths next to the bathtub, the tricolored bath bottles that she could see through the glass shower door, and the various boxes, glasses, bags, and small towels arrayed below the mirror in front of her—all these objects began to spin around. Her gaze became like pieces of mud stuck to a car's wheels, and through that mud-like gaze she heard her body fall to the ground and her head strike the tile floor. Then, everything went blank.

Yahui felt as though a bucket of cold water—square, round, wide, narrow, solid, liquid, opaque, and translucent—had been dumped on her head, and she became simultaneously blind and all-seeing. It was as though she could remember everything, but also nothing at all. Eventually the questions "Are you awake? Would you like some water?" reached her ears. Only then did she murkily realize that she wasn't lying on the bathroom's tile floor or on the hotel room's queen-sized bed, but instead she was lying on a rug positioned in front of the bed and leading to the balcony. A large bedsheet had been placed on the rug, and on it there were a couple of large bath towels. Her head was oriented toward the balcony, and the balcony's wooden door was open. The cool breeze blowing in streamed down from her head to her body, as though a silk cloth were being pulled down over her. It was only at this point that she realized that she didn't have an ounce of strength in her body. She was like an infant, lying naked in front of the balcony. Meanwhile, Nameless was still wearing the same silk robe as before, but whereas previously his belt had been knotted on the left-hand side, now it was knotted on the right. He was holding a glass of water and sitting in a chair, gazing at her like a father who has a child late in life watches delightedly as the naked newborn is brought out of the delivery room. When he saw her awake, he blinked as he looked at the light on the balcony. Then, he took a sip of tea and put his cup down on the television cabinet.

"You truly are a jade nun." He was beaming like a child who has just picked up a new toy. "I promise to have your Pastor Wang released from wherever he is being held."

Yahui suddenly realized something and instinctively recoiled and sat up, while placing the towel between her legs and holding her arms in front of her chest.

"You should practice good hygiene," he said, picking up her clothing from the bed and smiling as he stood next to her. "It was only after I forced open the door and carried you out that I noticed that your face, body, and breasts look exactly like those of the Bodhisattva in a painting—when the Bodhisattva was young, she must have looked just like you. I hadn't expected that you would actually be a jade nun, but upon seeing you naked, I now see that you are really just like a young Guanyin. When the Virgin Mary was seventeen or eighteen, she probably also looked like this.

"To tell the truth, in three days or so, or in a week at most, I will become an omnipotent deity and the chair of the National Religion Association. Catholicism, Protestantism, and Islam, as well as Daoism and Buddhism, will all fall under my direct oversight. Then, to celebrate my appointment to the National Religion Association and the announcement that I have been appointed to serve as the new association chair, I want you to come back here and bring your robe and take a bath. Then I want you to place your robe on the bed and lie down on it, like a young Guanyin or a young Mary. We will celebrate my promotion to a ministry-level position, whereby I will become a deity of all your deities!"

As he said this, he smiled at her, while she remained curled up, her arms hugging her chest. She listened to him as though using her ears to catch apples and pears falling through the air. She remained motionless, as though those words were directed to someone else and she were simply overhearing them. It was not until he once again mentioned Pastor Wang that those words finally seemed to enter her ears and approach her heart.

"You are a Buddhist, yet you treat that Protestant pastor very well." He said this in a strange tone of voice, as he gently placed her clothing in front of her. "Jesus would definitely thank you. You should get dressed. When you passed out, you made me miss a meeting." As he said this, he looked at her, then explained, "When it is announced that I am the new chair of the National Religion Association, your agent will notify you, and later, if you encounter any problems, you can contact me directly. However, in the meantime, you should preoccupy yourself less with other disciples' problems."

As he said this, he walked up to a dresser located between the living room and the bedroom, untied his belt, then stood there looking at her as he changed into his shirt and pants. As he removed his robe, she saw that the liver spots on his shoulders and back resembled the spots on his window curtains. After he was dressed and prepared to leave, he told her that if he went ahead and left first, he would still be able to make the end of his meeting. He told her to wait a while before leaving, and as he was walking out, he turned and asked, "Other than the matter involving Pastor Wang, do you have any other issues that need to be addressed?" Seeing her holding her clothes and sitting there without responding, he reassured her, saying, "In a few days, Pastor Wang's problem will be resolved." Then he opened the door and left.

Yahui was left alone in the room, huddled naked under the bedsheet.

14 Director Gong and Yahui

Yahui returned to the school before dusk.

Before nine that morning, she had left through the school's stone archway, and now, as the sun was approaching the western horizon, she returned through that same archway. It had been less than a full day, yet it seemed as though during that time there was nothing that she had not experienced, while the day also in some ways resembled a perfectly ordinary one. In a way, she had simply gone out to run some errands, and although some of those errands did not proceed as smoothly as planned, in the end she still managed to get everything done. She felt fatigued, but also felt relaxed after having finished her tasks. Yet despite feeling relaxed, when she walked it was as though she could barely lift her legs.

When Yahui emerged from the Shangri-La Hotel, she felt that everyone was staring at her, and specifically at the area between her legs. She hurried forward and periodically glanced down at the waistline of her skirt, as though afraid there might be a hole or a rip there. Eventually she was able to catch a taxi, and while sitting in the back seat she was able to confirm that her skirt was still intact, without any holes or rips, and only then did she gradually begin to relax. When she arrived at the school, she got out of the taxi and, to make sure no one saw her, lingered for a while at the columns by the main entrance, pretending she was waiting for someone to see if anyone was secretly observing her. She waited under one of the columns for several minutes, during which at least several dozen people entered or left the school, but no one noticed her and no one asked her anything. The entire world was calm and peaceful, as though nothing at all had happened—and it goes without saying that no one knew where she had gone or what she had done. Pastor Wang would return in a few days, and the property tax issue had been resolved. Thinking of this, Yahui left the column in the entranceway and proceeded onto the campus. The setting sun was shining down on the campus's road and trees. It was as though she had recovered consciousness and seen the light falling on the twenty-second-floor balcony, without a trace of dust, and the sky as blue as the waters of Qinghai Lake in autumn. Meanwhile, the students were emerging from their classrooms and walking down the road like recently released prisoners, each of them taking such light steps that it seemed as though they were about to float away.

Yahui's pace also lightened. She wanted to immediately go find someone and explain that although she was only an eighteen-year-old Buddhist nun, she had nevertheless managed to save the Protestant pastor, Pastor Wang. She wanted to tell them to wait and see that within three days, Pastor Wang would be released. But at the same time, she also felt deeply conflicted. Even though she had rescued Pastor Wang, she knew she couldn't tell anyone what she had done. She knew she was no longer a jade nun, yet she had not yet experienced the pleasure of ceasing to be a jade nun, nor had she experienced any regret or annoyance upon ceasing to be a jade nun. She only felt a sort of itchy ache in the area between her legs. With a measured pace, she headed into the school while wondering why she had been so nervous that she had passed out in the bathroom. She reflected that it was fortunate that Nameless had carried her out, and it was fortunate that he had placed her in an open area in front of the balcony, because otherwise, afterward . . . Yahui didn't dare think about what might have happened afterward. Naturally, she didn't love Nameless, but then again neither did she hate him. She just felt that it would be better if he were younger—if instead of being in his seventies or eighties, he were in his forties or fifties, or even in his sixties. That way, she could clearly experience what it felt like when he caressed her, wiped her body with a towel, and entered her.

At this point, the setting sun was no longer as hot as before, but as Yahui walked through campus her face became flushed and covered in sweat. As she wiped her face, a classmate from the philosophy department walked over and greeted her. Ordinarily she would have clasped her hands to her chest to return the greeting, but for some reason she forgot she was a Buddhist and instead returned his greeting with a simple wave. Another person she knew, a teacher, walked past and nodded to her, and she nodded back.

She reached the entrance to the religion building, and Director Gong suddenly appeared. He had gone somewhere, but when he returned and saw Yahui, he stood there excitedly waiting for her. In a loud voice, he asked her, "Have you completed the property transfer?"

"It will be completed tomorrow."

Yahui walked over and stood in front of him. She initially wanted to tell him how the property taxes had increased, and how in a few days Pastor Wang would be released and permitted to return, but just as she was about to speak, she ended up swallowing her words. Instead, she simply stood there looking at Director Gong while he looked back at her. Seeing that she had a relaxed yet serious expression, he suddenly lifted his hand and patted her face. Then, smiling, he asked her to follow him into his office.

Another group of students walked past them. As for the disciples, because their teacher had extended their class, they were all still in the classroom listening to a lecture on the changes that religious belief has undergone in the new society, and the new society's functionality. There was no one in the first-floor hallway and lobby other than the cleaning staff. Yahui followed Director Gong into his office, and he told her to shut the door, which she did. Then he asked her to sit down and, clasping her hands, she did so. The two of them were the only people in the room, and it was as though they were the only people in the entire world. At the same time, it also seemed as though if Director Gong were to simply hold out his hand, Yahui would immediately go over to his side. However, Director Gong, sitting at his desk in front of the window, merely watched her for a while, then laughed bitterly and sighed.

"I have some good news and some bad news."

She looked at his face and wanted to go over to him. In the end, however, she continued sitting there without moving.

"Pastor Wang committed suicide during his interrogation," Director Gong announced. "When Protestants take their own lives, they cannot enter Heaven. Yet he nevertheless made this choice." Director Gong paused, then looked again at Yahui. "You know, eighteen years ago, the year you were born, Pastor Wang was the province's youngest department director, but because of corruption allegations, he disappeared, ultimately becoming a residential disciple in one of Guangxi's most remote churches. Surprisingly, however, eighteen years later he became a senior pastor. Thinking that no one would recognize him, he agreed to come to study at the religious training center. What happened simply confirms the saying that the net of heaven ultimately catches everything." Director Gong paused to take a sip of tea. Then, while slowly turning the lid of his teacup, he continued: "So, the bad news is that he unexpectedly killed himself. The good news, however, is that before he died, he left a will specifying that he was grateful to those who recognized him, those who reported him, and those who detained him. In this way, he confessed before God and became magnanimous. Even without reading the Bible every day, or going to church and seeing other believers, he was still able to confess wholeheartedly, like a thief who encounters the owner of a house he has robbed."

The office was full of late-spring sunlight and quiet. Outside the window there was the sound of students' footsteps and voices. Through the window, a couple of students could be seen hugging and kissing, and while they saw Yahui and Director Gong in the office, the students didn't appear to give them a second thought. Director Gong gazed out the window, though it was unclear whether he even saw the students. Then he turned to Yahui. Her face was not pale from shock, but rather was flushed from confusion. The blood that accumulated under her skin did not pour out, but her face did become covered in a layer of sweat, just as it had a few hours earlier, when she was about to pass out in the bathroom of room 2210. Like before, her legs became weak and her head began to pound, as though all the cars and pedestrians on the nearby street were about to burst out of her skull.

Yahui felt she was about to collapse, but she knew how to avoid doing so. She bit her lip and dug her toes into the ground, then fixed her gaze on Director Gong's face and struggled to catch every word that emerged from his mouth.

"Even more surprisingly, can you guess how much money Pastor Wang managed to save up?" Director Gong looked at Yahui as he asked this, as though he were actually going to wait for her to guess. In the end, however, he promptly answered his own question, saying, "Well, we don't know how much he received in bribes, but aside from those corrupt funds, he had legally saved up eight million yuan. Can you guess to whom Pastor Wang left these eight million yuan?" As Director Gong asked this, his face had a trace of a smile, as though he were again waiting for Yahui to guess. Instead, he continued, saying, "He directed that this money be given to our center, to establish a fund to promote religious training." He took another sip of tea, put the lid back on the cup, sat up straight, and said, "His will also contained an unexpected provision—apart from the greeting that was addressed to all the center's students, he also specified that his own private funds be used to repay your mortgage.

Is your mortgage for an even two million yuan, or two million ten thousand? Either way, everything has now been resolved. Protestantism is different from other religions, and I think that only someone who reads the Bible every day would be able to compose this sort of will. Of course, this is also directly related to our center's practice of intermixing disciples from different religions. If we hadn't repeatedly emphasized the principle that disciples from all five major religions belong to the same family, then disciples who follow the Bible or the Quran definitely wouldn't think of Buddhists and Daoists when writing their wills."

With this, it seemed he had said everything he wanted to say.

Yahui's eyes opened wide with astonishment and sweat poured down her face. As she recalled what had happened that afternoon at the Shangri-La Hotel, and how that person had said that he would arrange to have Pastor Wang released within two or three days, her complexion shifted from bloody red to lotus white. Without realizing it, she clasped her hands together. She didn't bring them up to her chest, however, but rather brought them all the way up to her chin, and furthermore put her index fingers in her mouth and bit down. She stared at Director Gong just as she had previously stared at that person who had agreed to rescue Pastor Wang. How could Pastor Wang have died? How could he have killed himself? He was a pastor, so how could he not have known how sinful suicide is? And how, in committing suicide, could he have bequeathed her such an enormous sum of money to repay her mortgage? How could he have left her such a vast sum? Was it really because they had been classmates and fellow disciples? Was it because, after studying at the center, they had come to believe that every member of every sect and every religion, and indeed every human, ultimately belonged to the same family? Did Pastor Wang not have any relatives to whom he could leave his assets? Were his relatives so rich that they didn't need his money? Or did he do this simply because, before he was taken away, he had told her he wanted to lend her a hundred thousand yuan?

Illuminated by a ray of sunlight in the entranceway, Yahui didn't know what to say or do. She stared blankly for a long time, before eventually moving her clasped hands from her face and asking, "Pastor Wang . . . did he really kill himself?"

"I myself only heard two hours ago." As Director Gong replied, he pulled out his cell phone to check the time. His face had an expression of regret, but also an unexpected smile. He walked over and stood in front of Yahui, then patted her head and said, "You truly have good fortune. It is as though there is a deity up in heaven looking over you. You've managed to acquire a Beijing apartment for free."

Director Gong went to open the door, whereupon he and Yahui heard the hallway full of the sound of footsteps of disciples who had just gotten out of class.

15 Disciples and Yahui

For several days in a row, Yahui was in a state of bewilderment—she lived as though in a dream. For three days she didn't attend class, nor did she buy anything for her new apartment, much less make any papercuts or read any sutras. It seemed that during those three days, the place she went most frequently was the bathroom. She constantly felt that her body was unclean, and when she wasn't showering with scented soap and bodywash, she was using bottled water to rinse the area between her legs. At one point she even used an abrasive detergent, which she stirred until the solution was full of bubbles, and then sat in a tub to soak her lower body.

After learning that Pastor Wang had committed suicide, she continually felt that her body smelled of semen. It was as though Nameless were constantly inspecting her body, walking over it with his hands as though they were a pair of feet. She felt like a bag filled with water, and whether she was placed on the ground in front of the balcony or on her towel and white sheets, her body didn't seem to know how to fall asleep.

The person who was about to become a deity of deities had known that it wouldn't kill her if he left her in a drafty location. He had known that, since this was her first time to connect with a man's body, she had been so anxious that she had lost consciousness. Therefore, as though going to the birthing room to retrieve his child, he had carried her out of the bathroom and placed her in the sun and wind. Then, he had removed his robe, revealing a body that resembled an old tree. He slowly knelt down next to her and unfastened her buttons one by one. Each time he unfastened a button, his hand would pause in midair and his gaze would linger on her exposed flesh. He unfastened the first button, then the second—and upon seeing her soap-bubble-like breasts, his gaze froze. He quickly unfastened all her remaining buttons, then pushed her clothing aside and pulled down her bra. She lay naked on the white and red surface. He was seventy or eighty years old and knew that at this point, it was more important to see her than to enter her. He could derive an hour or two of excitement from seeing her, but if he were to enter her right away, he might not be able to do anything, and it was possible that the excitement might dissipate after a minute or two. Therefore, he half urgently and half leisurely lay down on her body, sucking on her breasts one after the other. He kissed her entire body, from her lips to her chest, breasts, belly, and groin. After reaching the area between her legs, he pulled her legs apart, then pressed his lips down. He licked again and again with the tip of his tongue. Like a man parched with thirst who sees a spring and doesn't care about the quality of the water, he had to first take several gulps—and only then could he sit down and appreciate the clarity of the water, and the Mother Earth and fairy world that had produced the spring in the first place. In this way, he used her body to quench his thirst before proceeding to examine her body from head to toe.

In his lifetime, he had had many encounters with women, but this was the first time he had a chance to carefully inspect the body of an eighteen-year-old jade nun. So, he stood in front of Yahui and took a step backward. As he was examining her pure white body, he suddenly noticed that she resembled a young Guanyin, with a round face, fluttering eyelashes, and a nose that was both straight and rounded. Her lips were so full that they looked like they might start bleeding at any moment. She wasn't as tall as Guanyin, and her shoulders weren't as broad, nor were her breasts as large, but this simply made her look like the Bodhisattva Guanyin when she was still a girl and had not yet become the Bodhisattva. She was a little-girl Guanyin, or a young Mary who had not yet married Joseph the carpenter. Her skin was as white as a cloud, and her face was also cloudlike. The smile on her lips looked as though she were talking to someone, while the tips of her fingers and toes were as beautiful as freshly ripened grapes.

The man stood motionless in front of her, as his blood began to surge through his veins. Suddenly, he became very agitated. That thing, which had not become erect for the longest time, sent him a gift.

He rushed over to her and knelt in front of her, separated her legs, and licked that area with the tip of his tongue. Then he placed his legs around hers and as he gently entered her, he thought, *God, oh God, I must be appointed director of the National Religion Association, and must become a deity of deities, and definitely must have all jade nuns be like her—becoming my food and gifts* . . .

Yahui kept smelling semen on her body, and constantly felt as though there were bugs crawling over her face, torso, and back. She wanted to wash off that stench and soak her crotch in that basin. While washing herself, she sometimes scratched and slapped her crotch. She first used bodywash, then laundry detergent, but when she found that she could still detect the stench of semen emanating from between her legs, she even wanted to pour sulfuric acid over that area. In the end, however, she went to buy a bottle of concentrated kitchen cleanser instead. The first day she washed herself three times, the second day she washed herself four times, and by the third day the area between her legs hurt so much that she felt as though the skin were going to peel off. She imagined she could hear agonized screaming coming from between her legs, and only then did she get out of the basin, pour out the water, put on her clothes, and emerge from her room.

By that point, it was already eight or nine o'clock at night. There wasn't a trace of movement in the entire religion building. The doors to every room were closed, the lights of each floor's activity room were turned off, and the building resembled a giant tomb, as it had since Pastor Wang's death.

Yet no one discussed Pastor Wang's suicide, and it was as though no one even knew that he had died.

However, even though no one acknowledged that they knew about the suicide, it was still true that today, yesterday, and the day before, none of the disciples were smiling and chatting when they attended class. Instead, they were all silent, as though gloomy weather were pressing down on the classroom and slowly permeating the entire building, the entire sky, and the entire world. One might have expected that after Pastor Wang's death something momentous would happen in the classroom, but in the end nothing did.

Even as Yahui was beginning to think that the situation had passed, a new situation quietly developed when she went downstairs. Because the insides of her thighs hurt, Yahui walked with her legs separated, and as she hobbled down the stairs and into the lobby, a voice wafted toward her.

"You appear jaundiced. Are you ill?"

As Yahui turned to the window of the reception office, she heard the voice again: "Go to the classroom and see what your classmates are doing."

Dazed, she headed to the first-floor classroom. When she arrived, she gently pushed the door open and saw several students from other institutes standing in the entranceway, while other disciples were standing on the classroom's stage, staring at the floor. Several tables had been pushed against the walls, leaving an open space the size of half the classroom. In the center of that open space, the yellow ceiling lamp resembled an enormous page from a wordless scripture, and as it shone down on everyone's faces it made them appear pale and bloodless. Under that yellow light, there were three desks, two of which were oriented vertically while the third was oriented horizontally. Wang Changping's blue shirt and pants were laid out on the desks. On the end with the shirt there was a mirrored frame with an enlarged photograph of Wang Changping, while on the other end there was his favorite pair of black leather shoes. This was Wang Changping's cenotaph, and every effort had been made to arrange it so that it would look like he was asleep on the desk.

At this time there wasn't a trace of sound in the classroom. This late-spring night was comfortably warm, which helped the funeral proceed as smoothly as rain that comes when it is prayed for. In front of Wang Changping's portrait, there was a brand-new Bible and a white bowl that was temporarily serving as a stoup. The bowl was half-filled with water, but the water was so clear that the bowl appeared empty. It seemed like it was filled only with air, but also like it contained nothing at all. Standing at the end with Wang Changping's pants were the Protestant disciples, and behind them were the Catholic disciples. Beyond them were the Buddhist, Muslim, and Daoist disciples. Meanwhile, standing even farther from the end with the portrait, there was Director Gong and two young people from the school's security office whom Yahui didn't recognize.

The classroom was as solemn as a church, or a tomb.

The funeral ceremony began. The old bishop picked up the Bible from the table and hugged it to his chest, and after making the sign of the cross, he quietly intoned "Amen," then recited a hymn in a voice so low that no one could hear him clearly. He intoned, "Heaven awaits, and the deceased can rest, while God, the angels, and other spirits are all waiting for Wang Changping at heaven's gate." Finally, he prayed that the soul of the deceased would ascend peacefully to heaven, leaving behind the frustration and suffering of the mortal world. Then he replaced the Bible in front of Wang Changping's funerary portrait. He picked up the bowl, sang several more hymns, then dipped his finger in the holy water and touched it to Wang Changping's portrait and clothing. He dipped his finger in the holy water again, and walked in a circle around Wang Changping's clothing. When he reached the left side, his gaze momentarily met the gaze of the figure in the frame, whereupon he bent over and grabbed Wang Changping's empty sleeve, as though shaking his hand. Then he went behind Director Gong and the two cadres from the security office.

Next, Wang Changping's fellow disciples came forward one by one. Each of them stood where the old bishop had been standing and placed a white flower on Wang Changping's clothing. Each of them gazed at the portrait in the frame, then bent over and shook hands with the left sleeve. Then they said goodbye, walked around the clothing, and stood behind the old bishop.

No one said a word, and it was so quiet that you could hear the droplets of holy water falling to the ground. After the Protestant disciples bid farewell and departed, the Catholic disciples had their turn. After the Catholic disciples finished, the Muslim disciples came over and lined up behind Imam Tian, each of them holding a copy of the Quran. Imam Tian slowly walked forward, stood next to the table, and then removed a letter from his Quran and gently placed it next to Pastor Wang's sleeve, as though placing it directly into his hand. The envelope was still sealed, and where the recipient's address would be, there was a sticker printed with a single line:

Recipient could not be located, return to sender.

In the middle of the envelope below the sticker, there were the names of the letter's two addressees:

Jesus

Virgin Mary

At the very bottom, there was the sender's address and signature. The address was National Politics University's religious training center, and the sender was Wang Changping. Everyone looked at the letter and then stepped away from the sleeve next to which the letter was positioned.

The final group to bid farewell were the Buddhist and Daoist disciples. They were led by the seventy-three-year-old Shuiyue *shifu*, who was wearing the black funerary robe prescribed by Buddhist ritual and holding a copy of the Heart Sutra and three incense sticks. But when she approached Wang Changping's cenotaph, it occurred to her that this was not a Buddhist funeral, and therefore, after she performed a farewell ritual at Wang Changping's feet, she did not place incense sticks at both ends of his cenotaph as prescribed by Buddhist practice. Instead, holding the incense sticks, she walked halfway around his clothing, then took the copy of the Heart Sutra and placed it next to his cenotaph.

As the farewell ceremony was about to conclude, the last person to pay his respects was Gu Mingzheng. Like his fellow Daoist classmates, Mingzheng bowed down before Wang Changping, and then, as he walked around his clothing bidding his farewell, he took the letter Imam Tian had left on the cenotaph table and looked it over. He glanced at the entrance of the classroom, where his gaze met that of Yahui, who was standing by the door. He waved to her, gesturing for her to come over. However, at that moment Yahui felt an intense pain between her legs, as though she were being stabbed by a knife. Her face became as pale as a sheet of paper and was covered in large drops of sweat. She grasped the back of a chair, as though without it she would fall to the ground. She saw Mingzheng gesturing to her, but due to the pain between her legs all she could do was simply stand there. She noticed that all the classmates were looking at her, but she continued leaning against the chair, not daring to move.

Imam Tian walked over. "Why don't you bid farewell?" he said. "The National Religion Association is going to appoint a new director, and after his appointment begins, even this sort of farewell ritual is likely to be forbidden."

Yahui stared at Imam Tian, wanting to ask him something. However, Director Gong and the two cadres from the security office interjected, saying, "How about this—regardless of whether it is a question of fellow disciples or classmates at the center, you have all taught, understood, and felt, haven't you?"

Then Director Gong collected Wang Changping's clothing, photograph, and letter, and placed them in a cardboard box, as though collecting props following a theatrical performance.

The disciples began heading out of the classroom. At this point, the hoarse sound of a Qin opera tune suddenly emerged from the throat of the imam who could sing opera:

> I let out a mighty cry—here I stand outside!
> Brave warriors all about cheer in great delight
> I, Shan, alone astride my horse, trampling the Tang camps in a
>   single stride
> Wreaking death and destruction until grown men cry
> Wreaking death and destruction until rivers of blood flow to the sea
>   and nigh.

Then, everyone began to sing along:

> Wreaking death and destruction until mountains of corpses pile high
> Those piddling Tang troops, cowering in terror from my might.

The song rolled through the classroom like thunder, as though it were about to make the building collapse. The disciples continued singing as they filed out, and finally Mingzheng came over and stood by Yahui's side. She asked him, "The National Religion Association is going to appoint a new director?"

"That's what I've heard," Mingzheng replied. "But it is apparently an administrative issue, not a religious one."

At this point, Director Gong, having collected Pastor Wang's effects, came up to Yahui, and she asked him the same question: "Will the National Religion Association have a new director tomorrow?"

Director Gong laughed and said, "Yes, and it will be a good thing. By changing directors, our center will be able to move to a new campus, and we will begin a new chapter."

Yahui suddenly felt that the area between her legs stopped hurting, and she instead felt bloated, as though a man's organ were inside and thrusting in and out. Stunned, she stood there, feeling as though that twitching organ were stealing all her energy, transforming her into a hollow shell. Meanwhile, the scene in front of her seemed to morph into the room on the twenty-second floor of the Shangri-La Hotel, and the door and windows, bed, and sofa appeared to spin around in front of her. She dug her toes into the floor and stared intently at Director Gong, then at Gu Mingzheng, who had been looking at her strangely, after which she turned and walked out.

In the hallway, she again heard several imams loudly singing the lyrics to *The Decapitation of General Shan*:

> *When Jingde captured me, that was as fate would have it*
> *But I do resent that the hearts of all the braves were his to buy*
> *Thinking back to how we sealed our brotherhood with blood, and*
>   *all bonded as one,*
> *Yet now, one after another we bend to the Tang—should that be right?*

Yahui left behind that hoarse singing and proceeded to the lobby. When she looked up, she saw the agent hurry over and wave at her with a mysterious smile. With this, Yahui knew that Nameless was really going to become the person who oversees deities, a deity of deities. She knew that the agent was summoning her because Nameless, wanting to celebrate having become a deity of deities, was again waiting for her on the twenty-second floor of the Shangri-La Hotel. Yahui remembered he had told her that the next time she came, she should make sure to bring her Buddhist robe, because he wanted her to strip naked and lie on that robe so that they could do the same thing as before. Upon seeing the agent's smiling face, Yahui immediately ran away.

She turned instead to the elevator, at which point she heard Gu Mingzheng and the agent calling out, "What's wrong?! What's wrong?!" But the elevator seemed to be waiting for her and immediately opened its doors. She dashed in and pressed the "close door" button, leaving Gu Mingzheng and the agent outside. When they ran up the stairs to catch up to her, Gu Mingzheng, who was in front, heard a heartrending cry like the one that emerged from his throat when the blade came down between his legs three months earlier.

16 Mingzheng and Yahui

The hospital was a burn unit in the Haidian District, and most of the center's disciples didn't even know where it was located. But Mingzheng knew about it, and it was he who rushed Yahui there. She had poured half a bottle of sulfuric acid between her legs, such that her thighs had second-degree burns and her crotch had third-degree burns. The closer to the center of her crotch, the more severe the burns became. The acid had even seeped into the area between her legs, but the doctor, when discussing her internal injuries, did not specify the degree of the burn and instead simply asked, "How distressed must she have been to have done something like this?"

As the companion who had brought Yahui to the hospital, Mingzheng accepted the doctor's invitation to view her crotch, and saw that it was covered in red and black splotches like a burnt hornet's nest. Yahui had already passed out from the pain, and therefore no longer felt anything. At the hospital, she was bandaged, given an IV, and had the area between her legs cleaned. She was also given anesthesia, and as it took effect, she turned pale, her forehead became covered in sweat, and she bit down on her pillow and blanket.

"Whenever you feel any pain, we can give you more anesthesia," the doctor said.

"No need," she replied, looking at the doctor. "This is punishment from the deities, which I must accept."

Later Mingzheng spoke to the doctor, who said that Yahui needed treatment not only for her burns but also for mental illness, explaining that anyone willing to do this to herself must have serious mental health issues. He told Mingzheng where Beijing's depression treatment center was located. After ten days or so, when Yahui was able to sit halfway up in bed and the searing pain in her lower body had eased somewhat, she and Mingzheng were together in a small hospital room. They looked at one another, then Mingzheng solemnly told Yahui that the doctor had recommended that, after being discharged from the hospital, she go to a depression treatment center. Upon hearing this, a pallor flickered over Yahui's face, after which she calmly looked at Mingzheng and said, "If I'm mentally ill, that means I've become a true disciple."

Mingzheng didn't reply.

Yahui smiled wanly, and added, "My *shifu* always said that religion is the domain of the mentally ill, and whoever is perceived as being mentally ill on account of their religious belief is a true disciple."

Mingzheng stared at her, and asked, "Having undergone this ordeal, do you feel that you've achieved enlightenment?"

"I feel I've achieved enlightenment—it's as though I've managed to see something," Yahui replied. "It's as though I've glimpsed the Heart Sutra's proverbial other bank of the river."

"Yes, it is the other bank," Mingzheng affirmed. Then he sat down next to her, took her hand, and held it in his. From that moment, at ten o'clock that morning, they became siblings.

A few days earlier, it had rained in Beijing, but afterward the weather had been so good that it didn't even resemble weather. Similarly, the clouds visible through the window weren't clouds but rather translucent sheets of misty silk. The hospital was not very large, since it was a specialty unit, but whenever there was a fire in a nearby residential quarter, numerous burn victims would arrive at once. However, this wasn't something that happened every day, and consequently the hospital was very peaceful at the moment. Soon, Yahui would no longer need to use a urinary catheter, and would simply need to take her medication, have her dressing changed, and rest. When changing Yahui's dressing, the nurse would occasionally let Mingzheng watch, and he would stand there and look at the area between her legs. Yahui didn't mind Mingzheng watching. On this day, after the doctor and nurse left, Yahui asked Mingzheng how it was doing.

"What do you mean, how is it doing?" Mingzheng asked in return.

Yahui said, "I mean, down there."

Mingzheng blurted out, "It's healing well, like a blooming flower."

"I also saw your area down there." Yahui stared at the ceiling, then similarly blurted out, "Yours resembles a field capable of growing grass and flowers."

Mingzheng stared at Yahui's face and saw that below her eyes there were two streaks of tears. They both looked away, but after a while Yahui turned to Mingzheng and said she wanted to relieve herself, so he led her to the bathroom. The bathroom was in a corner of the room across from the bed. Mingzheng held her catheter and urine bag, both of which were half-filled with crystalline yellow liquid. Mingzheng saw this color and remarked, "Your interior is hot; you should drink more liquids." Leaning against his shoulder, Yahui replied, "Could you bring some fruit tomorrow?" Mingzheng nodded, then helped her unfasten her pants and supported her as she sat down on the toilet. He wanted to give her the urine bag, but she stuffed it back into his hand, saying, "The Buddha says that in a former life you owed me something, so now you must repay me." After this there was silence, as Yahui squatted over the toilet and Mingzheng held the urine bag.

Conversing openly like siblings, Mingzheng asked Yahui, "If you were still able to get married, whom would you marry?"

"I'd marry Pastor Wang," Yahui replied. "You mustn't get angry, but if I were still a woman when it came time to leave the hospital, and if Pastor Wang were still alive, I would definitely be willing to convert to his religion and live with him."

"But if you couldn't marry him, but also had no choice but to obtain a marriage certificate?"

Yahui gripped Mingzheng's hand, as though afraid he would run away. As though they were both still ignorant children and he were her elder brother, he squatted down next to her and relieved himself while explaining that two weeks earlier the regulations on purchasing real estate had changed again. Originally, outsiders could purchase apartments in Beijing as long as someone from a high-level personnel department issued a certificate attesting to the buyer's qualifications, and religious figures enjoyed the preferential rights accorded to individuals with special talent. Now, however, the government wanted to calm Beijing's real estate market, and specified that to purchase real estate you not only had to pay higher property taxes, but must also hold a Beijing ID card and a local household-registration certificate. After making these observations, Mingzheng continued squatting in front of Yahui, who stood up, fastened her belt, and took the urine bag from him, then carried it as she slowly returned to her bed. She sat on the bed and was silent for a moment, then said, "I feel that it is really true that there are no deities in the world."

"Of course there are!" Mingzheng retorted loudly. "I explicitly asked, and was told that, according to current regulations, if someone is a Beijing resident, then his or her spouse can also purchase real estate, take out loans, make transfers, and enjoy all of Beijing's policies and benefits."

Mingzheng pulled his stool over to Yahui's bed and once again held her hand. He told her what Director Gong had proposed: "We can use the money Pastor Wang left you when he died and apply for a marriage certificate. You can then transfer to your account the full amount for the apartment, and after having secured the marriage certificate you'll be able to purchase the apartment under your own name. Once you have a marriage certificate and a Beijing apartment, your household registration can be officially reassigned to Beijing. That way, you'll be able to leave Qinghai and become a Beijinger. At that point, we can get divorced, and each of us can pursue our own path and follow our own religion."

Yahui reflected for a moment, then removed her hand from Mingzheng's grasp.

"Would this work?"

Mingzheng said, "Yes, many people do it."

By that point, it was lunchtime. Yahui said she wanted dumplings, so Mingzheng went out and bought two servings of vegetarian dumplings. After they finished, they agreed that the shop made good dumplings, and that they would make sure to buy more in the future.

17 A Different Nameless

One day followed another, and one month followed another. After April came May, and after May came June.

In June, it was time for the graduation ceremony.

Yahui was discharged from the hospital in the first half of June. While she was in the hospital, each religion's class monitor had come to visit her, and when they returned to the center, they all reported that she had suffered a case of acute appendicitis and needed to have her appendix removed. An appendix is a useless organ to begin with, so removing it isn't a big deal. After Yahui was discharged from the hospital, many classmates went to visit her in her dormitory, and upon seeing her so thin and pale, they remarked that it appeared she had gotten a little carried away with trying to lose weight. The classmates offered her their prayers and blessings, brought her nutritious snacks to eat, and prayed to their respective deities that they watch over her. With the help of these deities, Yahui quickly began to recover her health. She began making papercuts and attending class again, and also began going to work at the office of the director's assistant every day. However, Director Gong was busy with the final preparations for the printing and cover design of his book, so when Yahui went to the office and didn't see him there, she took the opportunity to leave campus with Mingzheng and go buy some furniture and kitchenware. Another day, she also deposited the funds from Pastor Wang's bequest in the bank in order to transfer them to her mortgage account.

June did not arrive quietly, but rather with a bang. Students who planned to return home to see their families began to cry abjectly because they couldn't bear to leave, while those who planned to go out and work in the world would find that the world had prepared formidable obstacles for them to overcome. The disciples at the center, however, were not anxious at all, since the question of where they were coming from had already been determined by their previous lives, and the question of where they were going was controlled by the deities. Therefore, they simply continued their daily routine of getting up, performing rituals, lighting incense, attending class, and taking their exams. Thanks to Director Gong's instructions, most classes had open-book exams, and only the political events class was treated as a serious matter in which everyone had to close their textbooks and try to obtain a high score.

At the end of the semester, an expert from the national religious studies center was brought in to offer tutoring. This expert was several years older than Director Gong, but physically resembled him—tall with a large head, square face, high nose, and thick eyebrows. The only difference was that the expert had long hair that was parted on the side, while Director Gong kept his cut short all year round.

To get the desired high scores, Director Gong asked all students to come to the classroom on the day the expert visited. At 8:50, the classroom was still completely dark, but the expert who looked like Director Gong entered the room at 8:58 and stood next to the front podium, and for a long time he silently counted the assembled students. At 9:00, the bells in each institute's classrooms began to ring. The expert stood on the dais with his gaze directed at the students in front of him, and his lips closed as tightly as a sealed account book.

This was an overcast day in the middle of June. Above the clouds there were still more clouds, but some areas of the sky were clear. Outside, it constantly looked like it was about to rain, but in the end it never did. As the rain was holding off, a disciple with a pale face suddenly stood up and shouted, "Let's just start class already! Daoist master Gu Mingzheng and Buddhist nun Yahui aren't coming—they went to get a marriage certificate today, and won't be attending anymore!"

A stillness suddenly descended on the classroom.

In this stillness, someone began to applaud their classmates' marriage. A handful of other students began applauding as well, which left the pale student very embarrassed, as though he couldn't understand what was happening. In that moment of applause and embarrassment, the expert who had come to offer supplementary instruction walked to the middle of the dais and lowered his hands to ask everyone to cease their applause. "Let's start class! Let's start class!" he shouted with a smile. The classroom slowly quieted down, until all that remained was an air of confusion and emptiness.

"I am going to give everyone a question on religious political events to see whether you can answer it correctly . . ." the expert announced in a relaxed fashion. "You report that this religious masters class, after two semesters of study and training, has permitted two youths from different religions, who previously didn't know each other, to break the rules and fall in love, and even get married. With respect to this inter-sect marriage, we have the following three options:

1. The marriage between these two youths from different religions is entirely the result of their mutual affection.
2. The marriage is the result of the mutual tolerance and integration of socialism and religious belief.
3. The marriage is the result of both their mutual affection and the mutual tolerance and integration of socialism and religious belief."

As the expert was speaking, he looked down at the disciples in front of him. He saw that one disciple had raised his hand, but he waved him away and continued. "This multiple-choice question might appear simple, but it is actually very tricky. All three answers could be wrong, so you must simply try to select the response that is most correct. But which answer is most correct? In the brackets following the question, should you add something to make the answer not simply the most correct, but rather *absolutely* correct?"

As the expert said this, he once again cast his gaze over the disciples in front of him, and upon confirming that they were all looking up at him, he raised his voice and said, "Let me offer an essay question that might appear complex, but which is actually rather simple, and let me use Buddhism as an example. Buddhism is the world's largest religion and is also the first of China's five great religions. Regardless of whether someone is a Muslim, Catholic, or Protestant—much less a Daoist—they will be familiar with the general parameters and essence of Chinese Buddhism.

"It is said that because the Buddha's followers were increasing so steadily while he was in India promoting the Dharma in the south, he was so tired when he reached Uruvilvato that he decided to stay there for a while. One night while the Buddha was meditating on Lingjiu Mountain, someone hiding behind a tree tried to assassinate him. However, the Buddha already knew that the man was there, and while watching the tree's shadow he said, 'If you want to kill the Buddha, you should show yourself!' The other man emerged and placed his sword at the Buddha's feet. The Buddha asked, 'Who sent you to assassinate me?' The other man knelt down and, in a trembling voice, replied, 'I don't dare reveal my master!' The Buddha asked him to leave his sword and recommended that he use a safe path to finish climbing the mountain, and then use another safe path to come back down the other side. He told the man to return home and fetch his elderly mother, and then proceed with her to the neighboring state of Shakya to look for his younger brother. The Buddha knew that if the man had indeed succeeded in assassinating him, others would surely have killed the man on his way home, but conversely, if the man failed to assassinate the Buddha, then his own life would be even more at risk. Accordingly, the Buddha told the man to take a different road home.

"In this way, the person who wanted to assassinate the Buddha fled with his mother to Shakya. Everyone, please note: as a result of this failed attempt, the person who wanted to assassinate the Buddha instead came to realize the Buddha's greatness and sagacity, and therefore began to believe in Tathagata. Meanwhile, based on new evidence and research, it has been revealed that, around that same time, Emperor Ming of the Eastern Han had a dream in which he saw a gold-colored figure who could project sunlight from his neck. The next morning, the emperor asked the officials: Who was this deity that had appeared in his dream? One official told him that the deity was the Bodhi of Tianzhu. Accordingly, in the seventh year of the Yongping reign era—which is to say the year 64 CE—the emperor sent an envoy to Tianzhu to seek the Dharma. However, the Bodhi whom the envoy encountered at Tianzhu was none other than the person who had previously been sent to assassinate the Buddha and subsequently been reformed by him. It was he who ended up being the first to transmit the Buddhist teachings to China. Meanwhile, the Baima Temple in contemporary Luoyang, Henan, was originally constructed by Emperor Ming to house the sutras and the Dharma brought back by that person who tried to assassinate the Buddha. At the time, Baima Temple was a national guesthouse used by people translating sutras and disseminating the Buddha's teachings. Accordingly, the first Buddhist to enter China was that person who wanted to assassinate the Buddha, and the first sutras to enter China were the ones brought back by that same person after he achieved enlightenment.

"Now, we have four essay questions. Please select one and provide an argument and explanation:

1. From your understanding of China's revolutionary history, what do you think of the possibility that Chinese Buddhism originated from the person who tried to assassinate the Buddha?
2. What is the relationship between the tolerance and integration of each religion within socialism's great family, on one hand, and the Buddha's act of rescuing the person who tried to assassinate him, on the other?
3. From the perspective of Buddhism's relationship to the world, do you think that if the planned assassination had in fact succeeded, today's world would still have Buddhism? If not, then what would the world now be like?
4. In today's world, humanity is divided into four races: yellow, white, black, and brown. At the same time, however, the world has thousands upon thousands of religions, large and small. In this mortal world with its countless different schools of religious teachings, do you think that there should be one deity who is able to oversee all the others?"

18 Guanyin and Laozi

1. Thousands upon thousands of years ago, there was one day—either yesterday, today, or tomorrow—when two auspicious entities met in the sky and became entangled with one another.

2. Were these auspicious entities the spiritual essence of Laozi and Guanyin? Yes, and no. However, it isn't important whether they were or not. What is important is that Laozi ultimately became Laozi, and Guanyin ultimately became Guanyin.

3. Their souls are interlinked, though one soul cannot become interlinked with another. Only souls that cannot become interlinked are true souls. Only souls that can become interlinked are true souls.

4. They meet and have an argument. Guanyin asks
   Laozi: Li Ran, what is it that has permitted us to
   meet again?

5. Laozi replies with a smile: The person I see today
   is not the you from before, and the person you see
   today is not the me from before.

6. Laozi: Why didn't you go to
   Jerusalem to wait for me that day?

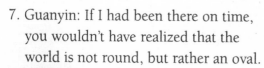

7. Guanyin: If I had been there on time,
   you wouldn't have realized that the
   world is not round, but rather an oval.

8. Laozi: Do you know how far
   I walked to reach Jerusalem?

9. Guanyin: Because it is
   so distant, you must
   have observed vast
   stretches of heaven
   and earth, and
   discovered countless
   patterns and secrets!

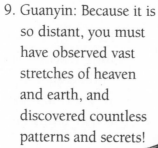

10. At this point, Laozi smiles: Fortunately, by the time you reached Jerusalem, I had already left. If you hadn't used your own body to rescue the tigress, and if you hadn't entered the brothel twenty-seven times in one day, rescuing twenty-seven children, mothers, and young girls who were themselves about to enter the brothel, and if you had in fact arrived at Jerusalem on time to see me, then you wouldn't have encountered the ten Eastern nations on the road back from Jerusalem.

11. Guanyin smiles:
    Yes, that is true. Go on.

12. Laozi: If you hadn't encountered the ten nations and rescued tens of thousands of people, then you wouldn't have become a Buddha and acquired this world of believers.

13. Guanyin: You should thank me
for not arriving there on schedule,
because if I had, you would not
have achieved an enlightened
understanding of heaven and earth.

14. Laozi: I want to thank heaven and earth,
not you. It was heaven and earth that
were responsible for your failure to arrive,
which in turn enabled me to learn the
rules and mysteries of heaven and earth.

15. Guanyin replies angrily: It had nothing to do with heaven and
earth! It was humans who prevented me from arriving there!
    Laozi replies with equal anger: It was heaven and earth that
prevented you from arriving, and it had nothing to do with
humans!

16. Guanyin and Laozi begin to argue—arguing like the wind, water, and primal chaos.

17. They argue like light in darkness, and like darkness in light.

18. After they have argued for a long time, Laozi finally begins to calm down: On the surface it appeared as though the masses of people prevented you from arriving on time, but the people's disaster was a result of their not having abided by the rules of heaven and earth. Therefore, it was indeed heaven and earth that prevented you from arriving on time.

19. Guanyin: Heaven heaven heaven, earth earth earth. Then you tell me, how high is heaven? How broad is the earth?

20. Laozi: Heaven does not have a fixed height, and the earth does not have a fixed size. However, if you want to know how high heaven is or how large the earth is, don't start measuring from just any territory or edge of a territory. Instead, to measure the height of heaven, you must start from the surface of the ocean, and to measure the size of the earth you must start from the ocean's edge. This is because the ocean under heaven is all the same height, and it is the ocean that abuts onto the land.

21. Guanyin: Although it is true that the earth does not have a fixed size, if someone stands on the earth, there will be level ground beneath her feet, and there will be the heavens above his head. The size of the earth can be measured from the edge of the ocean, but it can also be measured from a person's heart. This is because all measurements must begin from a person's heart.

22. Guanyin believes: Between humanity and heaven and earth, humanity is superior. Laozi believes: Between heaven and earth and humanity, heaven and earth determine humanity.

23. In the end, Guanyin and Laozi both agree that the world is constituted by heaven and earth and humanity, but as for whether it is humanity that determines heaven and earth, or heaven and earth that determine humanity—this question must be temporarily set aside.

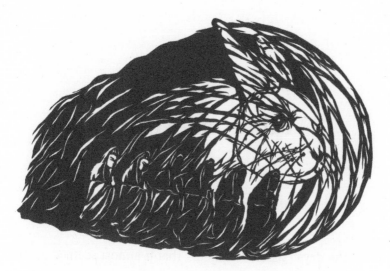

24. In this way, they decide that from now on Laozi will focus on understanding the harmonious integration of heaven, earth, and humanity.

25. Meanwhile, with respect to the relationship between heaven, earth, and humanity, Guanyin will take life as the center and will focus on rescuing human life from suffering between heaven and earth.

19 Yahui and Mingzheng

In June, the days passed so quickly that it almost seemed as though they didn't exist at all. If someone is quiet on one day and active on another, several days—or even a week or two—can pass in the blink of an eye. The students spent most of their time reviewing their notes, taking exams, purchasing cardboard boxes, and packing their bags. As they were preparing to leave campus by the end of the month, the students took their bags to shipping agencies and the post office, or to the consignment areas at the train station or the airport.

In a few breaths' time, graduation day arrived. After their last exam, for their class on the relationship between individual belief and humanity, the classmates recognized that separation was imminent.

The graduation ceremony for this master-level class was scheduled for that evening, and the school specified that after the ceremony, all graduates had to return their room keys and leave campus during the final three days of the month. The first of July was designated as the day the school would check and close the dormitory rooms of all recent graduates, and this regulation was enforced as strictly as a religious precept.

Yahui visited the examination hall one final time, and this time she was taking the exam not for Jueyu *shifu*, but rather for herself. Director Gong said it would be possible to quietly change the name on the diploma from Jueyu to Yahui. With this master training certificate issued by the National Religion Association and National Politics University, perhaps one day Yahui could become a religious master—at which point she might earn a monthly salary of more than twenty thousand yuan and be able to live a life in Beijing that would be as relaxed as burning one incense stick a day.

Therefore, Yahui took this examination extremely seriously. Several days earlier, however, she had purchased some furniture and decorated her apartment, after which she and Mingzheng invited their classmates out to dinner. With the followers of each religion sitting at different tables, Yahui and Mingzheng treated their classmates to an elaborate wedding banquet, and everyone drank quite a bit. The hosts spent twelve thousand yuan on the banquet, but they received more than one hundred two thousand yuan in gifts, meaning that their profit was almost ten times their investment, which could be considered a rather respectable business transaction.

Since Yahui had spent so much time preparing the banquet, when it came time for her to take the exam, she couldn't find the correct responses in her textbooks. Fortunately, the exam's supervising faculty member was the same Associate Professor Huang who had previously quarreled with Director Gong. Associate Professor Huang was chatting with some students as they turned in their examination booklets, and didn't ask Yahui about her copying. Even after Mingzheng turned in his own booklet and then asked Yahui for her pen and proceeded to fill out her examination booklet for her, Associate Professor Huang made a point of looking the other way.

The final question was "Who should a disciple love more: his divine ancestors or a beggar who happens to pass by the entrance of his house?" If one responded that the disciple should love his divine ancestors more, the deities would lose their love for humanity. On the other hand, if one responded that the disciple should love the beggar more, then the next question would be, "What if the beggar is a criminal and is carrying a cleaver he has just used to kill someone?"

354

Most disciples, when they encountered this question, would select the option "I would love my divine ancestors more." While Mingzheng was filling out Yahui's examination booklet, however, he happened to see Tian Dongqing going up to submit his own booklet. Mingzheng pulled Imam Tian aside and pointed to the multiple-choice question, whereupon Tian Dongqing, in a voice as soft as a stream of water, said, "I'd respond that I would love the beggar, but that I also love Muhammad. Therefore, I would not only give the beggar food and clothing, I would also give him a copy of the Quran."

Mingzheng followed Tian Dongqing's lead and checked the "I would love the beggar more" option, while also checking the "I would love my divine ancestors more" option. In the blank space for an explanation, he wrote, "Because I love the beggar, I would give him food and clothing; and because I love my divine ancestors, I would include a copy of the Altar Sutra of the Sixth Patriarch with that food and clothing."

Yahui was the last disciple to turn in her booklet. By that point, it was already five in the afternoon, and when Yahui emerged from the examination hall, not only was the hall itself empty, but so were the hallway, the lobby, and the area outside the religion building. All the other disciples were busy shipping their belongings, going shopping, or saying goodbye to their friends. The end of June was afoot, and the early-summer heat lay ahead. The students who were about to graduate were standing under the trees of the campus road selling their old textbooks, clothing, and other items, thereby transforming the school into a virtual market or temple fair.

Since Mingzheng didn't need to immediately ship his belongings and leave campus, he moved his things to Yahui's new apartment. Meanwhile, Yahui's entire class knew she had bought an apartment in the Yujian residential quarter, and that she would never again return to Jing'an Temple in Xining. As Yahui and Mingzheng strolled through campus hand in hand and shoulder to shoulder, discussing many solemn topics, she remarked at one point, "It's strange—but yesterday I once again dreamed that Tathagata had fallen seriously ill and had become so confused that he forgot what he originally looked like." Mingzheng suddenly stopped and said, "What are you talking about?" Yahui replied, "It's true. I also dreamed that the Virgin Mary was lying on her sickbed, and when her son Jesus went to see her, she didn't even recognize him." Mingzheng quickly looked around, covered Yahui's mouth, and frantically led her forward. They went to the school's shopping area, where the graduating students had already packed up their stands and left, leaving behind trash and random items everywhere. Yahui and Mingzheng proceeded to pick up the cardboard boxes and twine that had been left on the ground, and placed them next to the trash can. Then they picked up the old books and newspapers and took them to the recycling area. When they finished, they noticed that they still had some time before the graduation ceremony began at seven, so they proceeded to stroll through the campus, picking up trash along the way and reflecting: If today the campus were allowed to become a garbage heap, by tomorrow might it not grow into a mountain of garbage?

What about the day after tomorrow? Or the day after the day after tomorrow? Or the day after the day after the day after tomorrow? After collecting many random and miscellaneous items, Yahui and Mingzheng sat down in a remote area where there wasn't anyone else around and proceeded to eat some bread and drink some water. When the campus's streetlights came on, Yahui and Mingzheng finished their meal and headed toward the auditorium where the graduation ceremony was being held.

20 Director Gong, Leaders, and Disciples

The graduation ceremony was held in a small auditorium in the art institute. Below the stage there were approximately two hundred brown leather seats, and on the first row of tables there was an assortment of fruit, teacups, and printed programs. The walls were covered in soundproofing cloth that was decorated with different sorts of light-colored striped paper. The seats were in a stadium arrangement, with each row positioned higher than the one in front. The stage was crescent-shaped and a meter high. Red curtains were hanging on either side of the seats, and the spotlights positioned in front of and over the stage were all directed toward the carpet in the center of the stage.

While one might have expected that some students would be out shopping and unable to make it back in time, it turned out the entire class arrived punctually, before seven o'clock. Some students were still wearing their school attire while others were wearing street clothes. The temperature in the auditorium was comfortably warm. In front of the stage, there was a banner with a row of yellow characters that read: *Third annual religious-master training class graduation ceremony*. Of the first disciples to arrive, some were taking photographs in front of the banner while others were chatting with each other. Each student was holding a program listing and a bottle of mineral water they had picked up at the entrance. One asked, "What did you buy at Wangfujing?" Another remarked, "The Xidan market is simply too big and too crowded; as soon as you get there, you dissolve into the crowd." In the commotion, there were many lingering farewells. Even the old abbots and hosts were holding insulated cups imported from Japan, skin creams imported from South Korea, and mobile-phone power banks from specialty stores—all of which had been purchased for them by other disciples. Shuiyue *shifu* was holding a pair of dolls. Still wrapped in plastic, the boy and girl dolls were almost life-size and were hugging each other, and when Shuiyue *shifu* gave them to Yahui and Mingzheng, someone shouted, "Kiss! . . . Let's see a kiss!" Everyone else turned to look, and as they were waiting for the couple to kiss they instead saw Associate Professor Huang rush in. He lowered his hands to ask everyone to quiet down, then said loudly, "Everyone please sit down . . . Everyone please sit down . . . The leader has arrived, so everyone please have a seat!"

The disciples all sat down in the sections assigned to their respective religions, as their gazes were riveted on the entrance to the auditorium. The first person to enter was Director Gong. He marched in and then stood next to the walkway, bowing in greeting. Next to enter were the director of the United Front Work Department and the chairman of the National Religion Association, followed by the school's leaders. The chairman was in his nineties and needed support when he walked. He belonged to the first generation of religious leaders to emerge after the founding of modern China, and he had also attained a high position within Buddhism, having previously served as the host of an important temple. Now he was the chairman of the National Religion Association. Ordinarily each religion's leaders and disciples would only be able to see him on television and in newspapers, just as Catholics around the world usually can only glimpse the Pope on television, and therefore no one had expected that he would attend this graduation ceremony in person, nor did anyone expect that the director of the United Front Work Department would also be in attendance. Everyone stood up and applauded when these two elderly leaders entered, as though applauding the arrival of the prime minister. The first disciples to stand up were several octogenarian abbots and bishops, followed by each class's class monitor and fellow students. They all stood together and applauded energetically until the auditorium sounded as though it were filled with gunfire. The applause continued until the two elderly leaders reached the first row of seats, whereupon they turned around and gestured for all the disciples to sit down, and only then did the applause slowly begin to ebb.

Then the ceremony began.

The ceremony was hosted by Director Gong. He was wearing a gray suit with white stripes, and his tie was a shade of dark red. After saying a few words about needing to open the door to see the mountain, he invited the school's principal to join him on stage. As the principal passed Director Gong on the steps, for some reason he smiled and patted Director Gong's shoulder. Once on stage, he earnestly thanked the department director and association chairman for attending, then suddenly announced that he had two pieces of good news. As he said this, he held up a book with a title in gold and a gray leather binding. This was Director Gong's *Synthetic Treatise on Tug-of-War and the Contradictions Between Religions*, and he said that the book had been published by a prestigious national press and had even been awarded first prize by the National Scientific Research Project. He said that he had received inside information that this book would definitely win another prize, and added that all of the disciples attending this evening's ceremony would receive a signed copy. Then he asked that everyone give Director Gong a hand, whereupon the area below the stage exploded with applause, interspersed with snapping and whistling.

After the applause began to subside, Director Gong handed the principal an envelope, from which the principal removed a document with several large red seals. He lifted the document for everyone to see, and said loudly, "Students and fellow believers, today you officially conclude your studies and graduate. But today is also the day our National Politics University's religious training center is officially promoted to the level of institute. This religion institute is the first school of religious studies in one of the nation's universities, and its establishment, promotion, and development have been made possible by the efforts and support of the department director and association chairman, who are both here with us. Without their efforts, not only would our center—which we've been running for nearly a decade now, including several years before we started the master training classes—not have been able to become an institute, but it would have been fated to remain a marginal section-level unit within the university. Beginning today, however, not only has your center become an institute comparable to the university's law, literature, economics, finance, and journalism institutes, it has even overtaken them, having become a vice-department-level academy. Moreover, from now on, our institute will have full control over its student enrollments, employee training, housing allotments, salaries, and appointments, as well as instructors' promotions and retirement—the same way that other institutes do!"

At this point, the principal paused and gazed down at the disciples assembled before him. This gesture resembled a tacit warm-up notice, and as all the students stared in shock at Director Gong—who had already been promoted to institute director and was planted at the front of the stage like a tree and applauding heartily—they realized that the significance of this ceremony lay in their inheritance from the past and the future opening of the world, like the ceremony commemorating the day when each religion was established. Therefore, there was another wave of applause, as the disciples once again broke into shouts and laughter, combined with loud whistles coming from the mouths of fellow disciples or of other students who had come to watch the excitement. In the middle of this ruckus, the principal invited the elderly department director and association chairman to come on stage and say a few words. They, however, merely stood below the stage smiling as they protested, "But we agreed that we wouldn't speak! We agreed we wouldn't speak!"

Thus, the principal approached the microphone and said, "In accordance with the central leaders' instructions, we should economize and keep things simple. I now announce the start of this year's religious-master training class graduation ceremony!"

Under a wave of applause, the principal descended from the stage. His descent was accompanied by music that was cheerful and melodious, but also broad and strong. The tune was "My Motherland," which often plays at the opening of Chinese events. After the music concluded, an art institute graduate student—who would later go on to become a television host—offered some opening remarks as though reciting a poem, whereupon the crowd once again erupted in applause. Then the student announced the evening's first event: an eight-person singing performance by members of the Buddhist class. The eldest monk was forty and was already an abbot, while the youngest was thirty and was preparing to become a sagacious monk positioned beneath an abbot. The eight monks stood up and waited for a moment in front of the stage, then walked up onto the stage, resembling a Buddhist typhoon. The monks were all wearing new yellow robes and new pointed-toe cloth shoes, and they all had closely shaved pates marked by the white dots they received after being ordained. The monks stood in a row on stage, holding four microphones between the eight of them. They were standing in pairs and appeared happy and relaxed, smiling childlike smiles. After a short musical introduction performed by a combination of ancient and modern instruments, the monks began to sing. This Buddhist song was originally meant to be sung by a female singer, but now was being sung by eight male monks. The song was originally intended to elicit joy, but when the monks sang it, they appeared a bit embarrassed yet also affectionate. That harmonious sound of monks' voices, which were raspy and hoarse, immediately attracted the attention of the crowd as they gazed up at the monks:

> Let the Buddha take my hand
> And lead me out of the fog
> A Buddha light is shining on me
> As I walk this path to the other shore
> Let the Buddha take my hand
> And let me finish my life's journey
> The benevolent Buddha smiles
> And is waiting for me on the other shore.

The slow melody and pious lyrics immediately inspired the disciples assembled below the stage. No one had expected that the monks would be able to sing a woman's song, nor that they would sing "The Buddha Is Leading Me by the Hand" while swaying with inter-linked arms, like in every performance that every Chinese person has watched of "Our Workers' Strength Is Great." Moreover, before going on stage, each of the monks had been holding a copy of *Biography of the Buddha*, but when they turned around after singing two stanzas and stood at the front of the stage, the original golden title had disappeared from the volumes they were clasping to their chests, and instead had been replaced with a single character. Each of the eight volumes now had a different character on the cover, and they combined to form the phrase: *Constructing a Harmonious Society with Bricks and Tiles.*

As loud as a thunderstorm, the applause began anew, and it continued until the monks, still holding their books, descended from the stage.

The second event was a Daoist troupe's martial arts performance and featured a competition between some disciples belonging to the southern Wudang school and others belonging to the northern

Taishan school. The performance included sparring, individual practice, leaping, and midair fighting, and although the disciples had previously practiced many of the moves in class, when they performed them on stage, their flying fists, astounding leaps, and contorted bodies won applause that was as dense as the clouds of dust that the performers were kicking up on stage.

After this martial arts performance, the third event was a Protestant woman's song. The performer was a high-level accountant, and although her fellow Protestants knew why she had converted while working in the world of high finance, the other disciples didn't know why she had suddenly decided to attend church every week to lead others in singing hymns. Most of the students in her class had heard her sing "My Lord Jesus" before, but today, after she finished, the applause was thunderous and interminable. Some audience members even began calling for an encore. The singer initially demurred, but eventually smoothed back her hair, which resembled that of a young teacher, and said with a smile, "How about if I sing the school song, 'My Beloved Deskmate'? What do you think?"

The audience fell silent, as though they were afraid they had misheard her. They all gazed up at the stage with a quizzical look, and then, before their doubts had been fully dispelled, someone filled the silence with applause, which was followed by shouts of "Sing the song, sing the song!" Initially these shouts were accompanied by a single raised fist, but soon a veritable forest of fists filled the room. Therefore, the Protestant disciple, who had previously attended college, proceeded to sing "My Beloved Deskmate." A slow, crisp guitar sound emerged from the orchestra pit, accompanying the hurt, hopeless, and deeply nostalgic voice that poured soulfully out of the disciple's mouth:

> *Tomorrow will you still recall*
> *The diary you wrote yesterday?*
> *Tomorrow will you still recall*

The you who used to love to cry?
The teachers already don't remember
The you who couldn't guess the correct answer
I also occasionally look through old photographs
And only then do I remember you, my deskmate
Who married the sentimental you?
Who read your diary?
Who braided your long hair?
Who sewed your wedding gown?

. . .

Following this song with guitar accompaniment, a silence descended on the auditorium. The students and disciples were captivated by the melancholia of parting. Everyone began to clap along with the music, and when the former student sang the lines *Who braided your long hair?* and *Who sewed your wedding gown?*, some disciples' eyes became bloodshot, as teardrops streamed down their faces like morning dew.

During the ceremony, Yahui and Mingzheng were sitting in the right-rear section of the auditorium, and the gifts Shuiyue *shifu* and other classmates had brought them were placed next to the chairs in the hallway. Originally, the fifth event on the schedule, "Wedding," should have featured three wedding bows that Yahui and Mingzheng were going to direct to the deities, leaders, disciples, and classmates as they went on stage, at which point they would take the candy and chocolates the center had prepared and toss one handful after another into the crowd. Yahui and Mingzheng imagined how, as those colorful candies rained down, the disciples would applaud and discuss how this was the first mixed-faith marriage to emerge from the center. When the daughter of Jesus unexpectedly began to sing "My Beloved Deskmate," however, Yahui was deeply moved by the melancholic lyrics and transported by the celestial guitar playing. Someone began singing along, and Yahui also began singing along.

Someone stood up and began to clap, whereupon Yahui—together with several Daoist masters, Buddhist nuns, and Muslim imams— also stood up and began clapping and humming.

> *You have always been very careful*
> *And when asking me if you could borrow half an eraser, you*
> *Never inadvertently said*
> *That you liked being with me.*
>
> *At that time the sky was always blue*
> *The day always passed too slowly*
> *And you always said that graduation was in the distant future*
> *But in the blink of an eye, we each went our separate ways.*
> . . .

Yahui had never heard this song before, but for some reason she found she could already hum along, and furthermore was able to quickly memorize the lyrics. The spotlights were all focused on this daughter of Jesus, and even the teardrops that fell on her face as she sang were clearly visible. Meanwhile, below the stage there was a couple from the Catholic class who, as they were singing, suddenly began hugging one another and crying loudly. In the Protestant class there were two female disciples who didn't sing along or stand up, and instead merely stared blankly throughout the song, their faces pale as they gripped each other's hands, as though they wouldn't separate on pain of death. Meanwhile, Mingzheng originally shared Yahui's sensibility, as he sat there listening and watching.

As the event host Institute Director Gong started speaking again, Yahui looked around and remarked to Mingzheng, "It looks like Imam Tian didn't come after all."

Mingzheng got up and asked after Tian Dongqing in the Islamic seating area, then returned and said, "No, he hasn't come. No one knows where he is."

Everything proceeded as usual, with the only difference being that in the afternoon there had been an exam, and that evening there was the graduation ceremony. However, who could have expected that after the performance of "My Beloved Deskmate," Mingzheng would also be staring at the stage? As everyone stood up and began singing along, Mingzheng remained silent and bit his lip, as though placing a piece of meat under a blunt knife that wasn't sharp enough to draw blood. He bit his lip more forcefully in response to the song's melancholia—as though the force were produced not by his upper and lower teeth, but rather by the music emerging from that electric guitar and the mouth of that daughter of Jesus. When she reached the lines *And you always said that graduation was in the distant future / But in the blink of an eye, we each went our separate ways*, a streak of blood appeared in the corner of his mouth—reminiscent of how, six months earlier, blood from his shoulder had flowed along his belt prong and down his back, as though in a dream. Mingzheng sat there in silence, gazing through the crowd while staring at the daughter of Jesus up on stage, and as the blood—which was the result not of pain but rather pleasure—dripped down from his lips to his chin. When the blood reached his jaw, he once again heard the song and melody, and could smell the warm scent of blood. Just as he was about to get up to go wipe the blood from his chin, Yahui stopped singing along with the song, and instead turned to Mingzheng and asked in alarm, "What's wrong?!"

Mingzheng replied, "Nothing."

Yahui took out her handkerchief and handed it to him, and with a sallow smile said, "Don't forget that you are an enlightened priest, and I am an enlightened nun!"

At that moment, Institute Director Gong appeared before them. In the lamplight below the stage, he had an expression of excitement and satisfaction. In a very soft voice he asked them, "Did you bring your marriage certificates?"

Yahui and Mingzheng didn't reply, and instead they simply gazed at Director Gong, who was now a department-level institute director. Mingzheng held the handkerchief up to his face, as though his tooth hurt. However, Director Gong did not notice this gesture, and instead simply gazed at the couple in the lamplight, then continued, "If you didn't bring the certificates with you, then you should quickly go back and get them. The elderly department director and association chairman are very pleased with our center's recent work and achievements, and they said that in the years they have been overseeing the United Front Work Department and the National Religion Association, this is the first time that they've encountered disciples from the academy who have returned to secular life and gotten married. They would like to see your marriage certificates, and when you have your wedding, they would like to personally present the certificates to you onstage and say a few words, congratulating you on your marriage while celebrating the unity, harmony, and great integration of our nation's religions."

With this, the institute director turned and walked away. As he disappeared into the music and song, he resembled an enormous musical note.

21 Yahui and Tian Dongqing

Yahui emerged from the auditorium to fetch her marriage certificate. She wanted to hear the final portion of "My Beloved Deskmate" before going to the religion building, so she lingered in the entranceway for a while. By this point, all the seats in the auditorium were filled, and in addition to students from the religion classes there were also first- and second-year students from the music academy in attendance. Because there were no empty seats, new arrivals stood either in the back row or in the hallway. The air conditioner was blowing hot air, which, combined with the music, made the audience feel as though they were in a tropical rain forest. Meanwhile, in the June evening outside the auditorium, she could hear the people singing mournfully on and below the stage,

> Who encountered the you who is very sentimental?
> Who comforts the you who likes to cry?
> Who saw me write you a letter?
> And who threw the letter into the wind?
>
> . . .

The remaining lyrics dropped syllable by syllable, like autumn rain dripping onto Yahui's body. There was a bone-piercing comfort and chill, which made Yahui's entire being plummet into the depths of the elegy and melt into the boundary between life and death. At this moment, she was distracted by the sound of someone approaching her. The person approaching was Tian Dongqing. He walked quickly, with his head turned, and when he reached Yahui he abruptly came to a stop.

Ordinarily, he would have asked, "Has the performance been going on for very long?" or explained why he was late. However, when he saw her this time, he didn't say either of these things, and instead he urgently declared: "Today I went to the Miyun cemetery to visit Wang Changping's tomb. Although he and I didn't belong to the same faith, we were still classmates."

Surprised, Yahui stood on the crescent-shaped steps outside the building entrance. Both the overhead lights and Yahui's face were milky white, and the broken shadows of pagoda trees between nearby buildings covered Tian Dongqing's face such that Yahui couldn't even make out his expression when he was speaking. She could only hear his voice, which sounded as though it were traveling through a wall. If it weren't for the fact that Tian Dongqing was standing directly in front of her, Yahui wouldn't have known that the voice she was hearing was coming from his mouth.

"Do you know what is inscribed on Wang Changping's tombstone?" Tian Dongqing said in a very soft and level voice. "The inscription contains six characters: *I am the disciple Wang Changping!*"

Imam Tian enunciated the phrase *I am the disciple Wang Changping* as heavily and brightly as though he were excavating gold nuggets, then added in a strange voice, "Did you know? I hear that that person who almost became a deity of deities—he was actually Director Gong's foster father! I hear that last month he almost became the director of the National Religion Association, but the deities subsequently appeared and didn't permit the directorship to be changed. Consequently, the former director remains the director."

Yahui and Tian Dongqing both stood there silent and motionless. They gazed at one another, as though having just noticed something mysterious but not particularly extraordinary. They stood there as though separated by a river, and given that they were unable to hear one another, all they could do was let their gazes rest on each other's faces. The sound of song and music coming from the auditorium emerged through a crack in the door, and after drifting into the late-June night, it condensed into starlike lights overhead. *Who encountered the you who is very sentimental? Who braided your long hair? Who sewed your wedding gown?* . . . Even after the final guitar notes had faded away, the singer and the disciples in front of the stage continued to vocalize, "*Lalalalala . . . lalalalala.*"

For some reason, Yahui suddenly started sobbing, as though an inexplicable and irrepressible sorrow were welling up in her breast. Tears streamed down her face like rain, and she wanted to turn and leave. However, when Tian Dongqing saw that she was about to depart, he stopped her and said, "Tell me, isn't it true that the center was promoted to an institute only after it sent off half of the money donated by the religious masters—combined with the money that Pastor Wang bequeathed the center? You know, I hear that now that he is institute director, Director Gong will also be appointed to the National Religious Affairs Bureau. I am standing before you and requesting: If he is in fact appointed and either you or Mingzheng end up becoming his secretary, could you please ask him to relax the regulations pertaining to us Muslims?" As Tian Dongqing said this, he gazed at Yahui, like a child begging his mother for something. Tian Dongqing saw that Yahui seemed confused and befuddled, as though someone had mistaken her for someone else. In the lamplight, her face appeared flushed and panicked. Therefore, he smiled and said, "Did they announce the exam scores at the graduation ceremony? Did I have the highest scores? I told Zhisu I would receive the highest scores, and that way I'd be able to earn a little extra money to help restore the mosque where she is based."

Yahui shook her head and said that they had not yet announced the scores, whereupon Imam Tian left and continued toward the auditorium.

After staring blankly for a while, Yahui continued toward the religion building. Because she had been delayed while speaking to Tian Dongqing, she increased her pace, to the point that soon she was half walking and half running. However, even as she was rushing away, she turned and shouted, "Imam Tian, Brother Tian, you still haven't come to see my new apartment." She continued walking away, then started running. To get back to the dormitory and retrieve her marriage certificate from under her pillow as quickly as possible, she didn't take the same route she had followed on her way in, but instead she selected a path that cut between several buildings on the way to the religion building. The evergreens next to the path kept reaching out to grasp her arms and legs. From a poplar behind the evergreens, wave after wave of evening cicada cries rained down onto her head. The next event was the awards ceremony. It was reported that the total purse was more than eight million yuan, of which two million had been allotted for the student with the highest average score out of the five religion classes. There were also awards for the winning teams in tug-of-war, ping-pong, and badminton, for those who were most active in organizing athletic events for each religion, and for the "Most Popular Instructor," which was decided every year by votes from disciples and students, the Religious Harmony academic-paper award, and so forth and so on. After the prize ceremony, it would be time for Yahui and Mingzheng to go on stage for their "wedding." Now that the religious training center had become a religion institute and Director Gong had become an institute director, perhaps he would indeed be appointed to serve as director of the National Religious Affairs Bureau, where he would oversee the country's religious affairs, like Tian Dongqing had said. Who knows? Although these developments would ultimately be arranged by the organization and deities, they still filled Yahui with a sense of horror and dread.

Half walking and half running, Yahui arrived at the entrance to the religion building, where she used the weight of her body to push open the door. There was no one in the lobby when she arrived, only several bags of trash. In one partially open bag, she could see various items that students had thrown out—including old clothes, winter scarves, tattered shoes, and a monk's dirty robe and an imam's ripped skullcap. Next to that bag of old clothing, there were several bundles of old books, newspapers, and magazines that the cleaners had tied together. The newspapers were copies of *The People's Daily*, *Guangming Daily*, and the National Religion Association's *Chinese Religion Daily*, of which the center had purchased subscriptions for each floor of the religion building. In addition to the magazines, which included political journals, literature journals, and religion journals such as *Religion Study* and *New Faith Stories*, there were also three bundles of books. Yahui knew that these were instructional materials that the students had dumped as they were moving out. During each graduation period, although it might appear that the students are the busiest, it is really each institute's cleaning staff that works the hardest. Throughout the university, each dormitory's trash was piled as high as fruit in an orchard following a thunderstorm, and every day the cleaning staff had to collect the trash, transport it, and clean up afterward.

As Yahui was passing the piles of trash, one book attracted her attention. This was a small copy of the Heart Sutra, only as big as a fist and half as thick as a finger. The volume, with its red title and yellow cover, resembled a book of quotations from a certain year. Because of its small size, it couldn't be placed with the larger volumes, and therefore had been tossed into a pile next to them. Nevertheless, this copy of the Heart Sutra attracted Yahui's attention. She looked at the volume, then forced herself to turn away, since she still needed to retrieve the marriage certificate from under her pillow. The ceremony's fifth event was about to begin. Feeling as though she were in a mud pit, Yahui waded through the trash bags to the elevator. As the elevator was ascending, she saw a discarded copy of the Annotated Daodejing on the dust-covered floor. The cover was curled up like the leg of a discarded pair of pants, and just as Yahui was bending down to pick it up, the elevator arrived at the seventh floor.

The elevator came to a stop, and after the doors opened, Yahui glanced again at that copy of the Daodejing before hurrying back to her room. Her task was as simple as picking up a cup and taking a sip of boiled water. She entered her room and retrieved the marriage certificate, then she stuffed the document into her pocket. She quickly left the room and locked the door, but at this point, things took a strange turn, as though she had just noticed an ant hole that was about to cause a dam to collapse.

At the base of the wall in the hallway outside her door there was a discarded brick-sized copy of the New Testament with a hard black cover and gold title, and below the title there was a line that read "Chinese Protestant Association Internal Publication." This was a brand-new book, and it looked as though it had just been printed. In the lamplight, the black cover was shimmering with the light of Christ. Yahui was puzzled as to why she had not noticed this volume when she first entered, and she half suspected that the deities might have placed it in the entranceway after she went in. Perhaps they had done so to test whether she was pretending she hadn't seen it? Perhaps it was to test how she felt about other people's deities?

She leaned over to pick up the book. Then, she naturally also had to pick up the Daoist scripture. So, upon entering the elevator, she picked up that copy of the Annotated Daodejing that was lying in the corner. She felt that when she was picking up another religion's scriptures, she obviously couldn't leave her own religion's Heart Sutra lying in the trash. Therefore, when she got out of the elevator, she reflexively glanced over at the copy of the Heart Sutra that was lying next to that pile of discarded books. However, where there had originally been three bundles of discarded books, now there were six or seven, not to mention several additional bags of discarded clothes and other items.

Yahui knew that the center's cleaning woman was somewhere in the building picking up trash, and when she went upstairs to fetch the marriage certificate, the cleaner had been taking trash and discarded books back to the auditorium. Yahui looked around now but didn't see her. It occurred to her that she should leave the scriptures she was holding with these other bundles of books. She picked up the copy of the Heart Sutra, and as she did so she saw that in another bundle of books there was a newish copy of the Altar Sutra of the Sixth Patriarch. She tried to remove the latter volume from the knee-high bundle, and as she tugged at it the bundle fell apart, whereupon copies of the Bible and the Quran tumbled out. After picking up both scriptures, she opened another bundle, in which she quickly found a copy of the Diamond Sutra as well as a volume of collected Bible stories. She put these scriptures in a pile, then opened another bundle, and another. She even checked in a trash bag filled with old newspapers, as though a jewel had gotten thrown away and she had no choice but to rummage through the trash to look for it. Each time she opened another bundle, she found scriptures that her classmates had thrown out along with the training center's instructional materials. These included Buddhist, Daoist, Islamic, Protestant, and Catholic scriptures—scriptures from the five major religions that had all been discarded along with ordinary trash, like sacred fruit tossed into a wastebasket. These sacred books were still books—printed words on paper, like any other commodity that can be thrown away after being used. A book's fate is like a person's life, and no one can escape this inexorable path toward death, as Yahui's *shifu* had demonstrated. However, how could the Buddha, the Bodhisattva, Siddhartha, Laozi, Christ, and the Virgin Mary, as well as Muhammad and Allah, not to mention the celestial deity she had imagined in her heart, in whose image she had made a papercut, and who oversees everything—how could they all be like ordinary people? They are not like ordinary people, and similarly, the scriptures that record and praise their words and actions are naturally not like ordinary books.

The light in the lobby seemed to be exhausted, as muddled as an octogenarian's gaze. The dusk light permeated the entire building, and the terrifying stillness was reminiscent of Imam Tian's description of Wang Changping's tombstone. Yahui took all the scriptures and arranged them in a pile with the largest on the bottom and the smallest on top, so that they resembled a miniature pyramid, and then tied them together with some twine she had found lying on the ground. She knew that most of these volumes were scriptures that disciples had discarded because they belonged to other faiths: Daoists would throw out their copies of the Bible and the Quran, and Protestants would throw out their copies of the Altar Sutra of the Sixth Patriarch and the Annotated Heart Sutra. If a disciple happened to have two copies of the Bible or the Daodejing, they might throw out the older one and keep the newer edition. What had been thrown out were all scriptures pertaining to other faiths, which had been issued to the students for the center's class on Selected Readings of Scriptures from Other Faiths. Now that the students had graduated, they had discarded these volumes the way one might throw out an ill-fitting article of clothing that one has received as a gift.

The air was filled with dust, and as Yahui picked through the trash, her back and legs became so sore that she had to stand up and stretch. Only after she had tied up several dozen scriptures did she remember the ceremony and performance that were still unfolding in the auditorium.

She froze for a second, then picked up her bundle of scriptures and headed to the main door. Just as she reached the entranceway, before she even had a chance to open the door, the religion building's main gate suddenly opened inward, and a twelve- or thirteen-year-old boy appeared before her. He was covered in sweat, as though he had just run dozens of li to find her.

"Are you Nun Yahui?"

Yahui looked at that boy as though she were looking at a holy child. Staring at him in astonishment, she nodded.

"You must quickly go home—your apartment has been broken into!"

Yahui almost dropped the bundle of scriptures that she was holding. After relaying his message, the boy ran back out of the religion building like someone who goes to report a fire and immediately rushes back to the burning house. However, as the boy was leaving, he turned and said, "I'm going to get Gu Mingzheng. You should immediately return home. If you don't hurry, the thieves might steal everything!" Then he headed toward the art institute's auditorium, following the same path Yahui had taken when she arrived. It was as though after reporting that his master's house was on fire, he was now rushing to report to the firefighters, running as fast as thunder and rain.

Yahui paused for a couple of seconds in front of the religion building, and then, without a word, began running toward the university's east gate.

22 Deities

In the eighteen years since Yahui was born in the entrance to Jing'an Temple, she had never rushed so anxiously. She began to run, and the roadside trees fell behind her as she passed, as did the streetlamps. As she was dashing through the school's main gate, Yahui resembled a leafless branch buffeted by the wind. She didn't even remember that she was still holding that bundle of scriptures until she was climbing the stairs to the skywalk, and she regretted she hadn't left it in the religion building lobby or in an isolated part of the campus's tree grove. But now it was too late, and on that summer night, both the skywalk and the street were full of people, so she couldn't very well leave a bundle of scriptures on the side of the road or next to a trash can. She had no choice but to continue carrying it as she ran up the skywalk on one side of the road, and then back down the other side. Each time she took a step, the bundle would jostle and hurt her knees, and she also felt a tearing sensation in the area between her legs. Sweat began gushing out of her pores, and soon the front and back of her pink-collared blouse were completely soaked. The passersby under the streetlamps all stared at her, as though she were being chased because she had just stolen something. She alternated between holding the bundle in her hand and hugging it to her chest. She should have put the books down and asked someone to watch them, but as she looked at the shops and the people in the Yujian

Street night market, she was afraid that asking someone would waste precious time, so she continued running until she couldn't run anymore, at which point she switched to loping along with large strides.

Her new apartment was about two thousand meters from the entrance to the Yujian residential quarter, and it seemed as though it took her ten years to cover the distance—but then again it also seemed as though she managed to cover the distance in the blink of an eye. As Yahui entered the residential quarter through a side door next to the main entrance, she almost fell over. After regaining her balance, she started to take another step but realized that her legs were so weak that she was about to collapse. In the end, she managed to stumble over to building number two, and after entering the elevator she immediately crumpled to the floor.

The otherwise empty elevator began ascending to the twenty-second floor. As the elevator was passing the fifteenth floor, she managed to stand up, and when it passed the twentieth floor, she picked up the bundle of books and hugged them to her chest. When the elevator reached the twenty-second floor, she stepped out.

The scene that greeted her was exactly as the boy had reported. The lights between the elevators were a creamy yellow, and the anti-theft door of her neighbor's apartment across the hall was still securely locked. Yahui's apartment's newly installed anti-theft door, however, was unlocked and ajar, leaving an opening between the metal door and the doorframe. For a moment Yahui remained frozen in place, her heart beating so hard it seemed as though it were about to knock the bundle of books out of her hands. Then she rushed over to her apartment and opened the outer door, but before she had a chance to touch the lock of the inner door, the door swung open on its own.

The light in the room rushed toward her like water from a reservoir. Waves of light buffeted her face, as sweat droplets froze into beads of ice and stuck to her face and eyelashes. The light in the room was so bright she almost couldn't open her eyes, and when she did finally manage to open them, she saw that the light was tinted with red, yellow, and flaming white. The room resembled a pool of color made from mixed pigments. For this new apartment, Yahui had made countless different-sized papercuts of Buddhist and Daoist temples, Protestant and Catholic churches, and Islamic mosques. Based on images of the world's most famous religious sites that she had seen on television or in books, she had made papercut reproductions of Saint Peter's Basilica in the Vatican, Milan Cathedral in Italy, and Seville Cathedral in Spain, as well as Masjid al-Haram in Mecca, the Prophet's Mosque in Medina, and the Dome of the Rock in Jerusalem, not to mention the Baima Temple in China, the Kinkakuji Temple in Japan, and the Daoist Baiyun Monastery in China. She had taped these papercuts behind her door, over her bed, on her window, and over her dresser, as well as on her refrigerator door and the chopping board hanging on the wall. In this way, her apartment resembled a conference hall or a warehouse full of all the world's religions. The scene was simultaneously chaotic and refined, and this was particularly true of the wall over her bed, where she had posted papercuts of a variety of different deities.

Positioned in the middle and above the others, there was a papercut of China's celestial deity, who oversees all the other deities. Below this celestial deity, there were papercuts of the Buddha, the Bodhisattva, Laozi, Jesus, Mary, and Allah. Because of the prohibition on making images of Allah, Yahui had made a papercut of the great mosque in Nanguan, Yinchuan, to stand in for him. Behind this mosque standing in for Allah, there were images of Siddhartha, Bodhidharma, Moses, and Muhammad's first wife and first disciple, Khadijah, who was always by his side. Apart from the celestial deity, who was positioned above all the others, the deities and disciples were different sizes and were displayed in no particular order. They seemed to have been posted at random based on the size and color of the paper, and whether the image had been made using a fake cut, a real cut, a knife cut, or a hollow-and-blank cut. One side of the bed was dominated by red papercuts of deities who were all sitting quietly, smiling and peaceful, not one of whom appeared solemn, melancholy, or angry. Yahui didn't like melancholy or angry deities, and she was even less fond of those who were solemnly meditating. Instead, she liked deities who were smiling peacefully like the Bodhisattva Guanyin, and her papercuts of Jesus, Mary, and Khadijah were all smiling. Because she liked the way that the Buddhist monk Jigong was always drinking and laughing, and the Daoist master Iron Crutch Li was always playfully riding a donkey backward, she made a pair of comical papercuts of Jigong holding a gourd and drinking wine and Iron Crutch Li riding a donkey while eating roasted chicken. She placed one of these papercuts next to one of the ever-suffering Jesus and the other next to a papercut of the mosque that stood for Allah grieving for Islam.

Under the colored lights of these deities, and next to her bright red sofa and her new bed with its water-blue sheets, Yahui saw the intruders who had broken into her apartment—Guanyin and Laozi were sitting on the bed, Jesus and Mary were sitting on the sofa, and Muhammad was sitting on the chair directly across from them. They were all sitting around a tea table with cups of hot water and the peanuts, candies, and sunflower seeds Yahui had bought for her wedding. The candies and sunflower seeds were in green and red plastic dishes that Yahui had placed in the middle of the tea table. Although Guanyin, Laozi, Jesus, Mary, and Muhammad were sitting around the table, none of them touched a single peanut or candy, and only Laozi was sipping from his cup of water. Instead, they were all quietly waiting for something, as though they had just discussed an important matter and were waiting for the outcome.

Then Yahui arrived.

Yahui immediately froze in the entranceway, then peered inside, as the bundle of scriptures she was holding fell to the ground. Her eyes widened, her jaw dropped, her face turned pale, and sweat covered her forehead. The deities, however, did not appear at all flustered, as though they had known that she was going to appear at that exact moment. They looked at her calmly, and only after she dropped the scriptures she had been clutching did they finally move. It seemed they initially wanted to try to catch the books, but in the end they simply remained seated. The room appeared small, and its occupants all had a restless expression. The television behind Guanyin and Laozi wasn't turned on, but the spotlight on the television cabinet was shining bright. The window was open as the balcony and the late-June sky merged, and the wind blowing in through the window seemed to contain a whistling sound from the sky.

At that moment, the stillness in the room resembled a blue-white stretch of sky, and Yahui's own mind was as empty as the sky. She stood in the doorway with her hands by her side, without even making an *Amitābha* mudra. Among the deities, Guanyin was the first to stand up, and with light steps she approached Yahui. Then she stopped, caressed Yahui's face, and tucked a strand of hair back behind her ear, like a mother combing a stray strand of hair on her daughter's head. She whispered into Yahui's ear, saying, "I was afraid you might leave this bundle of books somewhere, because if you did the other deities wouldn't believe you were a true disciple and wouldn't be willing to come." After glancing at the deities behind her, Guanyin squatted down to pick up the Bible and Quran that had fallen to the ground and then placed them on a table between the doorway and the kitchen. She opened a copy of the Sunnah and smoothed out the pages, and as she did so Yahui noticed that Guanyin's fingers were unusually elongated and her fingerprints resembled delicate ripples on a pool of water. Guanyin's shiny black hair was in a bun, but if you looked carefully you could see flowers blooming at the end of each strand, the same way that every road ends in a fork. Her skin was light yellow, and although it also had a hint of red, it was still unable to conceal her exhaustion. As Guanyin leaned over to pick up the copies of the Altar Sutra of the Sixth Patriarch and the Annotated Heart Sutra, Yahui also leaned over to pick up the same volumes. As a result, Yahui and Guanyin knocked heads, which startled Yahui, who appeared panicked. Yahui wanted to stroke the area of her forehead that had knocked against Guanyin's head, but when she extended her arm, her hand suddenly froze. It occurred to her that what she had bumped into was the head not of a human but rather of a deity. She stared at Guanyin, waiting for Guanyin to reproach her. At this point, Laozi, Jesus, Mary, and Muhammad also stood up, as Guanyin picked up the remaining dozen or so volumes from the floor and placed them on the table. Guanyin then led Yahui over to the other deities, who thanked her for having collected these scriptures that had been discarded by the other disciples. As the deities were thanking her, Yahui offered them a seat in her room and in her heart. The deities turned to Yahui, then turned to Guanyin as though waiting for her to say something.

Guanyin looked back at the other deities, then shifted her gaze to Yahui, who was still standing there frozen. Guanyin saw that Yahui's earlier panic had begun to fade, as her previous pallor changed to excitement—as though a red veil had suddenly fluttered over her face. There was a bright light in her eyes, as though they had absorbed some of the night's starlight.

"May I say something to *Shifu*?"

Guanyin gazed at Yahui and replied, "We are all here to hear you speak."

Not understanding, Yahui gazed blankly at Guanyin's moonlike face, and Guanyin explained, "Before dusk, we all heard you tell the Daoist Mingzheng that last night you dreamed Tathagata had fallen seriously ill. Isn't that correct?" Guanyin stared at Yahui's face, as though trying to find in it the answer to her question. "Is it true that you also said that Tathagata was delirious, to the point that he had forgotten what he himself looked like?"

Yahui turned pale, and a layer of sweat appeared on her forehead. She slowly nodded, then lifted her hands and clasped them to her chest.

Guanyin asked, "Did you indeed have this dream?"

Yahui again solemnly clasped her hands and nodded, as though the act of solemnly clasping her hands could prove that she had indeed had the dream.

Guanyin asked, "Who else did you see in the dream?"

Turning to Jesus and Mary, Yahui saw that they were both nodding. She said softly, "I dreamed that God was suffering from a very strange amnesia. He could remember everything, except for how to rescue humanity from its suffering."

Guanyin, Laozi, and Muhammad turned to Jesus and Mary. After finding something in their faces, they turned back to Yahui, waiting for her to continue. Meanwhile, Yahui was still gazing at Guanyin.

Guanyin said, "Go on, tell us."

"I also dreamed of Allah," Yahui said. "Allah was also suffering from amnesia and had forgotten how to rescue his sons and daughters. Whenever he was reminded of his amnesia, he would weep. Gazing out at his sons and daughters throughout the world, he wept tears that were as red as blood."

Everyone looked over at Muhammad, who was silent for a moment, and then eventually nodded to them.

Finally it was Laozi's turn. Laozi looked at the other deities, then stepped forward and asked, "And Daoism?"

"You were OK," Yahui said. "But I dreamed that not only was Heavenly Master Zhang so sick that he was on the verge of death, but furthermore he even forgot how to read and write the Chinese characters for heaven and earth that appear in the Daodejing."

At this point, everyone fell silent as they gazed at one another. It was as if they finally realized that it was not only their own divine ancestors who were suffering from amnesia, but also the divine ancestors of all religions and all sects. All these divine ancestors were suffering from dementia-induced amnesia, and while they could remember some other things, they had completely forgotten how to rescue humanity from its suffering. These memories had disappeared without a trace. At this point, Guanyin, Laozi, Mary, Jesus, and Muhammad silently stood up. They each had an uneasy expression, and a layer of sweat appeared on their foreheads and cheeks, as though their secret were about to be revealed. It was as though the disasters the deities would encounter in the mortal world were about to come to pass. They silently gazed at one another, then looked at Yahui the same way she had looked at them when she first came in. After this long silence, the deities turned to Guanyin, as though thinking that since Yahui herself was Buddhist, Guanyin should therefore step forward and take care of the situation.

Guanyin asked Yahui, "Do you know about Gilgamesh?"

Yahui stared in shock and shook her head.

"Have you heard of him?" Laozi asked, and Yahui nodded.

Then there was a silence, whereupon Mary explained, "Long, long ago, Gilgamesh knew many things involving the deities in heaven. He could have become a deity in his own right, but instead chose to remain a man, and it was as a man that he aged and died. Now you too know the affairs of deities. You are the only individual from the human realm who knows that all the divine ancestors have developed amnesia, and you are the only one who knows that they have forgotten how to rescue humans from their suffering. Because you know this, the deities are afraid you will reveal their secret in the mortal world, and therefore they want to give you an opportunity to become a deity in your own right, just like Gilgamesh. So, now you have a choice of whether to become a deity or to remain human."

After Mary finished, the deities turned to Yahui, looking at her the way they might look at a book they already know by heart—as though they already knew every character but still needed to see the page, as though through this act of looking, the words and sentences might undergo a transformation and new holy words might appear. Under the deities' collective gaze, Yahui felt like she was in a real-life dream—but even though she knew it was a dream, she nevertheless treated it as though it were real. Yahui shifted her gaze from Muhammad, past Jesus, Mary, and Laozi, and finally brought it to rest on Guanyin, who was standing next to her. Guanyin realized that Yahui was hesitating, so she discreetly nodded, encouraging Yahui to consider carefully before replying, while also indicating that Yahui shouldn't casually pass up this opportunity to become a deity.

This entire time, Yahui kept her hands clasped to her chest and was constantly biting her lower lip. Eventually, a breeze blew in from the balcony, as the sound of moonlight shining in through the door resonated throughout the room. This seemed to remind the deities of something. They glanced at one another, whereupon Guanyin said more firmly, "This will be your only chance, so once you have thought it over, please tell us your decision."

Yahui replied in a soft voice, "Let me remain human—if it is my decision, I'd like to remain human."

Stunned, the deities stared at Guanyin and Yahui, the same way that when Gilgamesh rejected the goddess Ishtar's advances, the earth and heavens had seemed shocked and baffled, while also knowing all along that this eventuality would come to pass. The late-June sky outside the balcony was crystalline indigo, and repeated bursts of cold air passed through the balcony into the room. The papercuts on the wall rustled in the breeze and fell to the ground, like footsteps in the Beijing night. At this point, in a corner of the building there was a sound and shadow that only the deities could hear and see. During this rustling, Guanyin looked toward the door and asked Yahui, "Are you sure you want to remain human?"

Yahui nodded.

"But why?!" Guanyin's voice hardened.

"I'm still only eighteen." Yahui raised her voice slightly. "I'm only eighteen!"

At this point, no one said anything. It was as though the deities suddenly remembered that Yahui was only eighteen and was a mortal girl who lacked a deity's enlightenment, wisdom, and understanding, and realized that this accounted for her reckless decision to remain human and reject deification. The deities looked at one another, and a childlike smile appeared on Laozi's face. After glancing at Guanyin, Laozi stepped forward and hugged Yahui as though hugging a child. He said, "I should thank you on behalf of my disciple, Mingzheng." Then, he released Yahui and returned to Guanyin's side with a content and relaxed expression. Meanwhile, Mary, Jesus, and Muhammad stood there with a look of loss and regret, until eventually, like the deities, Yahui too could hear the rumbling of the elevator motor. Guanyin sighed and asked Yahui in an even more serious tone, "If you remain human, can you keep the deities' secret? Can you refrain from telling other humans about the deities' memory loss, and how they have forgotten how to rescue humanity from suffering?"

Yahui nodded emphatically, and Muhammad asked, "How can we believe you?"

Yahui reflected for a moment, and after biting her lip for a while, she opened her mouth and slowly said, "I think I remember— I think my *shifu* did mention someone called Gilgamesh, who chose to remain human and then told his fellow humans about many of the deities' faults and secrets—and isn't that why his name is now inscribed on a human's headstone, and not a deity's?" As Yahui asked this, she gazed at the deities gathered around her. "So, if I choose to remain human and don't reveal any of the deities' secrets and faults, will my name be inscribed on a human's headstone, or on a deity's?"

Now it was the deities' turn to stare in surprise, as though it had never occurred to them that there might be any difference between headstones for humans and those for deities. They looked at one another, and finally, just as Muhammad, Jesus, and Mary were about to speak, they saw the shadow of a Daoist appear behind Yahui. This angelic child briefly showed his face and then, like a shadow, disappeared again. He seemed to bump into the apartment's anti-theft door, whereupon the door, which had originally been ajar, was locked shut.

The locked door was indeed locked.

Muhammad looked at the door in alarm, then walked over and pushed the handle, but the door remained as immobile as though it were welded in place. He once again tried to turn the handle, but it wouldn't budge. A look of terror crossed his face, and after trying the handle several more times, he glanced at the other deities, who also appeared alarmed and fearful. They also came over and tried to open the door, but none of them was able to open it. Even when Yahui repeatedly stuffed the key into the brass cylinder lock, she was still unable to turn it.

At this point, Laozi suddenly said: "Isn't this the deity-luring site where, seventy years ago, disciples' decapitated heads were mounted on posts in order to lure and capture deities?"

Everyone silently looked at Yahui.

Yahui's face turned pale and became covered in sweat as she remembered how this apartment was on the site of Beijing's prison and execution grounds. She remembered how Nameless had told her that during the Republican era the authorities would often tie disciples to posts and use them to lure, capture, and execute deities. Laozi continued, "How could you, as a disciple, think of purchasing an apartment here? Weren't you afraid that if you ended up bringing deities with you, they might be detained, seized, and executed?!"

Yahui began to tremble, as sweat covered not only her face but her entire body. She looked around at Jesus, Guanyin, Mary, Laozi, and Muhammad and wanted to kneel in front of them, but at the same time she also looked over at the balcony. Several beams of light suddenly appeared in the sky outside the balcony. These beams happened to be shining directly onto the building, and specifically the building's east wall. It even seemed as though they were shining directly onto Yahui's balcony.

Jesus was the first to follow Yahui's gaze and head over to the balcony.

He leaned over the railing and peered down at the base of the building, then slowly returned and said in a measured tone, "Several decades ago they used disciples' decapitated heads to lure me here, and today you will join me in suffering." The deities all gazed at Jesus, then they too rushed over to the balcony and peered over the railing. After several seconds, they returned to the center of the room. It was the middle of the night and outside everything was perfectly still, though the room's lamp appeared even brighter than before and, combined with the beams of light shining in from the balcony, the room was illuminated as brightly as though it were the middle of the day. The anti-theft door was welded in place by a piece of rebar as thick as a man's thumb, and was covered on all sides in a thick black iron sheet. Meanwhile, apart from the balcony and a small window in the kitchen, the rest of the apartment was cut off from the outside world. Moreover, the window and the balcony happened to be on the same side of the building, and both were positioned beneath the spotlight beam. The deities found themselves locked inside this iron cage of an apartment. They knew that it might well be impossible for them to leave, because otherwise upon returning from the balcony, they wouldn't have stood in the center of the room gazing at one another as silently as a windless mountain covered in a thick cloud just before a thunderstorm.

As the deities stood there, Yahui walked past them and leaned over the balcony railing. She saw that the courtyard of the Yujian residential quarter was full of people. There were three spotlights positioned above the flower garden in the middle of the courtyard. Meanwhile, in front of the entrance to the building there was a row of armed police, beyond which there was a kneeling man and a crowd who had come to watch the excitement. The police blocked the road to prevent the crowd from rushing toward the building, while opening a path to allow a stream of plainclothes police to jog up to the building. Farther away, it appeared that Yujian Street was also full of people. In the center of that crowded street, there were two rows of troops who were rushing toward the residential quarter. Yahui knew that the whole residential quarter and building number two were surrounded by police, soldiers, and atheists, and even if she were to sprout wings it would still be difficult to escape. Sweat poured down her chest and back, and the weakness in her legs made her feel as though she were about to fall from the balcony. To stabilize herself, Yahui gripped the railing with both hands while pushing backward. She wondered if there might be a rifle pointed at her balcony and kitchen window from the roof of a building across from hers or in some window. As she looked across the way, she saw that on the heads of the crowd of people kneeling under the lamplight, there was a white area, which turned out to be an array of Muslim skullcaps. Yahui looked beneath the caps and could vaguely make out Imam Tian kneeling there, his cap resembling a white circle over a grave site after the Qingming grave-sweeping festival. It appeared that Tian Dongqing's wife, Ruan Zhisu, and the old imam Ren Xian were kneeling next to him and praying. Then Yahui stretched her neck and peered down at the base of the building, and noticed that the group of people kneeling there were all her former classmates. She saw Shuiyue *shifu*, Monk Dade, and someone else she couldn't make out clearly, who had led the other monks to kneel behind the Muslim disciples. The Protestant and Catholic disciples were kneeling directly to the north of the Muslim ones, and the Daoist disciples were kneeling behind the Buddhist ones. In all, more than a hundred disciples were kneeling and praying in accordance with the customs of their respective religions. Meanwhile, up in the building, Yahui could only hear the shouts and murmurs of the people down below. She scanned the crowd of kneeling figures trying to find Mingzheng, and when she couldn't find him, she turned to the crowd standing behind them. Eventually, directly between the first two searchlights next to the pond in the middle of the residential quarter, she saw Mingzheng holding a large sign with two lines of text.

The first line had four words: *Do not come out!!*

The second had five: *You must not come out!!!*

Mingzheng kept waving the sign in Yahui's direction, as though trying to communicate a warning to her and to the deities. Yahui stared in shock, then quickly went back inside. At this point Guanyin, Laozi, Mary, Jesus, and Muhammad were all sitting on the bed, sofa, and chair, just as they had been when Yahui first arrived. They were all silent and appeared as peaceful as the unchanging sky. It seemed that Yahui had finally calmed down as well, as the sweat was gone from her face and back.

She stood next to them.

They all turned to look at her.

Muhammad had an odd expression, and there was a hint of reproach in Guanyin's gaze. Meanwhile, Laozi, sitting on the bed, was looking up at the ceiling, as though waiting for some highly anticipated event to quickly come to pass. At this point, they heard the elevator come up, and after the elevator door opened, there was the sound of muffled footsteps, whereupon everyone turned toward the doorway. They knew that on the other side of the door there must be quite a few people, who were also probably armed. The only reason the people outside hadn't already broken down the door was because they needed to wait for the elevator to return with another group or two. By this point, there was nothing more to say or do, other than to let the silence remain for a while longer. The room became so quiet that when human and deities looked around, their movements sounded like bursts of rain.

In the middle of this explosive silence, Jesus suddenly said, "Those of you who want to leave should go ahead, but please let me stay behind."

Everyone looked at him.

Muhammad asked, "But how can we leave?"

Jesus replied, "If you truly want to leave, there will always be a way."

At this point, Mary and Guanyin stood up. They looked at one another, then Guanyin walked over and grasped Yahui's hand. "Do you have anything with a soul in your room?" As Yahui stared in surprise, Mary came over and grasped her other hand, and added, "Something that isn't human, but has a human soul." Laozi and Muhammad seemed to have the same thought, and they also came over and stood in front of and behind Yahui, respectively. Jesus also stood up, straightened his back, and gazed eagerly at Yahui. Outside, there was the sound of the elevator returning to the twenty-second floor, followed by the sound of whispering and muffled footsteps. From the beginning of the universe up to now, time has only been as long as a single chopstick. At this point, all the deities were gazing expectantly at Yahui's face and body.

Yahui stood in the middle, biting her lip and looking at something.

"Take your time and think about it," Laozi said, simultaneously reassuring Yahui and urging her on. Guanyin brought Yahui's hand to her own chest and wiped the sweat from her palm.

Outside, someone bumped against the iron door, producing a loud *kang dangdang* sound. Then, the areas inside and outside the room fell silent.

It was as though at this moment the entire universe had become as still as death.

"The papercuts . . ." Yahui suddenly exclaimed. "The papercuts contain human souls!"

The deities all turned to look at the papercuts on the walls.

"Let's free them!" Guanyin released Yahui's hand. "You must quickly free whichever papercut contains your soul!"

Mary, Laozi, Jesus, and Muhammad simultaneously grasped Yahui, who was heading to the bed to take down the papercuts, and said, "You mustn't go onto the balcony. Instead, stand in the doorway and toss out the papercuts one by one." Then, each of the deities proceeded to take down the papercuts of themselves and of their temples, churches, and mosques from the bed, the dresser, and the walls, as well as from the refrigerator in the kitchen and the cupboard's glass doorframe. One after another, they brought over the papercuts and placed them in Yahui's hand. Yahui then stood in front of the balcony and tossed out the papercuts of Guanyin, Laozi, Mary, Jesus, and Muhammad, as well as of various temples and churches. She watched as some of the papercuts spiraled downward while others hovered for a moment in the lamplight, then began slowly drifting upward. The farther they drifted, the more they picked up speed, like a flock of enormous birds and butterflies flying away from the lamplight and into the vast, distant moonlit sky.

Each deity was thereby able to ride his or her papercut and escape.

They all escaped the mortal world and returned to the realm of quiet sky and blue moon. When Muhammad left, he told Yahui, "Please tell Imam Tian on my behalf that he and his wife don't need to renovate that mosque. Given that all mosques are poor and dilapidated, it simply means that souls have an even greater need for me, and therefore I will frequently appear there." As Laozi was leaving, he told Yahui, "I thank you on behalf of the Daoist master Mingzheng. You have cultivated a blessing for him that will last three lifetimes." As Guanyin was about to fly away, she whispered into Yahui's ear, "I can see everything you think and do. You have already been enlightened and become a Buddhist deity."

Jesus's papercut first drifted downward and was the last to rise again, and as he was waiting for it to return, he said to Yahui, "Please give my regards to Pastor Wang—tonight, on behalf of humanity, you helped the deities once again become deities. However, I also ask that you promise not to reveal that God, Allah, and the Daoist patriarch all suffer from amnesia and have forgotten how to rescue humanity from its suffering. If you make and keep this promise, then Guanyin, Laozi, and I, as well as Mary and Allah, will ensure that your name is eternally inscribed on a headstone—a female Chinese disciple's name, forever inscribed on a deity's headstone!"

23 Yahui and Mingzheng

1. Image: A Paean to a Deity

Another semester came to an end.

A new day arrived, and on this day the religious masters in National Politics University's high-level religious research class graduated and bid each other farewell. They returned to their respective temples, churches, and mosques, to begin a new routine of burning incense, chanting sutras, worshipping, and praying. Meanwhile, Yahui and Mingzheng remained in the Yujian residential quarter, where they got married and lived together.

Yahui never told anyone the secret that the deities had forgotten how to save humanity from its suffering, and therefore her name was forever inscribed on a deity's headstone.

Afterword

This *Heart Sutra*—this mutual reflection of inner and outer belief—is not the short 260-character-long Heart Sutra that appears in the Mahaprajnaparamita Sutra.

Each of the 260 Chinese characters in that other Heart Sutra is like a precious diamond, but when I speak here of a mutual reflection of inner and outer belief, I am referring to the story about the mutual reflection between the departure from holiness and the entry into secularity that appears in this fictional *Heart Sutra*. This latter work contains a combination of solemnity and vulgarity that corresponds to that 260-character sacred text—capturing the touching, caressing, and kissing that occur at the instant when an egg and a rock collide.

I did not wish (nor, for that matter, was I even able) to relate this story the way Nathaniel Hawthorne wrote *The Scarlet Letter* or Fyodor Dostoyevsky wrote *The Brothers Karamazov*, nor the way that Isaac Bashevis Singer wrote *The Magician of Lublin* or Graham Greene wrote *The Power and the Glory*, nor the way that Shūsaku Endō wrote *Silence* and *Deep River* or Zhang Chengzhi wrote *History of the Soul*. I didn't even want this work to resemble Yukio Mishima's *The Temple of the Golden Pavilion* or Salman Rushdie's *Satanic Verses*—where the former takes the beauty of the Temple of the Golden Pavilion and then gives it a strange glow, while the latter takes a set of apocryphal Quranic verses introduced by Satan and develops them into an earth-shattering narrative. These earlier religious novels have already fully explored the twin extremes of humans and deities, the same way that a stonemason might with impeccable precision inscribe a stone stele with images of branches and flowers, sand and diamonds, feces and food, secularity and holiness.

Given that devout people are also human, the religious world is richer and fuller than our secular world, and given that people with religious feelings have all scaled spiritual peaks, their world is even stranger and purer than that of strictly secular people.

More than twenty years ago, I visited an old temple in the Henan town of Ruzhou with a brother from my hometown of Luoyang. We arrived to autumn sunlight, night sparrows, and the zither-like sound of golden rain pattering on the surface of a drum. We followed the sound of the zither, and in the evening light we saw a group of five or six cassock-wearing monks (both young and old). The monks had placed two mats on the ground in front of the temple, between which there was a mountain of money taken from donation boxes in front of the temple god—including assorted hundred-yuan, fifty-yuan, twenty-yuan, ten-yuan, and one-yuan bills and coins. The monks were sorting the bills and coins into piles based on their shape and value, then slowly counting them and neatly placing them in front of their crossed legs—like shepherds separating sheep from goats, or farmers separating barley, wheat, and blighted grain from soybeans and black beans. The setting sun shone copper yellow, the music was like warm oil, and the monks all had calm, simple smiles and natural, relaxed expressions.

Even today, I still clearly remember the secret beauty of that scene. Perhaps it was at that moment that the seed of this book about the mutual reflection of inner and outer belief was first sowed. However, because the seed did not receive a springtime shower, for a long time it remained locked beneath the soil's hard, thin crust.

One day more than two decades later, a fellow author told me about a friendly tug-of-war competition between different religious sects. At the time, both of us were shocked by the existence of this sort of inter-sect competition, but later I purchased the story from him for the price of a cup of wine.

This story of the tug-of-war competition and the earlier scene with the monks counting money immediately became grafted together, and the effect was as though a rainstorm had suddenly fallen where that seed was buried, after which the seed swelled and sprouted, and several years later it broke through the earth's surface and grew to its current form.

I repeatedly reread the great novels mentioned above, and in this way I reached an important understanding. The reason I reread those other works was because I didn't want to write this novel the way others would have written it—even as I simultaneously realized that this meant my voice might appear less familiar. Nevertheless, I asked myself, "If others have already written works like that, why would you want to do the same?"

I didn't write about why humans are humans and deities are deities, nor about humans ascending to divinity or deities descending to humanity, nor did I write about souls caught in the interstitial region between humanity and divinity. This is because those earlier great works blocked my literary path like tall mountains. Given that other authors have already written extensively about these majestic topics, I was left with mere disordered fragments; given that those heavy topics already belonged to others, I therefore had to try to write about lighter ones; given that the long annals of history are filled with literary mountains of humans and deities scattered along the road, I was therefore left with the instant when humans and deities glimpse one another as humans enter divinity and deities emerge from humanity. Of these humans and deities, one may proceed from inside to outside while another proceeds from outside to inside; or one's body may go inward while his or her heart goes outward, and another's heart may go inward even as his or her body goes outward. Meanwhile, I hoped I could find and grasp this instant when they pass one another. I wanted to write about how they smile when they see each other, about their silence and coldness, their applause and laughter, and about the nonrecognition, silence, and bitterness they experience when they pass one another.

What I wanted was very minimal and very minute.

Against my own past and my own habits, I only wrote about the simple and secret love they experience in that instant when they pass through that door of faith and see one another.

Of the 320,000 Chinese characters I originally wrote for this novel, fewer than 160,000 now remain. Of the discarded 160,000 characters, there were 50,000 that one could say were full of lust, passion, and desire, but the instant my young granddaughter entered my writing studio to tell me it was time to eat, I immediately decided to delete them.

At that moment, I decided that only half of this 320,000-character novel still lived. I settled on the work's rhythm and tone, its holiness and secularity, and the plotlines that emerged from points of contact between humans and deities, then I endeavored to compose the work within the sliver of light that appears when you slowly open a door in darkness, and in the sliver of darkness that appears when you close the door in light. I hoped to write about the beauty and secret love that emerge when light and darkness meet—like the instant of mutual gazing, caressing, and kissing that occurs when an egg and a stone collide at high speed. Prior to this instant, regardless of whether the stone is rolling toward the egg or the egg is hurtling toward the stone, the entire process is neither center nor core. Instead, the center and core lie in the mutual gazes, caresses, and secret love that the egg and the stone experience in the instant before they collide.

I hoped to write a light novel about the kisses and secret love that appear in that instant when holiness and secularity meet.

I hoped to write a small self-aware novel about how, when holiness and secularity meet, they have no choice but to kiss.

I hoped to write a shallow novel about Chinese-style religious belief that anyone could easily understand—the same way that we all have a general understanding of and confusion about the Prajna-paramita Heart Sutra itself.

In reality, this work was not produced by me, but rather it was produced by three other individuals and one cohort. The three individuals include the brother who took me to visit Ruzhou's Fengxue Temple, the author who told me about the inter-sect tug-of-war competition, and the papercut expert Shang Ailan, who spent a year and a half producing more than two hundred exquisite papercuts to illustrate this volume, while the cohort consists of all the colleagues at the publishing house where this book was published.

Meanwhile, I am merely the intermediary connecting these three individuals and this cohort—like a worthless piece of thread holding a string of precious pearls.

Translator's Note

Relatively early in its reimagining of the journey of the seventh-century Buddhist monk Xuanzang (a.k.a. Tripitaka) to the "Western regions" (i.e., Central and South Asia) to collect Buddhist scriptures, the beloved sixteenth-century Chinese novel *Journey to the West* features a pivotal scene in which Tripitaka hears an oral recitation of the Heart Sutra and immediately commits it to memory. The novel adds that it is through Tripitaka that the sutra "has come down to us this day. It is the comprehensive classic for the cultivation of Perfection, the very gateway to becoming a Buddha."*

The historical Xuanzang was responsible for the first Chinese version of the sutra, and a 661 CE stone inscription of his 649 CE translation is the earliest extant dated version of the sutra available in any language. Seductively short at only 260 Chinese characters and filled with seemingly paradoxical assertions such as "form is emptiness, and emptiness is form," the Heart Sutra has since become Buddhism's most popular sutra. Just as the sutra was translated into Chinese from Sanskrit,** Buddhism itself was introduced into China

---

* Anthony Yu, ed. and trans., *Journey to the West*, vol. 1 (Chicago: University of Chicago Press, 2012), 390.

** There is no extant version of the sutra that definitely antedates the earliest Chinese version, and some scholars have argued that the Heart Sutra may have originated as a Chinese text. See, for instance, Jan Nattier, "The Heart Sūtra: A Chinese Apocryphal Text?" *Journal of the International Association of Buddhist Studies* 15, no. 2 (1992): 153–223.

from Central and South Asia, though over time it has become an integral part of Chinese culture and society and recognized as one of China's "Three Teachings," along with Confucianism and Daoism.

Organized religion has had a rocky trajectory in China in the twentieth and twenty-first centuries. In modern China religious practice was restricted and suppressed for more than a quarter of a century, with religious faith being partially replaced by political belief. Since the beginning of the Reform Era in 1978, however, the practice of the nation's five officially recognized religions—namely, Buddhism, Daoism, Catholicism, Protestantism, and Islam—has experienced a significant revival.* According to a 2018 government white paper, "China's Policies and Practices on Protecting Freedom of Religious Belief," China currently has nearly 200 million religious believers, including approximately 20 million Muslims, 6 million Catholics, and 3.8 million Protestants. The white paper notes that it is difficult to calculate the much larger number of Buddhists and Daoists with any precision, though if one focuses more narrowly on professional clergy, the nation currently has approximately 222,000 Buddhist and 40,000 Daoist clergy members.**

Set in a religious training center located on the campus of the National Politics University in Beijing, Yan Lianke's novel *Heart Sutra* focuses on a cohort of disciples and clergy who have enrolled in the center for periods ranging from three to twelve months. Most of their courses focus on religious and political topics, but in addition to their formal studies, the disciples also engage in activities such as a series of tug-of-war competitions between teams belonging to different religions. One of the novel's notable fictional conceits, these athletic competitions dramatize a set of internal conflicts

* Ian Johnson, *The Souls of China: The Return of Religion After Mao* (New York: Pantheon, 2017).
** The State Council Information Office of the People's Republic of China, "China's Policies and Practices on Protecting Freedom of Religious Belief" (April 2018). http://www.scio.gov.cn/zfbps/32832/Document/1626734/1626734.htm.

within the training center, while also symbolizing a broader set of tensions between religious and secular life that underlie the work as a whole. Of the five religions represented at the center, Yan's novel gives particular attention to Buddhism, embodied by the nun Yahui, and to Daoism, embodied by the monk Gu Mingzheng. In contrast to the training center's other disciples, who are all senior clergy, Yahui and Mingzheng are rather young. Yahui is eighteen and is attending classes at the center on behalf of her mentor, or *shifu*—an older nun known as Jueyu, who has been hospitalized with a health crisis brought on by the tug-of-war competitions.[*] Mingzheng, meanwhile, has apparently managed to enroll in the center thanks to his high-ranking father—though Mingzheng himself is not entirely sure who his father is, and one of the novel's subplots involves Mingzheng's efforts to find and identify him. As the center's two youngest disciples, Yahui and Mingzheng quickly bond and fall in love, which helps catalyze their determination to leave organized religion and "return to secular life."

As Yan Lianke notes in his Afterword to the novel, *Heart Sutra* follows in the tradition of other religious-themed works such as *The Scarlet Letter*, *The Brothers Karamazov*, *The Temple of the Golden Pavilion*, and *The Satanic Verses*. Unlike those other works, however, *Heart Sutra* examines the dynamic religious environment of a modern state that is nominally areligious. Using a combination of realism, allegory, fantasy, and satire, the novel focuses on the interstitial space between religious and secular existence, using religion to reflect on a variety of secular concerns, while at the same time underscoring the degree to which secular issues permeate religious practice and belief. Moreover, like Yan's use of Biblical language in his earlier novel *The Four Books*, in *Heart Sutra* he draws on a variety

---

[*] In the original novel, Jueyu is named Yuhui, but given that the romanized name Yuhui and that of her disciple Yahui are visually very similar, we decided (with the author's approval) to change the name Yuhui (meaning "jade wisdom") to Jueyu (meaning "awakened jade").

of religious discourses to develop a unique new literary language and aesthetic vision.

Like *Journey to the West*, in which the fictionalized version of Xuanzang is accompanied and often amusingly upstaged by a group of supernatural disciples, including a pig, a horse, a river ogre, and an incorrigible monkey named Sun Wukong, Yan's *Heart Sutra* features an eclectic mix of realism and fantasy, history and allegory, and a complicated interplay between humans and deities. The novel's main diegesis is centered around the training center and combines quotidian descriptions with references to celestial deities, while the narrative of Yahui and Mingzheng's romance is interspliced with another romance between the Daoist sage Laozi and the Bodhisattva Guanyin—two very familiar deities in China who, under ordinary circumstances, are rarely discussed in the same breath.

Laozi is a sage figure believed to have lived in the sixth century BCE and is traditionally credited with having written the canonical Daoist text, the Daodejing. Guanyin, meanwhile, is the Chinese version of the Bodhisattva Avalokiteśvara and is also known as the goddess of mercy. Referenced in the first line of the Heart Sutra, Avalokiteśvara was originally gendered as male in South Asian Buddhism but was subsequently gendered as female after being introduced into China as Guanyin—a historical detail that resonates ironically with one of the plotlines in Yan Lianke's novel.

The illustrations featured in the Guanyin and Laozi plotline are intricate papercut images that were commissioned and created specifically for this volume by the artist Shang Ailan. Although the Chinese editions of several of Yan Lianke's earlier novels included similar papercut images, *Heart Sutra* is the first of his novels in which the papercut images are directly integrated into the work's plot. Not only is the novel's Guanyin and Laozi plotline narrated primarily through papercut images, but Yahui is also presented as a skillful papercut artist in her own right. Yahui's creations are discussed at various points throughout the novel, and even have a crucial significance in one pivotal scene.

The mixture of realism and fantasy in Yan's *Heart Sutra* can be viewed as an example of a contemporary narrative mode that Yan, in his book of literary criticism *Discovering Fiction*, calls "mythorealism," which he explains "is not a bridge offering direct access to truth and reality, and instead it relies on imaginings, allegories, myths, legends, dreamscapes, and magical transformations that grow out of the soil of daily life and social reality."*

Although in *Discovering Fiction* Yan Lianke identifies mythorealism as a relatively recent literary development that builds on earlier narrative practices ranging from Western modernism to Latin American magical realism, he simultaneously cites *Journey to the West* to emphasize that mythorealism "is not something that any one author created from scratch, but rather it is something that Chinese literature has possessed all along." With its combination of history and fantasy, religious allegory, and satirical humor, *Journey to the West* is a key antecedent of the approach that Yan Lianke adopts in *Heart Sutra* and also offers an intriguing commentary on how one might approach the text itself. In the final reference to the Heart Sutra in *Journey to the West*, Tripitaka and his disciple Sun Wukong are debating the sutra's meaning. Sun Wukong suggests that although Tripitaka may be able to recite the sutra, he doesn't necessarily understand it. In response, Tripitaka angrily asks Sun Wukong whether he understands the sutra, to which Sun Wukong replies, "Yes, *I* know its interpretation!" and then falls silent. Tripitaka's other two disciples proceed to raucously mock the simian disciple for his apparent ignorance, until Tripitaka interrupts them to specify that "Sun Wukong's interpretation is made in a speechless language. That's true interpretation."**

* Yan Lianke, *Discovering Fiction*, trans. Carlos Rojas (Durham, NC: Duke University Press, 2022).
** Anthony Yu, ed. and trans., *Journey to the West*, vol. 4 (Chicago: University of Chicago Press, 2012), 264.

Tripitaka is referring here to the Heart Sutra, but a similar point could perhaps be made about Yan Lianke's *Heart Sutra* itself—namely, that while its intricately allegorical structure might appear to invite or even demand an elaborate interpretation, a "true" interpretation might be one that simply appreciates the text on its own terms.

Yan Lianke concludes his Afterword by noting that the novel was produced by "three other individuals and one cohort," and I would like to conclude here by noting that this translation was similarly a collaborative effort. The quotes from the Daodejing were borrowed (with minor alterations) from Victor Mair's translation* and the elegant translations of the novel's excerpts from the opera *The Decapitation of General Shan* were proposed by Eileen Cheng-yin Chow. I am also grateful to my editors and copyeditors, Peter Blackstock, Emily Burns, Greg Clowes, and Kathryn Jergovich, for many detailed and very helpful suggestions. Finally, I would also like to express my appreciation to Yan Lianke himself, for being such an excellent collaborator on this and many other projects over what has now been a decade-long partnership.

* Lao Tzu, *Tao Te Ching: The Classic Book of Integrity and the Way*, ed. and trans. Victor H. Mair (New York: Bantam Books, 1990).

ABOUT THE JACKET ARTISTS: XU DE QI

Xu De Qi was born in 1964 in Jinan, China, and graduated in 1991 from Shandong Normal University where he is currently Professor of Art.

His work has come to represent a personal form of Chinese Pop Art, a blend of traditional Chinese realism, Pop Art and Western poster styling from the 1960s and 1970s. He brings a contemporary vision to events in China, and many of his paintings express a passion, openness and hope for the future. He embraces change and his paintings often communicate happiness and a desire to live and have fun.

Already represented in major international exhibitions such as the Venice Biennale and at prestigious events with the Journée Rencontre at the Centre Pompidou, Xu De Qi is considered one of the great Chinese masters of contemporary painting.

ABOUT THE JACKET ARTISTS: ZHONG BIAO

Zhong Biao was born in Chongqing in 1968, and graduated from Hangzhou Zhejiang Fine Arts Academy in 1987. Biao's paintings feature cultural symbols and human figures that seem to defy the limits of time and space. The rapid and dramatic economic, cultural and political changes that have taken place in China animate much of his work.

'I don't want to force my own understanding or interpretation of my paintings on the audience,' Zhong Biao has said of his approach. 'The mixture of images within each of my paintings is like a combination of controversial elements in life. We don't have to understand everything we see in each painting. Like life, we cannot understand everything that we have seen or experienced. In my paintings, Eastern and Western, historical and modern opposites coexist, reflecting the reality of today's lifestyle.'

Zhong Biao's style is highly recognisable, and he is considered one of the most influential modern Chinese artists in the world. Biao is an associate professor and master's advisor at Sichuan Academy of Fine Arts, and a member of the China Artists Association and Chongqing Association of Oil Painters.

ABOUT THE JACKET ARTISTS: WANG GUANGYI

Wang Guangyi was born in Harbin in 1957. He grew up in the propaganda-saturated environment of the Maoist regime and graduated from the Zhejiang Academy of Fine Arts in 1984. He is associated with the Chinese political pop movement that grew up in the 1980s as political and social change swept rapidly across China.

Wang Guangyi's billboard-sized paintings juxtapose Cultural Revolution-era motifs with the aesthetic of Western pop art to comment on the commercialisation of Chinese culture and highlight the tensions between past and present. 'I came to realise that the essence of art is its ancestry, its history,' Wang Guangyi has said. 'When creating a work of art, one's head is full of these historical considerations; an encounter with what has been and its entry into the process of rectification.'

Wang Guangyi has exhibited his paintings around the world. He currently lives and works in Beijing.

ABOUT THE JACKET ARTISTS: DUAN JIANWEI

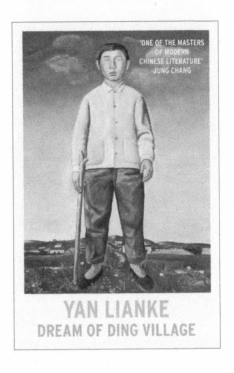

Born in Xuchang, Henan Province, in 1961, **Duan Jianwei** graduated from the Department of Fine Arts, Henan University. He is known for his idealised rural scenes, which convey the profound serenity of simple country life.

Duan Jianwei rose to prominence after the 1991 exhibition 'Oil Paintings by Duan Zhengqu and Duan Jianwei', the 'Two Duans of Henan'. The pair's 'new rustic' paintings established a new direction, departing from the radical style of China's '85 New Wave, and from the highly decorative and expressive rustic painting of the past. Duan Jianwei has also taken inspiration from ancient Chinese statues, wall paintings and, more recently, from the liberating simplicity of shape, volume and colour. Duan Jianwei currently lives and works in Beijing, and teaches at the College of Fine Arts, Capital Normal University.